THE HAPPINESS INDUSTRY

THE
HAPPINESS
INDUSTRY

How the Government and Big
Business Sold Us Well-Being

WILLIAM DAVIES

VERSO
London • New York

For Lydia

First published by Verso 2015
© William Davies 2015
All rights reserved

The moral rights of the author have been asserted

1 3 5 7 9 10 8 6 4 2

Verso
UK: 6 Meard Street, London W1F 0EG
US: 20 Jay Street, Suite 1010, Brooklyn, NY 11201
www.versobooks.com

Verso is the imprint of New Left Books

ISBN-13: 978-1-78168-845-8 (HC)
ISBN-13: 978-1-78478-272-6 (Export)
eISBN-13: 978-1-78168-847-2 (US)
eISBN-13: 978-1-78168-846-5 (UK)

British Library Cataloguing in Publication Data
A catalogue record for this book is available from the British Library

Library of Congress Cataloging-in-Publication Data
A catalog record for this book is available from the Library of Congress

Typeset in Fournier MT by Hewer Text UK Ltd, Edinburgh, Scotland
Printed in the US by Maple Press

Contents

Preface   1

1   Knowing How You Feel   13
2   The Price of Pleasure   41
3   In the Mood to Buy   71
4   The Psychosomatic Worker   105
5   The Crisis of Authority   139
6   Social Optimization   181
7   Living in the Lab   215
8   Critical Animals   245

Acknowledgements   277
Notes   281
Index   303

Preface

Since the World Economic Forum (WEF) was founded in 1971, its annual meeting in Davos has served as a useful indicator of the global economic zeitgeist. These conferences, which last a few days in late January, bring together corporate executives, senior politicians, representatives of NGOs and a sprinkling of concerned celebrities to address the main issues confronting the global economy and the decision-makers tasked with looking after it.

In the 1970s, when the WEF was still known as the 'European Management Forum', its main concern was slumping productivity growth in Europe. In the 1980s, it became preoccupied with market deregulation. In the 1990s, innovation and the internet came to the fore, and by the early 2000s, with the global economy humming, it began to admit a range of more 'social' concerns, alongside the obvious post-9/11 security anxiety. For the five years after the banking meltdown of 2008, Davos meetings were primarily concerned with how to get the old show back on the road.

At the 2014 meeting, rubbing shoulders with the billionaires, pop stars and presidents was a less likely attendee: a Buddhist monk. Every morning, before the conference proceedings began, delegates had the opportunity to meditate with the monk and learn relaxation techniques. 'You are not the slave of your thoughts', the man in red and yellow robes, clutching an iPad, informed his audience. 'One way is to just gaze at them . . . like a shepherd sitting above a meadow watching the sheep'.[1] A few hundred thoughts of stock portfolios and illicit gifts for secretaries back home most likely meandered their way across the mental pastures of his audience.

True to their competitive business principles, the Davos organizers had not just gone for any monk. This was a truly elite monk, a French former biologist named Matthieu Ricard, a minor celebrity in his own right, who acts as French translator to the Dalai Lama and gives TED Talks on the topic of happiness. This is a subject he is uniquely qualified to speak on, thanks to his reputation as the 'happiest man in the world'. For a number of years, Ricard participated in a neuroscientific study at the University of Wisconsin, to try and understand how different levels of happiness are inscribed and visible in the brain. Requiring 256 sensors to be attached to the head for three hours at a time, these studies typically place the research subject on a scale between miserable (+0.3) and ecstatic (-0.3). Ricard scored a -0.45. The researchers had never encountered anything like it. Today, Ricard keeps a copy of the neuroscientists' score chart on his laptop, with his name proudly displayed as the happiest.[2]

Ricard's presence at the 2014 Davos meeting was indicative of a more general shift in emphasis from previous years. The forum was awash with talk of 'mindfulness', a relaxation technique formed out of a combination of positive psychology, Buddhism, cognitive behavioural therapy and neuroscience. In total, twenty-five sessions at the 2014 conference focused on questions related to wellness, in a mental and physical sense, more than double the number of 2008.[3]

Sessions such as 'Rewiring the Brain' introduced attendees to the latest techniques through which the functioning of the brain could be improved. 'Health Is Wealth' explored the ways in which greater well-being could be converted into a more familiar form of capital. Given the unique opportunity of having so many of the world's senior decision-makers in one place, it is no surprise that this was also the scene of considerable marketing displays, by companies selling devices, apps and advice aimed at supporting more 'mindful' and less stressful lifestyles.

So far so mindful. But the conference went further than just talk. Every delegate was given a gadget which attached to the body, providing constant updates to the wearer's smartphone to assess the health of his recent activity. If the wearer is not walking enough, or sleeping enough, this evaluation is relayed back to the user. Davos attendees were able to glean new insights into their lifestyles and wellness. Beyond that, they were getting a glimpse of a future in which all behaviour is assessable in terms of its impact upon mind and body. Forms of knowledge that could traditionally be accrued only within a specialized institution, such as a laboratory or hospital, would be collected as individuals wandered around Davos for the four days of the conference.

This is what now preoccupies our global elites. Happiness, in its various guises, is no longer some pleasant add-on to the more important business of making money, or some new age concern for those with enough time to sit around baking their own bread. As a measurable, visible, improvable entity, it has now penetrated the citadel of global economic management. If the World Economic Forum is any guide, and it has always tended to be in

3

the past, the future of successful capitalism depends on our ability to combat stress, misery and illness, and put relaxation, happiness and wellness in their place. Techniques, measures and technologies are now available to achieve this, and they are permeating the workplace, the high street, the home and the human body.

This agenda extends well beyond the reaches of Swiss mountaintops and has in truth been gradually seducing policy-makers and managers for some years. A number of official statistical agencies around the world, including those of the United States, Britain, France and Australia, now publish regular reports on levels of 'national well-being'. Individual cities, such as Santa Monica, California, have invested in their own localized versions of this.[4] The positive psychology movement disseminates techniques and slogans through which people might improve their happiness in everyday life, often by learning to block out unhelpful thoughts and memories. The idea that some of these methods might be added to the curriculum of schools, so as to train children in happiness, has already been trialled.[5]

A growing number of corporations employ 'chief happiness officers', while Google has an in-house 'jolly good fellow' to spread mindfulness and empathy.[6] Specialist happiness consultants advise employers on how to cheer up their employees, the unemployed on how to restore their enthusiasm to work, and — in one case in London — those being forcibly displaced from their homes on how to move on emotionally.[7]

Science is advancing rapidly in support of this agenda. Neuroscientists identify how happiness and unhappiness are physically inscribed in the brain, as the researchers in Wisconsin did with Matthieu Ricard, and seek out neural explanations for why singing and greenery seem to improve our mental well-being. They claim to have found the precise parts of the brain which generate positive and negative emotions, including an area that provokes 'bliss' when stimulated, and a 'pain dimmer switch'.[8] Innovation within the experimental 'quantified self' movement sees individuals carrying out personalized 'mood tracking', through diaries and smartphone apps.[9] As the statistical evidence in this area accumulates, so the field of 'happiness economics' grows to take advantage of all this new data, building up a careful picture of which regions, lifestyles, forms of employment or types of consumption generate the greatest mental well-being.

Our hopes are being strategically channelled into this quest for happiness, in an objective, measurable, administered sense. Questions of mood, which were once deemed 'subjective', are now answered using objective data. At the same time, this science of well-being has become tangled up with economic and medical expertise. As happiness studies become more interdisciplinary, claims about minds, brains, bodies and economic activity morph into one another, without much attention to the philosophical problems involved. A single index of general human optimization looms into view. What is clear is that those with the technologies to produce the facts of happiness are in positions of considerable influence, and that the powerful are being seduced further by the promises of those technologies.

Is it possible to be against happiness? Philosophers can argue as to whether or not this is a plausible position to take. Aristotle understood happiness as the ultimate purpose of human beings, though in a rich and ethical sense of the term. Not everyone would agree with this. 'Man does not strive for happiness', wrote Friedrich Nietzsche, *'only the Englishman* does that.'[10] As positive psychology and happiness measurement have permeated our political and economic culture since the 1990s, there has been a growing unease with the way in which notions of happiness and well-being have been adopted by policy-makers and managers. The risk is that this science ends up blaming – and medicating – individuals for their own misery, and ignores the context that has contributed to it.

This book shares much of that disquiet. There are surely ample political and material problems to deal with right now, before we divert quite so much attention towards the mental and neural conditions through which we individually experience them. There is also a sense that when the doyens of the World Economic Forum seize an agenda with so much gusto, there is at least some cause for suspicion. The mood-tracking technologies, sentiment analysis algorithms and stress-busting meditation techniques are put to work in the service of certain political and economic interests. They are not simply gifted to us for our own Aristotelian flourishing. Positive psychology, which repeats the mantra that happiness is a personal 'choice', is as a result largely unable to provide the exit from consumerism and egocentricity that its gurus sense many people are seeking.

But this is only one element in the critique to be developed here. One of the ways in which happiness science operates ideologically is to present itself as radically new, ushering in a fresh start, through which the pains, politics and contradictions of the past can be overcome. In the early twenty-first century, the vehicle for this promise is the brain. 'In the past, we had no clue about what made people happy – but now we *know*', is how the offer is made. A hard science of subjective affect is available to us, which we would be crazy not to put to work via management, medicine, self-help, marketing and behaviour change policies.

What if this psychological exuberance had, in fact, been with us for the past two hundred years? What if the current science of happiness is simply the latest iteration of an ongoing project which assumes the relationship between mind and world is amenable to mathematical scrutiny? That is one thing which this book aims to show. Repeatedly, from the time of the French Revolution to the present (and accelerating in the late nineteenth century), a particular scientific utopia has been sold: core questions of morality and politics will be solvable with an adequate science of human feelings. How those feelings are scientifically classified will obviously vary. At times they are 'emotional', at other times 'neural', 'attitudinal' or 'physiological'. But a pattern emerges, nevertheless, in which a science of subjective feeling is offered as the ultimate way of working out how to act, both morally and politically.

The spirit of this agenda originates with the Enlightenment. But those who have exploited it best are those with an interest in social control, very often for private profit. That unfortunate contradiction accounts for the precise ways in which the happiness industry advances. In criticizing the science of happiness, I do not wish to denigrate the ethical value of happiness as such, less still to trivialize the pain of those who suffer from chronic unhappiness, or depression, and may understandably seek help in new techniques of behavioural or cognitive management. The target is the entangling of hope and joy within infrastructures of measurement, surveillance and government.

Such political and historical concerns open up a number of other propositions. Maybe this scientific view of the mind, as a mechanical or organic object, with its own behaviours and sicknesses to be monitored and measured, is not so much the solution to our ills, but among the deeper cultural causes. Arguably, we

are *already* the product of various overlapping, sometimes contradictory efforts to observe our feelings and behaviours.
Advertisers, human resource managers, governments, pharmaceutical companies have been watching, incentivizing, prodding,
optimizing and pre-empting us psychologically since the late
nineteenth century. Maybe what we need right now is not more
or better science of happiness or behaviour, but less, or at least
different. How likely is it that, in two hundred years' time, historians will look back at the early twenty-first century and say, 'Ah,
yes, *that* was when the truth about human happiness was finally
revealed'? And if it is unlikely, then why do we perpetuate this
kind of talk, other than because it is useful to the powerful?

Does this mean that the current explosion of political and business interest in happiness is just a rhetorical fad? Will it dissipate,
once we've rediscovered the impossibility of reducing ethical
and political questions to numerical calculations? Not quite.
There are two significant reasons why the science of happiness
has suddenly become so prominent in the early twenty-first century, but they are sociological in nature. As such, they are never
directly addressed by the psychologists, managers, economists
and neuroscientists who advance this science.

The first concerns the nature of capitalism. One of the
attendees at the 2014 Davos meeting made a remark that contained far more truth than he probably realized: 'We created our
own problem that we are now trying to solve'.[11] He was talking
specifically about how 24/7 working practices and always-on
digital devices had made senior managers so stressed that they
were now having to meditate to cope with the consequences.
However, the same diagnosis could be extended to the culture of
post-industrial capitalism more broadly.

Since the 1960s, Western economies have been afflicted by an acute problem in which they depend more and more on our psychological and emotional engagement (be it with work, with brands, with our own health and well-being) while finding it increasingly hard to sustain this. Forms of private disengagement, often manifest as depression and psychosomatic illnesses, do not only register in the suffering experienced by the individual; they are increasingly problematic for policy-makers and managers, becoming accounted for economically. Yet evidence from social epidemiology paints a worrying picture of how unhappiness and depression are concentrated in highly unequal societies, with strongly materialist, competitive values.[12] Workplaces put a growing emphasis on community and psychological commitment, but against longer-term economic trends towards atomization and insecurity. We have an economic model which mitigates against precisely the psychological attributes it depends upon.

In this more general and historical sense, then, governments and businesses 'created the problems that they are now trying to solve'. Happiness science has achieved the influence it has because it promises to provide the longed-for solution. First of all, happiness economists are able to put a monetary price on the problem of misery and alienation. The opinion-polling company Gallup, for example, has estimated that unhappiness of employees costs the US economy $500 billion a year in lost productivity, lost tax receipts and health-care costs.[13] This allows our emotions and well-being to be brought within broader calculations of economic efficiency. Positive psychology and associated techniques then play a key role in helping to restore people's energy and drive. The hope is that a fundamental flaw in our current political economy may be surmounted, without confronting any serious

9

political–economic questions. Psychology is very often how societies avoid looking in the mirror.

The second structural reason for the surging interest in happiness is somewhat more disturbing, and concerns technology. Until relatively recently, most scientific attempts to know or manipulate how someone else was feeling occurred within formally identifiable institutions, such as psychology laboratories, hospitals, workplaces, focus groups, or some such. This is no longer the case. In July 2014, Facebook published an academic paper containing details of how it had successfully altered hundreds of thousands of its users' moods, by manipulating their news feeds.[14] There was an outcry that this had been done in a clandestine fashion. But as the dust settled, the anger turned to anxiety: would Facebook bother to publish such a paper in future, or just get on with the experiment anyway and keep the results to themselves?

Monitoring our mood and feelings is becoming a function of our physical environment. In 2014, British Airways trialled a 'happiness blanket', which represents passenger contentment through neural monitoring. As the passenger becomes more relaxed, the blanket turns from red to blue, indicating to the airline staff that they are being well looked after. A range of consumer technologies are now on the market for measuring and analysing well-being, from wristwatches, to smartphones, to Vessyl, a 'smart' cup which monitors your liquid intake in terms of its health effects.

One of the foundational neoliberal arguments in favour of the market was that it served as a vast sensory device, capturing millions of individual desires, opinions and values, and converting these into prices.[15] It is possible that we are on the cusp of a new post-neoliberal era in which the market is no longer the primary tool for this capture of mass sentiment. Once happiness-monitoring tools flood our everyday lives, other ways of quantifying feelings in real time are emerging that can extend even further into our lives than markets.

Liberal concerns about privacy have traditionally seen it as something which needs to be balanced against security. But today, we have to confront the fact that a considerable amount of surveillance occurs to increase our health, happiness, satisfaction or sensory pleasures. Regardless of the motives behind this, if we believe that there are limits to how much of our lives should be expertly administered, then there must also be limits to how much psychological and physical positivity we should aim for. Any critique of ubiquitous surveillance must now include a critique of the maximization of well-being, even at the risk of being less healthy, happy and wealthy.

To understand these trends as historical and sociological does not in itself indicate how they might be resisted or averted. But it does have one great liberating benefit: of diverting our critical attention outward upon the world, and not inward upon our feelings, brains or behaviour. It is often said that depression is 'anger turned inwards'. In many ways, happiness science is 'critique turned inwards', despite all of the appeals by positive psychologists to 'notice' the world around us. The relentless fascination with quantities of subjective feeling can only possibly divert critical attention away from broader political and economic problems. Rather than seek to alter our feelings, now would be a good time to take what we've turned inwards, and attempt to direct it back out again. One way to start would be by turning a skeptical eye upon the history of happiness measurement itself.

1

Knowing How You Feel

Jeremy Bentham was sitting in Harper's Coffee Shop in Holborn, London, when he shouted, 'Eureka!' The prompt was not some intellectual inspiration from within, as it had been when Archimedes immortalized the exclamation from his bath, but a passage from a book, *Essay on Government*, by the English religious reformer and scientist Joseph Priestley. The passage was this:

> The good and happiness of the members, that is, the majority of the members, of any state, is the great standard by which everything relating to that state must finally be determined.

Bentham was eighteen years old and the year was 1766. Over the next sixty years, he took Priestley's insight and converted it into an extensive and hugely influential doctrine of government: utilitarianism. This is the theory stating that the right action is whichever one produces the maximum happiness for the population overall.

There is something telling about the fact that Bentham's 'eureka' moment was not a matter of great intellectual originality. Nor did he ever claim to be much of a philosophical pioneer. In addition to Priestley's influence, Bentham was content to admit that much of his account of human nature and motivation was lifted from the Scottish philosopher David Hume.[1] He had little interest in producing new theories or weighty philosophical tomes, and never took much enjoyment in writing. As far as Bentham was concerned, there was a limit to what any idea or text could hope to achieve when it came to the political or social improvement of mankind. Merely believing that 'the greatest happiness of the greatest number' should be the goal of politics and ethics was of little consequence, unless a set of instruments, techniques and methods could be designed to turn this belief into the founding principle of government.

Rather than as an abstract thinker, Bentham is best understood as half philosopher and half technician, and from this various contradictions followed. He was an intellectual with a classically English distaste for intellectualism. A legal theorist, who believed that much of what law rested on was simple nonsense. An Enlightenment optimist and modernizer, who scoffed at any notion of inherent human rights or freedoms. And an advocate for hedonism, who insisted that every pleasure be neurotically accounted for. Reports of his personality vary wildly, with some discovering a man of great warmth and humility, and others one who was vain and dismissive.

Bentham's relationship with his father caused him considerable misery. He was a weak, shy and often unhappy child, and appears to have been bullied into the status of a child prodigy by his father, who insisted on teaching him Latin and Greek from the age of five. He attended Westminster School but was made miserable by being the smallest boy there. Aged twelve, Bentham went to Oxford, where he was drawn towards chemistry and biology. If anything, he was even less happy at university than at school. He established

14

a small chemistry laboratory in his room and felt a strong affinity for the natural sciences, which he pursued throughout his teens. With a less domineering father, this would no doubt have provided him with the intellectual satisfaction that his mathematical mind was seeking. But his father was a lawyer and insisted his son follow in his footsteps in order to earn a decent income. Under duress, he became a barrister in London's Lincoln's Inn.

Practising law did not make Bentham happy, and nor did the continued influence of his father. His shyness made him dread having to stand up and speak in court. Perhaps he still longed for his homemade chemistry laboratory. He certainly pined for emotional and sexual intimacy, but when he fell in love in his early twenties, yet again his father stood in his way, vetoing the relationship on the basis that the woman in question wasn't rich enough. In this conflict between love and money, the measurable thwarted the immeasurable. Later in life, Bentham would be an outspoken advocate for sexual freedoms, including the tolerance of homosexuality, which he saw as an inevitable component of the maximization of human pleasure.[2]

His career, as it developed from his arrival at Lincoln's Inn, was always a compromise, between the professional and moral injunctions imposed by his father, and the scientific and political urges that drove him from within. The law would indeed become the field in which he made his name, but never as his father intended. Instead, he set about criticizing law, ridiculing its language, demanding more rational alternatives and designing policies and instruments through which government could finally escape the philosophical nonsense of abstract moral principles. This stance did not make him rich, and Bentham ended up financially dependent on a stipend from his father, whose disappointment in his failed barrister son never lifted.

There were times when Bentham the technician overshad-owed Bentham the philosopher. During the 1790s his activities were those of what we might now associate with a public sector management consultant. He spent much of this period designing exotic schemes and technologies, which he believed could improve the efficiency and rationality of the state. He wrote to the Home Office suggesting that the various departments of gov-ernment be linked up by a set of 'conversation tubes' for better communication. He drew up plans for what he termed a 'frid-garium', to keep food fresh. And he wrote to the Bank of England with the blueprint for a printing device that would produce unforgeable bank notes.

This engineer's vocation was integral to his vision of a more rational form of politics. It drove many of his more famous policy proposals, such as the 'Panopticon' prison, which was very nearly signed into English law during the 1790s before falling by the wayside. During the late 1770s, Bentham began to write on the topic of punishment, specifically because punish-ment seemed to offer a rational means of influencing human behaviour, if it could target the natural psychological propensity to pursue pleasure and avoid pain. This was never a merely aca-demic or theoretical issue, and very little of this writing was published until several years later. His goal was always to achieve reform of public policy. But this did require a little deeper thinking about the nature of human psychology.

The science of happiness

Bentham was a fierce critic of the legal establishment, but he was scarcely much more sympathetic to the radical and revolutionary

16

movements which were erupting elsewhere. Confronted by the political claims of the French and American revolutionaries, Bentham was scornful. 'Natural rights is simple nonsense', he declared, 'natural and imprescriptible rights, rhetorical nonsense – nonsense upon stilts.'[3] When radical philosophers such as Thomas Paine appealed to such ideas, they were making the identical mistake that monarchs or religious leaders made when they claimed some divine or magical sanction for their actions: they were talking about something which had no tangible existence.

Bentham's alternative was to ground political and legal deci-sion-making in hard, empirical data. In that respect, he was the inventor of what has since come to be known as 'evidence-based policy-making', the idea that government interventions can be cleansed of any moral or ideological principles, and be guided purely by facts and figures. Whenever a policy is evaluated for its measurable outcomes, or assessed for its efficiency using cost-benefit analysis, Bentham's influence is present.

The great advances of the natural sciences, as he saw it, derived from the ability to avoid the meaningless use of language. Politics and the law had to learn this lesson. In Bentham's view, every noun either refers to something 'real' or something 'fictitious' – but we often fail to notice the difference. Words such as 'goodness', 'duty', 'existence', 'mind', 'right', 'wrong', 'authority' or 'cause' might mean something to us, and they have come to dominate philosophical discourse. But, as far Bentham was concerned, there is nothing which these words actually refer to. 'The more abstract the proposition is', he argued, 'the more liable is it to involve a fallacy.'[4] The problem is that we often mistake such propositions for reality.

By contrast, the language of natural science is organized in relation to physical, tangible things, which each word is attached to. But how would government or law be organized in this fashion? It is one thing for a chemist to attach names to specific compounds, but it is quite another for a judge or a government official to be quite so disciplined in their use of words. In any case, what are the physical, tangible things which make up politics? If politics is no longer to concern itself with abstract problems such as 'justice' or 'divine right', what will it concern itself with instead?

Bentham's answer was happiness, thereby assuming that this entity was rooted in something 'real'. But how? In what sense is the term 'happiness' any less fictitious than, say, 'virtue'? To answer this, Bentham fell back on a form of naturalistic assertion. 'Nature has placed mankind under the governance of two sovereign masters, pain and pleasure', and that just happens to be a fact.[5] Happiness itself may not be an objective, physical phenomenon, but it occurs as a result of various sources of pleasure, which have a firm, physiological basis.

Unlike many other things that arise in our minds, happiness is prompted by something real, something objective. It reminds us that we are biological and physical beings, with urges and fears, not unlike other animals. We can be scientific about happiness in a way that we simply can't about virtually any other philosophical category. If such a science could be pursued, it would provide governments with an entirely new basis on which to design policies and laws, so as to improve the welfare of mankind in the only realistic or rational sense.

It's possible to spot elements of Bentham's own life experiences in this psychological theory of politics. Its premise was a tragic one, which spoke of its author's own unhappiness: the one thing which all human beings hold in common is their capacity to suffer. Optimism could only lie in a wholesale reorientation of the state, towards the relief of suffering and the promotion of pleasure. Bentham was known to be unusually empathetic, often to a fault. His sensitive nature made him highly attuned to the unhappiness of others. One of the great virtues of utilitarianism, as a moral philosophy, is this empathetic dimension, its belief that we should take all others' welfare as seriously as our own. Given that humans are not the only species that suffers, many utilitarians also extend this to animals.

With a better understanding of what motivates human psychology, policy-makers might be able to divert human activity towards the greatest happiness of all. The question of punishment captured so much of Bentham's time and energy because it appeared to be the most effective tool in the possession of law-makers when it came to steering individual activity in the optimal direction. 'The business of government is to promote the happiness of society, by punishing and rewarding', he argued.[6] The free market, of which Bentham was an unabashed supporter, would largely take care of the reward part of this 'business'; the state would take responsibility for the former part. To inflict pain on people, either via their bodies or their minds, was to bring politics into the realm of tangible reality, and to leave the world of linguistic illusions behind. As a vision of Enlightenment optimism goes, Bentham's had a darker edge than most.

Bentham's emphasis upon the brute reality of physical pain and his distrust of language can be seen as mutually reinforcing. The cultural historian Joanna Bourke has highlighted the fraught relationship between language and pain since the eighteenth century.[7] Either pain seems to defy description altogether, or it has been treated as a taboo subject to be experienced silently. There is a long history of viewing sufferers, especially those of suspicious character, as exaggerating or wrongly describing pain.

19

This assumes, as Bentham did, that there is an objective reality about pain which could be represented if only words or sufferers were better equipped to do so. This opens the way for experts to grasp or describe that reality, given the sufferer himself cannot, and for numbers to represent such feelings on the assumption that words cannot.

The science of happiness was therefore a critical component in achieving a rational form of politics and law. It could be used to divert behaviour towards goals that would be best for everyone. And as government became more scientific, so it would be able to predict how different interventions influenced individual choices. This is not 'happiness' in some ethereal or metaphysical sense, and certainly not in any ethical sense, as Aristotle had understood it. It was happiness in the sense of a physical occurrence within the human body. Contemporary neuroscience, which consummates this reduction of psychology to biological processes, would have looked to Bentham like the answer to all of our political and moral questions. Conversely, a great deal of contemporary scientific interest in the brain and behaviour has strongly Benthamite presuppositions.

This is well illustrated by one neuroscientific study published by a group of researchers at Cornell in 2014. Claiming to breach the 'last frontier' of neuroscience, namely the secrets of our inner feelings, the researchers argued that they had unlocked the 'code' through which the human brain deals with all different pleasures and pains. As the lead author explained:

It appears that the human brain generates a special code for the entire valence spectrum of pleasant-to-unpleasant, good-to-bad feelings, which can be read like a 'neural valence meter' in which the leaning of a population of neurons in one direction equals positive feeling and the leaning in the other direction equals negative feeling.[8]

This description of how pleasure and pain operate physically is more or less what Bentham had already assumed, posing questions as to how successfully neuroscience can ever hope to escape its protagonists' cultural presuppositions. For scientists armed with measuring devices to discover that a bodily organ is also armed with measuring devices sounds like a coincidence to say the least.

The study touches upon one of the great controversies of utilitarianism, of whether diverse types of human experience can all be located on a single scale. The Cornell neuroscientists clearly believe that they can: 'If you and I derive similar pleasure from sipping a fine wine or watching the sun set, our results suggest it is because we share similar fine-grained patterns of activity in the orbitofrontal cortex'. This is a relatively innocent remark when it is fine wine or sunsets that are at stake. But when profound experiences of love or artistic beauty are rendered equivalent to baser experiences, such as drug taking or shopping, the claim that all pleasures are computed in the orbitofrontal cortex in the same way becomes more problematic.

Philosophers refer to this argument, that all pleasures and pains can be located on a single scale, as 'monism'. Bentham was the monist par excellence.[9] He couldn't deny that we speak of different varieties of happiness and contentment using different words, but the objective underpinning of all these forms was always the same – that is, physical pleasure. We naturally seek 'benefit, advantage, pleasure, good or happiness, all of which ultimately comes to the same thing'.[10] Likewise, suffering, rooted in the physical experience of pain, represents an entity that varies in quantity, but not quality.

Once we accept that there is a single, ultimate and physical sensation underlying all 'good' and 'bad' experiences and actions, then it follows that this sensation varies only in terms of quantity. Bentham never conducted any scientific research on the question but proposed a psychological model, detailing the different ways in which pleasure could vary in quantity. In his most famous statement on the topic, 'Introduction to the Principles of Morals and Legislation', he offered seven of these, most of which were easy to conceive of in quantitative terms.[11] 'Duration' of pleasure was one relatively obvious quantitative category. 'Certainty' of future pleasure is something that we would now see as amenable to mathematical risk modelling. 'Extent' of the population affected by an action is another simple quantitative yardstick.

The main scientific stumbling block for Bentham's entire enterprise was one category of variation in particular, namely 'intensity'. How could a scientist, legislator, punisher or policy-maker know how intense a particular pleasure or pain was? Of course one might draw on one's own experience through introspection, but that is scarcely a very scientific approach. Or one might ask people to report on their experiences using their own words. But then wouldn't utilitarianism be drawn back into the hall of mirrors that is philosophical language, the 'tyranny of sounds' through which we describe what it is like to be human? Measuring the intensity of different pleasures and pains was the technical task on which the Benthamite project would stand or fall.

How to measure?

The eighteenth century was a time of great inventiveness in the creation of measurement tools. The thermometer was invented in 1724, the sextant (which measures angles between any visible objects, such as stars) in 1757, and the marine chronometer in 1761. The introduction of new measuring tools and standards was one of the first achievements of the French revolutionaries in the 1790s. This involved the commissioning of an original platinum metre, the famous *mètre des archives*, which was placed in a vault in the National Archives in Paris.

The need for reliable standardized measures cut to the heart of the Enlightenment, whose high point coincided with the first half of Bentham's career. As Immanuel Kant defined it in 1784, Enlightenment meant mankind escaping its 'self-incurred immaturity. Immaturity is the inability to use one's own understanding without the guidance of another'.[12] Unlike their predecessors, who would allow religious and political authorities to dictate truth from falsehood, right from wrong, the 'mature' and Enlightened citizen would draw on nothing but his own judgement. The motto of Enlightenment, Kant suggested, was *sapare aude* – dare to know. The critical individual mind was the only authoritative barometer of truth. But for this reason, it was equally important that everybody was using the same yardsticks of comparison, or the whole project would collapse into a relativist babble of subjective perspectives.

Bentham hoped to cast a similarly scientific, sceptical eye over the workings of politics, punishment and law. In place of unquestioned beliefs about justice or common values, Bentham insisted that we should know what will make people happier, and to treat every person's feelings as of equal value. He knew precisely how to frame the scientific question – does this policy, law or punishment create more or less pleasure across society as a whole?

But what type of measuring tool was available to gather the answers? It's all very well feeling empathetic to the suffering of others, as Bentham undoubtedly did, but without a standard through which different pleasures and pains can be compared, the utilitarian is exercising guesswork. On the other hand, surely the very nature of pleasant or painful sensations is that they are subjective. The search for a common measure of happiness is fraught with difficulty.

Despite being critical to the viability of his political project, Bentham dedicated surprisingly little attention to this problem. Occasionally, he suggested that the 'greatest happiness' principle of political judgement was just that, a principle, which could never realistically be converted into a quantitative science. But given the appeal to hard empirical reality that is threaded through Bentham's psychology, and his scathing remarks about all forms of philosophical abstraction, one has to take seriously the sense in which he did intend to rebuild politics and law on technical forms of measurement and calculation. If happiness were the only human good on which it is possible to speak scientifically, then it would be strange if we didn't then pursue it using scientific methods. So we return to the problem: How is the intensity of a pleasant or unpleasant feeling to be measured? How does utility manifest itself in such a way that it can be grasped by measurement?

Bentham suggests only two tentative answers to this question, neither of which he pursued in any practical or experimental way. Both involved the identification of proxies for happiness, rather than a claim that feelings themselves could be grasped. But in each case, he unwittingly hinted towards vast zones of scientific enquiry which would later be explored by psychologists, marketers, policy-makers, doctors, psychiatrists, human resources experts, social media analysts, economists, neuroscientists and individuals themselves.

The first of Bentham's answers was that the human pulse rate might provide the indicator of pleasure that could be used to solve the measurement problem.[13] He wasn't particularly taken with this idea himself, but he recognized that the body offered certain measurable symptoms of what the mind was experiencing. As happiness is ultimately an assemblage of pleasant feeling, the notion that one might be able to discover happiness levels via the body is not so surprising. In everyday life, we intuitively understand this, in how we read another's facial expression or body language. A science of such signs might therefore be possible. Pulse rate would appear to offer the possibility of a hard, quantitative science of well-being that transcends culture. Words can deceive, but our heart rate does not.

Bentham's second answer, on which he was far keener, was that money might be used. If two different goods can command an identical monetary price, then it can be assumed that they generate the same quantity of utility for the purchaser. By making this claim, Bentham was well ahead of his time. Economists would only catch up with this analysis some thirty years after his death, but since Bentham was interested in what governments could do to influence general public happiness, rather than what occurred in market transactions between private individuals, he had little concern with pursuing this idea as an economist. Nevertheless, by putting out there the idea that money might have some privileged relationship to our inner experience, beyond the capabilities of nearly any other measuring instrument, Bentham set the stage for the entangling of psychological research and capitalism that would shape the business practices of the twentieth century.

These were and remain the options: money or the body. Economics or physiology. Payment or diagnosis. If politics were to become scientific and emancipated from abstract nonsense, it is through economics, physiology or some combination of the two that the project would be realized. When the iPhone 6 was released in September 2014, its two major innovations were quite telling: one app which monitors bodily activity, and another which can be used for in-store payments. Whenever experts seek to witness our shopping habits, our brains or our stress levels, they are contributing to the project that Bentham had mapped out. The status of money in this science is intriguing. While political and moral concepts are attacked as empty, nonsensical abstractions, somehow the language of pounds and pence is viewed as having some firm and natural relationship to our inner feelings. The exceptional status attributed to economics from the late nineteenth century onwards, as closer to a natural science than a social one, is one legacy of this worldview.

The problem of measurement may seem like a nerdish matter of scientific methodology. Surely we all know what Bentham was getting at when he said that government should pursue the greatest happiness of all. Do we really need to get fixated on the details of how to calculate this? Of course, we can allow Bentham the status of a philosopher and ignore his inventive and technical aspirations. We can look at how utilitarianism works in the abstract, by playing analytical games in the philosophy seminar room.

It is not clear that Bentham would have been very happy with such a legacy. And it is less clear that this is what his most important legacy has actually been. The technical, calculative, methodological problems of Benthamism, in various guises, are arguably the most transformative in how they have come to structure our political, economic, medical and personal lives. For this reason, whether happiness is to be indicated via the body (such as through pulse rate) or via money may prove to be of the utmost importance for how utilitarianism has actually set about constructing the world around us. However, any systematic attempt to construct quantitative measures of sensation would not begin until a few years after Bentham's death in 1832.

Weight-lifting in Leipzig

On 22 October 1850, a second 'eureka' moment took place, this time in Leipzig, Germany. Gustav Fechner, a theologian-cum-physicist who had recently emerged from a protracted nervous breakdown, suddenly realized that the mind–body problem, which preoccupied so many German philosophers, might be solvable through mathematics. He recorded the date of this breakthrough in his diary.

The relationship of the mind to the physical world, including the body, is the foundational problem of modern philosophy. René Descartes' doubt about the reality of the physical world, combined with his certainty of his own existence, established a dualism between the realm of thought and that of physical things. Dualism is an unwieldy philosophical position to hold, which always runs the risk of a reductionism in one direction or the other. Either the entire world might get reduced to an effect of the thinking mind (idealism), or thinking can be reduced to a merely physical occurrence, subject to natural forces (empiricism), rather as Bentham had assumed. Various Enlightenment thinkers grappled with this, most notably Kant, who believed he had avoided either fate by systematically distinguishing matters of scientific knowledge from matters of moral and philosophical principle. The human mind was, for Kant, something which fell firmly into the latter category, rendering any science of the psyche impossible.

Fechner was a dualist, but of a peculiar sort. His ideas were formed by a highly eclectic intellectual background, which put him in an unusual position with respect to traditional philosophical problems. Fechner was the son of a pastor, who (like Bentham's father) taught him Latin when he was a small child. He registered to study medicine at the University of Leipzig, but took the opportunity while there to attend lectures in botany, zoology, physics and chemistry. At the same time, he was exposed to many of the excesses of German idealist philosophy, including Schelling's philosophy of nature, romanticism and Hegel. Early in his academic career, he carried out experiments with electricity, while also getting drawn into theological debates about the nature of the soul. The separate domains that we now know as 'science' and 'philosophy' remained entangled in the German universities of the 1830s.

Nowadays, Fechner might well be described as a new age thinker. His genius was to find a way of bringing his disparate intellectual interests together, remaining a philosopher and a scientist, a metaphysician and a physician. In the process, he brought questions of the mind (which Kant had stipulated lay beyond the realms of knowledge) into the purview of science. For this reason, Fechner represents one of the key figures in the development of what we now know as psychology.

In what way would mathematics be helpful in solving the mind–body problem? The answer derived from Fechner's engagement with physics. The principle of the 'conservation of energy' had been formulated by a number of German physicists over the course of the 1840s, with transformative implications for the understanding of basic matter. This stated that energy is indestructible: it can be altered in its form, but not its quantity. If heat turns into light, or coal into heat, so the principle states, then we can assume that a single quantity of energy has been conserved along the way. This might be seen as another variant of monism. In the context of the industrial revolution, this discovery was a source of tremendous optimism that there was no limit to how efficient technology could become.

The power of mathematics to explain all forms of change was greatly increased as a result of this breakthrough in physics. An underlying quantitative stability had been unearthed. Fechner's innovation was to extend this same principle to questions that had previously resided in the terrain of philosophy. If the physicists were right, then even the mind could be included in this mathematical framework. What is interesting about Fechner's breakthrough was that it didn't simply propose a form of biological reductionism. He was adamantly not suggesting that the mind was constituted by physical matter, but that 'the will, the thought, the whole mind may be as free as it may be, yet it will be able to exercise its freedom only by means of, not counter to, the general laws of kinetic energy'.[14] Energy, as Fechner understood it, traversed the border between mind and body, obeying laws of mathematics as it did so.

The doctrine that Fechner proposed, known as 'psychophysics', argued that mind and matter are separate entities but must nevertheless have some stable, mathematical relationship to one another.[15] In certain respects, Fechner's theory of psychology was similar to Bentham's. He too was convinced that people pursued pleasure, although less as a matter of natural cause and effect and more as a matter of spontaneous libidinous desire. (He coined the term 'pleasure principle', which Sigmund Freud later adopted.)[16]

Fechner distinguished himself from Bentham's English empiricism in two respects. Firstly, philosophy held no threat for him. Words such as 'soul', 'mind', 'freedom' or 'God' referred to real things, albeit not in any physical or measurable sense. This was evidence of Hegel's influence. The philosophical innovation of psychophysics was to suggest that these entities could become known via the physical body in certain ways. The conservation of energy, as it passed between physical and non-physical realms, meant that philosophical ideas must sit in some stable mathematical relation to material and bodily things.

Fechner was therefore a dualist, in the sense that he maintained a belief in two parallel realms, one of philosophical ideas, the other of scientific facts. What distinguished him from philosophical dualists, such as Descartes and Kant, was a somewhat mystical belief that the two were in some mathematical harmony. Industrial metaphors were helpful here, which speaks of the economic context in which he was working. A steam engine involves intangible forces at work within a physical entity; likewise, a human being must be understood as an alliance of the immaterial mind and the material body.[17]

Secondly, Fechner was intent on discovering how this mathematical relation actually worked in practice. From 1855, he set about this with a series of arcane experiments, in which he lifted objects of subtly different weights, to test how changes in physical weight correlated to changes in subjective sensation. If I lift two very similarly weighted objects, precisely how big must the difference between them be before I can tell for sure which is the heaviest? The unit of measurement that Fechner introduced to assess this was what he referred to as a 'just noticeable difference'.

Alternatively, if I am already holding a weight of one size, how much additional sensation does it cause me if someone adds another weight of half that size? Does it alter the sensation by half again (as one might expect), or by less than that? Once the relationship between psychic and physical realms was properly measured, the questions of philosophy would be scientifically answerable. The scale of ambition that drove psychophysics was vast, even if the experiments which it rested on were comparatively primitive.

Bentham may have designed various schemes and policies, blueprints for prisons, proposals for 'conversation tubes', and so on, but he had never set to work upon the human body itself or tackled the problem of measurement beyond his theoretical speculations about pulse rate and money. English philosophers tended to be biased towards privileging the physical, sensible world of things over the metaphysical world of ideas – but they maintained this bias from the comfort of their armchairs. It is interesting that it was Fechner – the idealist, mystical, romantic – who really dragged metaphysics down to earth, by probing the body, measuring sensations, conducting experiments.

Precisely because he didn't simply presume that the physical was prior to the psychological (as Bentham did), he needed to set about testing how one related to the other. This wasn't a theory stating whether mental processes were really driven by biological ones, or vice versa. It was the opening up of a new field of scientific enquiry, which, by the end of the nineteenth century, would be populated by psychologists, economists and a nascent industry of management consultants. The quantitative and economic psychology in which theories of mind would be replaced by scales and measures, and which Bentham had merely speculated about, was now being assembled. The idea that individual feelings and behaviour might be amenable to expert adjustment was also now a technical, mechanical possibility.

A democracy of bodies

In the age of the fMRI scanner, it has become increasingly common to speak of what our brains are 'doing', 'wanting' or 'feeling'. In many situations, this is represented as a more profound statement of intent than anything which we could report verbally. A 2005 article published by the Oxford neuroscientist Irene Tracey is titled 'Taking the Narrative Out of Pain'.[18] The marketing guru Martin Lindstrom, who has studied the brains of thousands of consumers using fMRI, has built his career on the notion that 'people lie, but brains don't'.[19] In the less high-tech reaches of mental management, such as mindfulness training, people are taught to notice what their minds and feelings are doing in the present moment, as a way of alleviating anxiety. Meditation helps them to observe and accept these silent processes.

This poses a number of questions. How can some particular part of our bodies or selves possess its own voice, and how can experts claim to know what it is saying? Underlying these types of claims are some of the arguments and techniques that were first introduced by Bentham and Fechner. First and foremost is the distrust of language as a medium of representation. Bentham's fear of the 'tyranny of sounds' casts doubt on the capacity of individuals to adequately express themselves. To be sure, Bentham recognized that each person was the best judge of her own private pleasures and happiness in her own life. But for the purposes of a public politics, some other means of knowing what was good for people needed inventing.

Variants of mind-reading technology are invented only to get around the apparent problem that language is inadequate to communicate feelings, desires and values. Whether that technology involves money and prices, or measurements targeted at the human body (such as pulse, sweat or fatigue monitors), the science of our inner sensations seeks forms of truth that might eventually bypass speech altogether. One of the most striking cases of this ideal in action was reported in 2014, with the news that scientists had successfully achieved 'telepathic' brain-to-brain communication for the first time, using EEG neuro-scanners. The final destination of such developments is a form of silent democracy, peopled only by mute physical bodies. Bentham had little idea of how extensive the measurement of pleasure and pain would become, while Fechner was limited to running experiments on his own body rather than anyone else's. But taken to their logical conclusions, the work of these two polymaths points to a society in which experts and authorities are able to divine what is good for us without our voices being heard.

Something important is lost along the way. In the monistic worldview of Bentham and Fechner, experiences differ in terms of their quantity, sitting on a scale between extreme pleasure and extreme pain. One thing that this necessarily discounts is the possibility that human beings may have their own considered reasons to be happy or unhappy, which may be just as important as the feelings themselves. In order to credit individuals with 'critiques' or 'judgments' or 'demands' (or, for that matter, with 'gratitude' or 'acclaim'), we have to recognize that they possess authority to speak for their own thoughts and bodies. This means understanding the difference between, say, 'despair' and 'sadness', and the ability of the person using those terms to do so deliberately and meaningfully. Were, for instance, someone to describe themselves as 'angry', a response focused on making them feel better might entirely miss the point of what they were saying. It might even be deemed insulting. Were someone to be unhappy about the fact that income inequality in Britain and the United States has reached levels not seen since the 1920s, the advice – as given by some happiness economists – that one is best off not knowing what other people earn would seem like a form of hopelessness.[20] In a monistic world, there is merely sentiment, experiences of pleasure and pain that fluctuate silently inside the head, with symptoms that are discernable to the expert eye.

This has profound implications for the nature of political and moral authority. The rational, enlightened society imagined by Bentham was one in which all institutions were designed in such a way that they were perfectly attuned to the vagaries of human psychology. The job of governing a modern, liberal society comes to appear as the confrontation between two types of material thing. On the one side, there is the mechanics of the mind, governed by the pursuit of pleasure and the avoidance of pain, which is no more deniable than the need to eat or sleep. And on the other, there are various material forces designed to influence that psychology. Monetary incentives, social reputation, physical punishment and confinement, aesthetic seductions, rules and regulations, and so on, serve no purpose unless they are geared towards the calculations of the individual.

In this society, political authority lies with those who are most expert to measure and manage individuals. There is no reason why administration of this nature should be handled by the state directly, as so many neoliberal regimes have more recently discovered. Anticipating Thatcherism and workfare nearly two centuries beforehand, one of Bentham's policy recommendations was for the state to establish a National Charity Company (a joint stock company, modelled on the East India Company), which would alleviate poverty by employing hundreds of thousands of people in privately managed 'industry houses'.[21] His proposal for the Panopticon also included a recommendation for private firms to build and run the prisons, with a license provided by the state. Not content with reconceiving the very basis of legal authority, Jeremy Bentham can be viewed as the godfather of public sector outsourcing.

Fechner pointed the way to a more intimate micromanagement of individuals. In representing the relationship between mind and world as a numerical ratio, he implicitly offered two alternative ways of improving the human lot. If a certain physical context (such as work or poverty) is causing pain, one progressive route would involve changing that context. But another equivalent would be to focus on changing the way in which it is experienced. Many of the experts who followed in Fechner's footsteps were psychiatrists, therapists and analysts, whose critical eye was turned upon the subject having the feelings, rather than the object that seemed to be causing them. If lifting weights becomes too painful, you're faced with a choice: reduce the size of the weight, or pay less attention to the pain. In the early twenty-first century, there is a growing body of experts in 'resilience' training, mindfulness and cognitive behavioural therapy whose advice is to opt for the latter strategy.

The job of intervening, to alter the psychological calculations and feelings of individuals, can be distributed across various types of institution and expert.[22] We classify some as 'medical' or 'managerial', others as 'educational' or 'penal'. But really, these terms are just further abstractions and fictions. All that matters is how effectively they administer their task, of offering the carrots and sticks which alter human activity and experience for the better.

The (in)visibility of happiness

In 2013, the Cheltenham Literature Festival in Britain introduced an innovative form of evaluation in an effort to capture the value that it delivered to its attendees. Using a technology developed by the company Qualia, it set up cameras all around the site to track the smiles on the faces of visitors as they wandered around. Computers were taught to interpret these smiles and to convert them into a form of value. This was a more high-tech version of an experiment undertaken in the town of Port Phillip, Australia, which carried out an experiment in happiness measurement by stationing researchers around the streets who sought to record how much smiling they witnessed on the faces of those around them. A 'smiles per hour' value was produced from one day to the next.

Qualia's technology is still clumsy; a computer's ability to tell an 'authentic' smile from an 'inauthentic' one is not nearly as good as a human's. However the science of smiling is advancing rapidly in various directions, both psychological and physiological. The physical practice of smiling has been shown to accelerate recovery from illness.[23] The experience of seeing smiling faces has been shown to lower aggression.[24] Experiments show that 'real' smiles achieve different emotional and behavioural responses from 'social' smiles.[25]

A smile is another potential indicator of (and influence on) what is going on under the surface, along with pulse rate, use of money or a 'just noticeable difference' between two weights. To these, a long list of recently developed measures could be added, from the 'smart' watches developed by Apple and Google to monitor stress, to psychometric affect questionnaires used to assess depression. These are all means of rendering subjective experience tangible and visible, and therefore comparable. Like the sonar technologies which are used to map the ocean floor from sea level, these tools aim to mine the depths of our feelings and bring them out into the daylight for all to see.

Yet there is a perpetual uneasiness about this project. With something as important as happiness, no measure ever seems quite adequate to the philosophical importance of the matter. We are generally content to accept that the map of the ocean floor is not the same as the ocean floor itself, but merely a representation with various advantages and disadvantages. But with happiness, there always remains a frustration. The sense that quantified smiles, heart rate, money and 'just noticeable differences' miss something crucial about the nature of emotional experience is overwhelming. A smile may indeed reveal something of the person – but surely not as a scientific representation.

Let's consider again the foundation of Bentham's political science. 'Nature has placed mankind under the governance of two sovereign masters, pain and pleasure'. By making this claim, Bentham hoped to strip out abstract, unscientific bases for political programmes. But in what sense is his claim about 'nature' really any less metaphysical? Since when did nature involve erecting 'sovereign masters' over certain species? That sounds suspiciously like metaphysics after all. No matter how scientific his portrait of motivation may claim to be, in its epic generality it is guilty of the same abstraction that Bentham deplored in philosophy. And if it weren't, then the notion of happiness as the ultimate purpose of government would not be able to hold.

Here's the paradox. If happiness is granted its grand, philosophical and moral status as a 'sovereign master', we might agree that this is ultimately what life is all about. But then how could such an entity ever be measured scientifically? Whereas if happiness is anchored firmly in the physical, sensory experience of pleasure and pain, who is to say that such a mundane matter carries any fundamental or political importance? It becomes just a grey mushy process inside our brains. Too often, the utilitarian route out of this dilemma is simply to duck it altogether. As the influential British economist and positive psychology advocate Lord Richard Layard writes, 'If we are asked why happiness matters we can give no further external reason. It just obviously does matter.'[26] Is happiness measurement really a way of resolving moral and philosophical debate? Or is it actually a way of silencing it? Once the technocrats are in charge, it is too late to raise any questions of intrinsic meaning or collective purpose.

Happiness science is a science like no other, because it is always reaching beyond a mere object. What it grasps for is something meaningful, but it grasps for it via tools and measures that are too cold to adequately capture that meaning. Fechner's bizarre efforts to access transcendent truths via weight-lifting have become an exemplar of how psychological management works today. Neurological, physiological and behavioural monitoring devices are clamped together with meditation practices and pop existentialism. The philosophical deficit in the science of happiness is dealt with by importing ideas from Buddhism and new age religions. Somewhere in between the quantitative science and the spiritualism sits happiness.

The cultural effect of this is that certain indicators and measures of happiness take on a moral luminosity of their own. While happiness itself may remain invisible, a smile or a diagnosis of positive health acquires a sort of iconic value. The material symptom or indicator becomes a doorway into some inner being, granting it a magical quality. When Bentham idly wondered whether pulse rate or money might be the best measure of utility, he could scarcely have imagined the industries that would develop dedicated to asserting and reinforcing the authority of particular indicators to represent our inner feelings. Among these, no indicator has acquired a greater authority than money, an object that straddles the abstract and the material like no other.

2

The Price of Pleasure

The accident and emergency unit of the Royal London Hospital in East London is never the most salubrious of environments. But on a Saturday night, it turns into a cross between a warzone and a Hammer horror movie. Drunk people stumble around, bruised and beaten from bar brawls. Ambulance staff and police officers compete for access to suspected drink-drivers. The fear or grief on the faces of visiting family members is the most disturbing sight of all.

It was into such a scene that my wife and I arrived with our screaming daughter when she was less than a year old. We actually had no idea if there was anything wrong with her or not. That's the problem with babies: they won't tell you. The question perennially asked by doctors of parents with babies – 'But does she seem OK in herself?' – is another way of saying, 'Trust your instinct.' On this occasion, she'd woken up at an unusual time and was screaming in a way we'd never heard before, coupled with a rash and a temperature. She really didn't seem 'OK in herself'.

Amid the predictable chaos of the waiting area at 2 a.m., I noticed three young men who appeared to be plotting something with urgency. They were clustered around a form, onto which one of them was writing details in consultation with the other two. They pointed at parts of it, advising him on what to write, checking with each other for agreement before encouraging him further. He scribbled away while his two friends appeared to debate what he should do next, occasionally looking up to check if they were being watched. There was a great deal of nodding and pointing, as if some plan were being hatched. This went on for about twenty minutes or so, while our by now infuriatingly cheerful daughter was enjoying playing with some NHS leaflets.

After a while, a nurse came out and called the name of the young man who was filling in the form. The effect this had on him surprised me. His shoulders drooped, his face went into a grimace and he very, very slowly got to his feet, while his two friends suddenly became a picture of concern and pity. As he inched towards the nurse clutching his form, he held his head angled sharply down to one side and supported his neck, to suggest that he was now suffering a great deal. He walked slowly and – apparently – painfully towards the nurse, who led him off to a treatment area. After he'd gone, his two friends cheered right up and returned to their furtive discussions.

The young man had clearly suffered a neck injury. Or at least, he had clearly experienced some mishap that could have caused a neck injury. Whatever had happened, it had resulted in slightly more enthusiasm among the three young men than one would normally associate with accidents or emergencies. From where I was sitting, this was an obvious case of an insurance scam being plotted. I immediately felt angry that these time-wasters were holding us up, quite apart from the apparent fraud going on. No doubt a car accident had occurred, and one of them had then immediately recognized an opportunity to make some money.

The only question was whether the 'injured' party could get through the necessary medical examination without fluffing his lines.

Maybe my reaction was grossly unfair. Maybe it wasn't. As with babies, so for whiplash: there is no possible way of knowing. Whiplash is a curious type of medical phenomenon for a couple of reasons. Firstly, the term itself technically refers to an event that has befallen the sufferer, and not to a medical condition as such. Thus, if someone has experienced sudden straining of the neck muscles, as often occurs with rear-end car collisions, it makes sense to say that she has 'suffered whiplash'. Secondly, to the extent that whiplash has any symptoms, they are only detectable to the sufferer. Evidence that 'whiplash' has occurred (other than a smashed car bumper) consists in the fact that the victim experiences long-term pain in the neck and back. But as with some psychiatric disorders, there is no identifiable disorder underlying this symptom.

Medical researchers have studied whiplash since the 1950s, in search of some physiological explanation for it, but without luck.[1] It first entered the Cumulated Index Medicus (the database of American medical journals) in 1963, as experts struggled to come to terms with this mercurial syndrome. During the 1960s, American scientists conducted a series of experiments on monkeys which simulated extreme rear-end collisions, in the hope of then being able to discover the precise way in which these accidents damaged neck tissue. Too many of these caused paralysis or brain damage to the monkeys, without doing much to unravel the mystery of whiplash in humans.

One thing which is well known about whiplash, however, is that it is very unevenly distributed internationally. Rates of whiplash diagnosis are far higher in the English-speaking world than in most other nations, and have been growing sharply since the 1970s. Given that whiplash is chiefly associated with car accidents, and that cars have been getting progressively safer over this period, this increase is clearly associated with other factors to do with insurance claims. In Britain, for example, whiplash is responsible for a 60 per cent rise in personal injury claims related to car accidents between 2006–13, to the point where whiplash payouts are now equivalent to 20 per cent of the cost of every car insurance premium.

In other countries, the syndrome is far less well known, and extracts far less money from the insurance industry as a result. While whiplash featured in 78 per cent of all personal injury claims made in Britain in 2012, across the channel in France the figure was only 30 per cent.[2] In the early 2000s, Norwegian neurologist Harald Schrader noticed that the incidence of long-term neck pain resulting from car accidents in Lithuania was zero. After studying this phenomenon and publishing his findings, he was met with fury from the Norwegian whiplash disability patient group (which boasted 70,000 members in a nation of 4.2 million people), who took umbrage with what they assumed he was implying.

The bizarre philosophical status of whiplash as a form of entirely invisible pain makes it unusually amenable to fraudulent insurance claims. Intuitively, this explains how rates of whiplash diagnosis vary so sharply from one country to the next: in countries such as Britain and the United States, where it is a well-known phenomenon, drivers who have suffered a rear-end collision will be that much more likely to spot the opportunity for some monetary reward. The three young men in the Royal London accident and emergency unit were a case in point. They obviously realized that they had to work out their version of events straight away and then get the victim to report the right sort of pain, even though a 'whiplash' diagnosis would require the pain to persist for some time. The number of lawyers specializing in representing such claims has grown dramatically since the 1970s. In the United States, lawyers can even attend specialist training seminars, organized by fee-hungry doctors, on how to construct a viable medical case.

Yet for the same reason that this syndrome is attractive to the fraudster, it is impossible to ever know how much fraud is really going on. Expert estimations of the rate of fraud vary wildly, between 0.1 per cent and 60 per cent, indicating the depth of the fog obscuring this issue.[3] Insurance companies are struggling to know how to cope. Some have introduced somewhat mediaeval-sounding 'Truth Statements', which accident victims and their lawyers are required to sign, to confirm the discomfort that they claim to be suffering.

Adding to the confusion is a further philosophical and cultural riddle. As even some critics of the whiplash industry will admit, it is perfectly possible that drivers in Britain or America will, on average, genuinely suffer greater long-term neck pain following a rear-end collision than those in continental Europe. An accident victim who is aware of whiplash, and its possible monetary value, will consult a doctor, wear a neck brace, take rest, recuperation and time off work, and generally act like a victim. The psychosomatic aspects of back and neck pain mean that this person may indeed find herself with long-term problems. Meanwhile, the accident victim who dusts herself off, swaps numbers with the other driver, and sets about getting her car repaired, is likely to feel far less discomfort over the long term. Observable behaviour and subjective sensation eventually bleed into each other.

The medical or neurological response to this sort of problem, encouraged by the insurance industry, is to carry on looking even harder for the physical reality of neck pain. Fraud will be eliminated once the truth of pain has been uncovered. Until that point, truth statements and the like will have to do. This assumes, as per Bentham's gambit, that accident victims experience a certain quantity of pain that could in principle be scientifically known to an observer, if only an appropriate method could be found. Such a method would likely have to focus on the body in some way. Bentham's preferred route for measuring utility – using money as a proxy for it – is ruled out on this occasion, seeing as it is precisely the pursuit of money that appears to be generating the problem in the first place.

But what if whiplash is necessarily entangled with the pursuit of monetary compensation? And what if fraud of this sort is not some unfortunate, exceptional and eradicable element of our compensation culture, but an entirely inevitable feature of how our sense of justice and injustice has been colonized by monetary calculation? Deep within the whiplash syndrome, there is the idea of equivalence between the sensations produced via the nervous system, and money. The principle states that a certain quantity of subjective feeling can be counterbalanced by an appropriate quantity of money. Admittedly, this principle may be widely abused, in some societies far more than others. But the very fact that it is impossible to know whether it is being abused, or by how much, tells us something about the absurdity of this presupposition. Maybe, instead of searching harder for the 'truth' of physical pain, we should explore if money could ever serve as some neutral, honest and mathematical representation of our feelings.

The authority of mathematics

Joseph Priestley, the man whose work had led Bentham to shout 'Eureka!' in Harper's coffee shop that day in 1766, was a strong influence over the emerging middle class of industrial England. In 1774, he helped to establish the first Unitarian church in the country, which was still an illegal religious movement at the time. Unitarians rejected the orthodox Christian belief in the Trinity of Father, Son and Holy Ghost, arguing instead for a single God. Varieties of Unitarianism had been in existence across Europe since the sixteenth century, though never politically accepted. The English practitioners had been an underground movement until Priestley formally established his church. Understandably, given the suppression they had experienced, they were avid Enlightenment optimists and campaigners who argued for freedoms of speech and religious association.

They were also scientific optimists who placed great faith in the power of mechanics and engineering to advance the progress of humanity. Popular among industrialists, this coincidence of faith with machinery was convenient. A number of Mechanics' Institutes were founded by Unitarians in the early nineteenth century, in an effort to connect engineering progress to the public good. Mathematics was viewed as especially valuable, where it helped to construct useful machinery and transform the physical world for the benefit of mankind. But it needed pushing beyond the study of the natural world or engineering and into social and political realms. It is scarcely surprising that they immediately viewed Bentham as a kindred spirit.

William Stanley Jevons was born into a Unitarian family in the outskirts of Liverpool in 1835. His father was a successful iron merchant, and the family was comfortably off. Unitarian principles dominated the family and dictated the young Jevons's education, within which mechanical devices and geometric reasoning were constantly recurring features. As a child, he played with a balancing device as a toy, and such instruments would retain a fascination for him throughout his later career.[4] He received his first introduction to economics as a nine-year-old, through the children's textbook Easy Lessons on Money Matters, authored by the Archbishop Richard Whateley, which was read to him by his mother.[5] Aged eleven, he attended the Liverpool Mechanics' Institution. Throughout this, he was taught to view mathematics as the mark of 'true' science, no matter what the object might be.

In the early 1850s, Jevons enrolled to study chemistry at Bentham's alma mater, University College London (UCL). This also gave him the chance to attend the lectures of another famous Unitarian, James Martineau, a Benthamite who taught a course on 'mental philosophy'. It was during the 1850s that a distinctive tradition of English psychology was emerging that had parallels with what Fechner was doing in Leipzig at the same time. The use of introspection, to study the inner life of the mind, gained respectability through the mid nineteenth century, especially following Alexander Bain's 1855 work, *The Senses and the Intellect*. Bentham's influence was important to this tradition too, but it was more the speculative, philosophical Bentham, who created theories of pleasure, rather than the technocratic Bentham, who wanted to actually ground politics in physical equipment. With his Unitarian and industrial background, Jevons was more naturally inclined to hard, geometric mechanics. Psychology was all very well, unless it could not be rendered mathematical.

Jevons would have remained at UCL for longer, but in 1853, with his family suffering financial difficulties, his father obliged him to accept a job in Sydney, Australia, as a gold assayer. This required the use of very finely tuned instruments and scales to test the quality and weight of gold, a practice that appealed to Jevons's mechanical sensibility. Here was a practical challenge, which involved the application of mathematics to the physical world and saw Jevons returning to his childhood hobby of using balancing devices. Not only that, but the object in question would prove to be the critical one in shaping Jevons's later intellectual career: money. It is interesting to consider that at precisely the same time as Fechner had begun his weight-lifting experiments to look at the mathematical relationship between physical objects and psychic feeling, 10,000 miles away Jevons was working with another form of weight-lifting instrument to test the monetary value of a precious metal. If the three different entities of mind, matter and money could be fixed in some mathematical relation to each other, the implications for the understanding of the market economy would be profound.

While in Australia, Jevons continued to read widely in psychology, exploring Bentham's work and discovering the writings of another English psychologist, Richard Jennings. He showed comparatively little interest in economics, which was at the time dominated by the figure of John Stuart Mill, and remained within the tradition of 'classical political economy' that had been initiated by Adam Smith in the 1770s. Classical political economists concerned themselves with weighty, material and political issues of how to increase the productive capacity of nations through free trade, division of labour, agricultural policy and population growth. They argued in favour of free markets, but principally because this was viewed as a way of increasing production. If wealth was the goal, they reasoned, then the resources that needed studying were physical ones: labour power, food, fixed capital, land. The classical economists had no discernible concern with psychological questions of feelings or happiness. As far as they were concerned, the problems of economics were ultimately those of how best to harness nature.

But while Jevons was in Australia, there were signs that the core assumptions of political economy were about to change. Jennings was a psychologist, but his 1855 work *Natural Elements of Political Economy* suggested that economists could not ignore psychology any longer. Given that labour was central to the classical economic view of capitalism, it must surely be relevant that workers suffer different levels of pain as they go through their day, which then influences how much they are able to produce.

It is often said in circumstances of boring or monotonous work that 'the last hour drags the longest'. Jennings made a similar observation, but specifically in relation to physical exertion: the longer one spends labouring on a task, the harder it gets. Fechner's observation, that weights feel heavier the longer they are held, picked up on the identical issue. Such insights spoke to an emerging concern among industrialists at the time, that workers were suffering from fatigue, and that the bourgeoisie's principal source of wealth, namely labor, was gradually becoming depleted. As the nineteenth century wore on, this worry led to an explosion of strange experiments on fatigue and possible ergonomic solutions.[6] And so it was via the subjective experience of work, as an exercise that gradually increases in painfulness, that capitalists became interested in how we think and feel for the very first time.

Jevons was drawn into reading economics, thanks to Jennings's pioneering work. In 1856 he was also drawn into a dispute over the funding of a railway in New South Wales, and his interest in economic theory was piqued further.[7] From Jevons's Unitarian perspective, economics, as passed down by Adam Smith, was not strictly speaking a science: it lacked the mechanical and mathematical rigor. But by starting from a different premise, much as Jennings had already suggested, perhaps this was a domain that was amenable to truly scientific reasoning after all. If the economy could be understood as a mathematical problem, to be solved through the attainment of quasi-mechanical balance, then economics would be placed on genuinely scientific foundations. He wrote to his sister in 1858 letting her know that he was now determined to focus on extending mathematics to the study of society. In 1859, he returned to Britain and re-joined UCL to study economics.

Markets as balancing devices

Money is an extraordinary thing which can cause psychological havoc. In some psychosomatic situations such as whiplash, it may even cause physiological havoc. The central fact about money is that it must perform two contradictory functions at once: to serve as a store of value and as a medium of exchange. When acting as a store of value, it becomes something we cherish and want to hang onto, often by placing it in a bank account. When acting as a medium of exchange, it is something that opens up infinite possibilities to attain other, much more useful and desirable things. This contradiction is manifest in the physical design of money itself, which has to combine a high level of symbolic appeal (in its insignia and shininess) and minimal level of actual physical usefulness.

Interest rates are the main way in which capitalist societies strive to balance these two functions of money. When interest rates go up, our desire to hang onto money increases accordingly; when they go down, our desire to spend it increases instead. Sometimes, we flip between viewing money as everything, and viewing it as nothing. The psychoanalyst Darian Leader has noted how money often plays a central role in the behaviour of bipolar disorder sufferers.[8] When they are manically happy, they view money in purely liquid terms, of infinite possibility, with no intrinsic worth of its own. They give it away, spend rashly, revel in the freedom it grants. When they are later depressed, they become weighed down by money's ubiquitous importance once more, only more so due to the debts and costs they ran up during their mania.

Thus one way of understanding the history of liberal economics, from Smith onwards, is as an ongoing attempt to deal with the bipolar character of money. As we all instinctively recognize, markets are places where goods or services are exchanged for money of some sort. But what we tend to overlook is how odd such an exchange actually is.

How is that a £10 note can be deemed equivalent to, say, a pizza? In order for this exchange to take place, money's dual roles as both medium of exchange (I am willing to get rid of it) and as store of value (the pizza seller is willing to accept it) have to function simultaneously. How can a piece of pure, numerical symbolism serve as equivalent to a doughy, cheesy meal, without either side feeling hard done by? For if it can't, then the market system itself becomes completely impossible, and we would end up each having to produce our own food, clothes and shelter. The constant risk is that people either value money too highly (cue hoarding and price deflation) or not highly enough (cue barter and hyper-inflation). The solution offered by economists is to invent a mysterious entity that lurks magically inside the pizza, which they term 'value'.

Often, we use the word 'value' to mean 'price', as when someone says, 'This painting is valued at £1,000'. But it's quite clear from other uses of the term 'value' that it doesn't mean price at all. If I describe the pizza as 'bad value for money', that suggests it really shouldn't have been exchanged for as much as £10. The value and price of the pizza were not, in fact, equivalent to each other, and the customer was being ripped off. The idea of value allows us to view markets as balancing devices, whose outcome should in principle be fair. By suggesting that value is a quantity like money, economists are able to show how both sides of an exchange are, ultimately, equivalent. When the market for pizzas is working correctly, they argue, ten of these pounds will buy you an equivalent quantity of value. Rather than exchange a quantity (money) for a quality (pizza), both sides of the equation can be represented in numerical terms. The market becomes imagined as a set of scales, which weigh money and value against each other, until the two are in perfect balance. What the idea of value really says is this: money itself is not the most important thing in life, but it is the perfect measure for anything that we do consider important.

So what is value? How is this ubiquitous quantity to be conceived? The classical political economists argued that the value of a good or service derives from the amount of time that has gone into making it. In this case, the pizza's real worth resides in the amount of time spent producing its various ingredients and cooking it. In principle, if markets are working fairly, the price of the pizza should be equivalent to this quantity of labour time in some way. This 'labour theory of value' dominated economics for nearly a century. By 1848, John Stuart Mill was confident enough to write that 'happily there is nothing in the laws of value which remains for the present or any future writer to clear up;

the theory of the subject is complete'.[9] But that particular version of the theory never interested Jevons.

On 19 February 1860, Jevons wrote the following entry in his diary:

At home all day and working chiefly at Economy, arriving as I suppose at a true comprehension of Value regarding which I have lately very much blundered.[10]

The book in which this 'true comprehension of Value' would be articulated, *The Theory of Political Economy*, would not appear for another decade. By then, two continental economists, Léon Walras in France and Carl Menger in Austria, had 'blundered' towards a similar discovery. In combination, these three economists unleashed a revolution within economics, eventually producing the narrower, more mathematical discipline that we recognize as economics today.

Shopping for pleasures

A number of English theorists, including Bentham, had wondered whether the mentality of consumers might actually be the decisive factor in determining the price of things. This idea even cropped up in Archbishop Whateley's children's book of economics that was read to Jevons as a child. But it took Jevons, Walras and Menger to establish this notion as the new foundation for economics. The question of value remained crucial, for how else could the market be represented as a place of fair exchange? Their novelty was to conceive of value from the perspective of the person spending the money, rather than the person producing the goods. Value would become a matter of subjective perspective.

What marks out Jevons was his determination to build such a theory directly upon the psychology of pleasure and pain. He described his project in sharply Benthamite language:

> To satisfy our wants to the utmost with the least effort – to procure the greatest amount of what is desirable at the expense of the least that is undesirable – in other words, to maximize pleasure, is the problem of economics.[11]

The centrifugal point of capitalism was being shifted. From Adam Smith through to Karl Marx, the factory and labourer were deemed to dictate the price things were sold for in the market. From 1870 onwards, all of this changed. Now it would be the inner 'wants' of the consumer where the all-important question of value would be established. From this perspective, work is simply a form of 'negative utility', the opposite of happiness, which is only endured so as to gain more money to spend on pleasurable experiences.[12] Subjective sensation, and its interaction with markets, was elevated to a central question of economics.

In keeping with his Unitarian roots, Jevons was only prepared to engage in economics if he could find a way of doing so mathematically. 'It is clear that economics, if it is to be a science at all, must be a mathematical science', he argued; 'our science must be mathematical, simply because it deals with quantities'. It's not clear that Jevons was ever particularly good at maths himself, but his prejudice in favour of such an analysis held nevertheless. Economics could be founded on a science of pleasure and pain, but only on the basis that these psychic entities also obeyed certain mathematical laws. For such a vision of economics to succeed, the mind itself would have to be treated like a calculator.

In the preface to the second edition of *The Theory of Political Economy*, Jevons expressed his regret that he had retained the term 'political economy' in the book's title and not used 'economics' in its place. The distinction is a significant one. He clearly saw his work as a new start for a more rigorous discipline than the political economists had been able to achieve. Once the correct mathematical foundations had been established, the study of the economy would be placed on new and objective foundations.

For Jevons, everything was a question of balance, gauged in terms of quantity. His fascination with the machine-like qualities of the mind made him a pioneer of the sort of cybernetic thinking that would later produce computer science. He even commissioned a Salford clockmaker to build him a primitive calculator out of wood, or what he termed his Logical Abacus, as a mechanical model for rational thought.[13] The mind resembled the toy balance he'd played with as a child, or the gold-assaying device he'd used in Sydney.

When deciding whether or not to eat a pizza, I am performing a balancing act, with the pleasures on one side and the pains on the other. How much pleasure will it give me, versus how much pain? Whichever quantity is greatest will dictate what I decide to do. As Bentham had proposed, our minds work like mathematical calculators, constantly trading off the pros against the cons.[14]

Jevons's landmark contribution was to plant this vision of a calculating hedonist firmly in the marketplace. Bentham was seeking mainly to reform government policy and punitive institutions, which acted on the public in general. But Jevons converted utilitarianism into a theory of rational consumer choice. The mechanics of the mind, where value resided, and the mechanics of the market, which generated prices, could be perfectly attuned to each other. As he suggested:

> Just as we measure gravity by its effect in the motion of a pendulum, so we may estimate the equality or inequality of feelings by the decisions of the human mind. The will is our pendulum, and its oscillations are minutely registered in the price lists of the markets.[15]

The market was a vast psychological audit, discovering and representing the desires of society.

This granted money an exceptional psychological status, as it allowed others to peer into people's private desires. Bentham had idly wondered if money might serve as a proxy through which to measure pleasure, but never quite extrapolated this into a theory of economics. Jevons was effectively turning the market into one vast mind-reading device, with prices – that is, money – as the instrument that made this possible. This being the case, money was no ordinary instrument, and economics was no ordinary science. The ideal of bringing the invisible realm of emotions and desires into the open was now bound up with the ideal of the free market.

The classical economists had studied capitalism in terms of toil, sweat and the physical produce that resulted. Jevons represented it merely as the play of fantasies and fears, rendered mathematical. This was partly an effect of historical context. Between his childhood in industrial Liverpool and his middle age spent living a comfortable scholarly existence in Hampstead, north London, industrial economies were exhibiting some profound changes, especially manifest in cities.

The world's first department store opened in Paris in 1852, introducing the experience that we now recognize as 'shopping'. Never before had products simply appeared on display, magically separated from their producer, with nothing but a price tag to represent the pain of acquiring them.[16] Nationwide rail networks meant that goods were now moving around further and faster than most people. Official bank notes or fixed prices would have been relatively uncommon in the 1830s, with many shops still maintaining their own ledgers of who owed what to whom, and at what agreed price. By the 1880s, retail culture, based upon widespread circulation of paper money and even some recognizable brands, was established. In the absence of such a culture, an economic theory founded on the premise of individual pleasure-seeking would have looked like crazed utopianism.

In short, capitalism could now be viewed as an arena of psychological experiences, in which physical things were merely props for the production of sensations, to be acquired through cash. A commodity, for Jevons, was simply anything that can 'afford pleasure, or ward off pain'.[17] Alfred Marshall, one of the giants of English economics who followed directly after Jevons, expressed this acutely:

Man cannot create material things. In the mental and moral world indeed he may produce new ideas; but when he is said to produce material things, he really only produces utilities; or in other words, his efforts and sacrifices result in changing the form or arrangement of matter to adapt it better for the satisfaction of wants.[18]

During the 1980s, it became fashionable to declare that capitalism had suddenly become based upon 'knowledge', 'intangible assets' and 'intellectual capital', following the demise of many heavy industries in the West. In truth, the economy was reconceived as a phenomenon of the mind a whole century earlier. Capitalism became oriented around consumer desire, directed by that most alluring spokesman for our silent inner feelings, money.

Measurement revisited

'I hesitate to say that men will ever have the means of measuring directly the feelings of the human heart', wrote Jevons in *The Theory of Political Economy*.[19] This must have been a difficult thing for him to admit. After all, he had made some strong claims about precisely how human beings take decisions. Like Bentham, he looked to the natural sciences in the hope that they might one day provide the empirical basis for his theory of individual choice. 'The time may come,' he suggested, 'when the tender mechanism of the brain will be traced out, and every thought reduced to the expenditure of a determinate weight of nitrogen and phosphorous.'[20] He even conducted some experiments of his own, very similar to Fechner's, in which he lifted weights to study the impact of objects on his own sensations.

For a cluster of British scholars, working between 1850–90, the challenge of psychic measurement would not be given up without a struggle. They drew on Bentham and Darwin in search of a theory of human behaviour that might confirm their largely aristocratic political prejudices, which often translated into a belief in eugenics. One of them, James Sully, had studied with the great German physicist Hermann von Helmholtz in Berlin and returned to England with the new psychophysical methods pioneered by Fechner. Another, Francis Edgeworth, became a neighbour and close friend of Jevons, through whom he was introduced to economics.[21]

Building on Jevons's example, Edgeworth pushed the case for psychic measurement even further.[22] He had high hopes for the science of feelings. We need 'to imagine an ideally perfect instrument, a psychophysical machine, continually registering the height of pleasure experienced by an individual'. Such a machine would be called a 'hedonimeter'. 'From moment to moment the hedonimeter varies,' he went on, 'the delicate index now flickering with the flutter of the passions, now steadied by intellectual activity, low sunk whole hours in the neighbourhood of zero, or momentarily springing up towards infinity'. Of course, in 1881, this was mere science fiction. Some would claim that in the twenty-first century, it is no longer so, that we are approaching the point when the inner feelings of consumers (for example, whiplash claimants) can be scientifically discerned. The more interesting question is why such a scientific fantasy has long exerted such a hold over our economic imaginations at all.

The question that Jevons was not able to answer was why, if markets are working effectively, such a science of pleasure and pain is necessary. If we can simply *assume* that individuals are broadly pursuing their own interests, and that they know how to do this, why not just let the market sort it out? Why would we also worry about how much 'nitrogen and phosphorous' is churning through their brains, or build 'hedonimeters' to represent their pleasures? For Bentham, as a public policy thinker, it was quite clear why such instruments were needed. Governments needed a science which informed them of what was the best use of their power and money. But wasn't the great advantage of the market price system that it would perform such a science of its own accord? Surely money was the measure of value, not psychology. Did economists really need to know what was going on inside people's heads?

For the economists who came immediately after Jevons, the answer was a firm 'no'. Following Jevons's death in 1888, economists began to distance themselves from his psychological theories or methods.[23] In place of Jevons's theory stating that each pleasure and pain has its own discernible quantity, a theory of preferences was introduced in its place. As economists such as Marshall and Vilfredo Pareto saw it, economists have no need to know how much pleasure a pizza gives me, but only whether I would *prefer* to have a pizza or a salad. The way I spend my money is determined by my preferences, and not by my actual subjective sensations.

Gradually economists discovered that they could say less and less about what goes on in the minds of consumers, to the point where it's enough to simply observe their use of money and assume the rest. By the 1930s, the divorce of economics from psychology was complete. Jevons would have been delighted to see how mathematical the science was becoming. But he may have been somewhat disappointed to discover that the basis for such science owed nothing to his theories of happiness. In which case, why, today, is happiness everywhere once more?

Economic imperialism

Jevons is one of the architects of what is often referred to as *homo economicus*, a somewhat miserable vision of a human being who is constantly calculating, putting prices on things, neurotically pursuing his own personal interests at every turn. *Homo economicus* doesn't have friends and doesn't relax. He is too busy looking out for number one. If he ever really existed, he would be deemed a psychopath. But of course that is partly the point – this theoretical construct doesn't actually exist. Jevons imagined the mind through *metaphors* of geometry and mechanics; he never went quite as far as suggesting that the brain is actually a physical balancing instrument.

At the end of the nineteenth century, *homo economicus* made sense as a scientific theory to help understand markets. There was never any sense that it should be applied outside of the monetary arena. The theory of utility maximization, as it was developed by Jevons et al. in the 1870s, was useful to the extent that it explained why people buy and sell things. That was all. But over the second half of the twentieth century this economic theory became increasingly expanded, until it came to serve the same broader public function that Bentham's original utilitarianism sought to achieve. What began as a theory of market exchange was gradually inflated until it became a theory of *justice*.

Consider the following example. On 24 March 1989, the Exxon Valdez oil tanker ran aground off the coast of Alaska, while carrying 55 million gallons of oil, resulting in what was then the largest oil spill in US history. Over one hundred thousand seabirds were killed, and the populations of various fish, sea otters and other wildlife were still below their previous level over twenty years later. Various reports emerged regarding the negligence of those on board, inadequate staffing, and poor equipment that might otherwise have prevented the disaster. The legal consequences of this took several years to be worked out. But beyond Exxon's liability for the cost of the clean-up, there was a broader moral question: how to punish the company for the damage they had done to a thousand miles of beautiful coastline? How to counterbalance what they'd done?

One of the answers to this question was produced by the state of Alaska. Using a technique known as a 'willingness to pay survey', a representative sample of citizens in all of the other forty-nine US states were interviewed on how much they would be 'willing to pay' for the Exxon Valdez disaster not to have taken place.[24] They were each provided with information about the extent and impact of the disaster to inform this mental calculation. The answer, so it turned out, was an average of $31 per household. Multiplied by 91 million households, this produced the calculation that Exxon owed the American public $2.8 billion. This figure was used to help calculate the final legal settlement of what Exxon had to pay as a fine.

What we witness in this sort of example is economics becoming used as a basis for broad public agreement, well beyond the limits of the marketplace. Techniques invented for the study of equilibrium in small private market exchanges are extended to deliver judgements over major public moral controversies. And think what a strange activity is at work at the heart of this: citizens scattered across America were required to close their eyes and imagine what they personally would pay in order for some distant event not to have happened. They must reach down inside themselves, in search of some number which they believe to be equivalent to the 'value' of a clean coastline. How odd it is that a technique based on wild introspection, whose veracity is entirely impossible to prove one way or the other, should attain higher authority than, say, the testimony of judges or elected officials or wildlife experts.

And yet the political authority of such techniques is growing all the time. Wherever the capacity to reach publicly acceptable agreements recedes, so the recourse to economics to settle disputes has increased. To find out whether it is worth spending money to protect beautiful landmarks, making cultural resources freely available to the public or increasing transport safety, policymakers increasingly use techniques such as 'willingness to pay surveys' to work out what the hypothetical price of those goods might be.[25] Other techniques include studying the effect of a beautiful park on local house prices, to understand the park's value in money terms. In health care, where limited resources must be spent in the best way possible, the question of 'value for money' is a constant problem. Once again, psychological introspection plays a role, with the public being surveyed to discover their numerical evaluation of cancer or blindness, despite typically having no experience of these hypothetical syndromes.

These techniques represent a fudge between a democratic worldview, which demands that the voice of the public be heard, and a Benthamite science, which states that only numbers can be trusted. The unwieldy outcome is that the public may speak, but on the condition that they adopt metrics and prices as their language. In order to have their say, they must mimic a calculator.

In the early 1990s, economics and psychology experienced something of a reunion. Data on 'well-being', drawn from surveys, began to be used by economists. New techniques for measuring 'experienced' utility (as opposed to 'reported' or 'anticipated' utility) were introduced, such as the 'day reconstruction method', in which participants try and record how they actually felt at various times during the day, or smartphone apps which prompt the user for an update on their current feelings throughout the day. Appropriately enough, one of these apps, developed at the London School of Economics, is referred to as a 'hedonimeter'.

If economists can establish precisely the link between psychological pleasure and money (through comparing the well-being of people with different incomes), and they can then study the relationship between well-being and various non-market goods (such as safety, clean air, health and so on), a series of correlations can be traced in order that a price can then be put on anything. The British government has used just such a technique to establish the monetary 'value' of art galleries and libraries: find out how much happiness these places create, and then find out how much income would be required to produce the equivalent amount of psychological benefit.[26] This enables decision-makers to put a price on public culture. The same technique has been suggested as a basis on which to calculate damages payments to those who have been victims of some intangible or emotional harm, such as the loss of a child.[27]

None of this is to say that such techniques are not useful. Spending on health care, for example, requires *some basis* on which to navigate dilemmas. Money has become the moral lingua franca through which this is now done: different health outcomes are given different monetary values by specialist health economists. But as economics is drawn into more and more public issues and moral disputes, so the psychological question of valuation becomes more problematic. In order that money and economics can stand up as viable means of dealing with public controversies, Jevons's question of how we experience pleasures and pains becomes harder to ignore.

So long as economists were only dealing with market exchanges, they were able to operate without any concern for what we felt inside. Jevons's dabblings in utilitarian psychology were not really necessary for what he was trying to achieve. It is only when economists start to spread their calculative tentacles further into public life, into the settling of moral and legal disputes, that they start to wonder what we're feeling. Outside of the market, the question returns: what is this quantity of money equivalent *to?* How much well-being is it actually delivering? Money tries to stand on its own as the measure of everything, but ultimately, given its bipolar character, always fails. And it's only for this reason – the perilous vacuity of cash – that happiness has returned as a preoccupation for economists once more.

Back to Jevons?

Jevons wondered if the 'tender mechanism of the brain' would eventually be brought to light, resolving the truth of our pleasure-seeking once and for all. Just over a century after his death, some believed that this breakthrough had arrived. Nitrogen and phosphorous were not quite as central as Jevons had guessed. Instead, the economic mechanics of the mind appeared to come down to a single brain chemical: dopamine.

The notion of a neurological 'reward system' first appeared in the 1950s, as scientists began to probe the brains of rats to see how they altered their behaviour in pursuit of pleasure.[28] The very idea of such a system has clear echoes of the psychological theories as proffered by Bentham and Jevons. It implies that animals are governed by pleasures and pains, repeating the actions which reward them, and avoiding those which punish them. Only now, there is no longer any need for metaphors of balancing devices, along the lines entertained by Jevons – the real biological substrate of our calculated hedonism is allegedly being revealed.

In the early 1980s, it was discovered that dopamine is released in our brains as the 'reward' for a good decision. To economists, this posed an enticing question: could value in fact be a real, chemical substance, varying in quantity, inside our brains?[29] When I decide to spend £10 on a pizza, might this actually be because I will receive an *exactly equivalent* quantity of dopamine, by way of reward? Some perfect balance is imagined, with cash on one side of the scales, and a commensurate dose of neuro-chemical on the other. Perhaps it might be possible to identify the exchange rate through which these dollars-for-dopamine trades are undertaken.

Elsewhere, neuroscientists believe they have identified the precise region of the brain, the nucleus accumbens, which triggers decisions to buy a product. Confirming the theory of psychology as a balancing act, one paper claims to have located the specific neural circuits which deal with pleasure and price respectively, the scales, as it were, on which every consumer decision depends.[30] For the more optimistic disciples of Jevons, this is the brave new world that is dawning today.

Common sense suggests that these are absurd propositions. The sheer unlikeliness that the brain would 'naturally' operate according to principles first developed by economists in the 1860s seems overwhelming. Why would anyone believe that, in our fundamental biological nature, we operate like accounting machines? The answer to that question is simple: to rescue the discipline of economics and, with it, the moral authority of money.

After 2008, which witnessed the largest financial crisis since 1929 leading to the longest recession since the 1880s, this was the terrain in which a large number of apparently intelligent people believed political economy should be debated. Peering inside the brain would reveal what exactly had gone wrong. Thus it was not the strategic lobbying of banks against financial regulation from the 1980s onwards that was to blame. Nor was it the revolving door between the White House and Goldman Sachs. Neither was it the fact that investment banks were able to bribe credit-rating agencies into praising financial products that were full of junk. No. The problem that had struck the financial world was one of *the wrong kinds of neurochemicals*.

Explanations were legion. There were too many men in Wall Street, driven by too much testosterone![31] Too many of the bankers were high on cocaine, which led to dopamine being released when it shouldn't have been![32] Bankers had simply forgotten about the biological flaws in their brains, which led them to be overconfident at the wrong moment (blame cavemen for not having evolved out of that one). They were victims of evolutionary malfunctions.[33] In response, traders have discovered meditation practices as ways of trying to calm themselves to a state of better-calculated risk-taking. A medicine is offered by the company truBrain, a neurosupplement developed on the basis of EEG brain scans run on traders while trading, which promises better decision-making in the market. Some are simply fortunate to be endowed with brains that 'tip them off' when a financial bubble is about to burst.[34]

The neuroeconomic prejudice is that the mechanical, mathematical view of the mind ought ultimately to be correct. Of course there are anomalies, when neurochemicals are produced in the wrong quantity, or at the wrong time. But by tracing when these occur and building them into our calculations, the mind can be relied upon to perform its balancing act once more. The truth is that whenever policy-makers, economists or business leaders start to dabble in the neuropsychology of reward or incentives or dopamine, their agenda is really a different one altogether: to ensure that money retains its privileged position as the measure of all value.

A financial crisis represents an acute threat to the public status of money, raising the urgency of placing 'value' on firm foundations. The brain is simply the latest locus for these foundations, in a history that snakes back to the 1860s. Much of our interest in pleasure and happiness today derives from a tradition of economics that only requires sufficient theory of the mind, as is required by a free market economy. To suggest that such theories can be divorced from that political and cultural context is like trying to understand a set of kitchen scales without any understanding of what cooking involves. When the three young men in the Royal London Hospital recognized that neck pain equals compensation payout, they were simply exploiting an idea that is integral to our contemporary trust in markets. Unless the idea of fairness can be disentangled from the notion of 'value for money', with all of the psychological questions that the notion poses, philosophical quandaries such as whiplash will proliferate.

Markets are one context in which such ideas have been developed in the broader service of capitalism. But they are far from being the only one. Other economic and political institutions require quite different ways of imagining and measuring our pleasures and well-being. After economists shut the door on psychology during the 1890s, psychologists were free to engage in economic activity on their own terms, with their own paymasters. Different metaphors and assumptions about our minds came into play, with their own implications for how capitalism would develop. Our current preoccupation with quantities of inner happiness is as much a legacy of these, as it is of Jevons and those who followed him.

3

In the Mood to Buy

A sheet of metal with two square holes cut into it lies on a table-top, with a piece of rope attached to it. At the end of the rope, dangling from the table, there is an iron weight. At a given moment, a lever will be pulled, releasing the sheet of metal, which is then pulled violently across the tabletop by the weight. As it moves, the square holes quickly pass over an image drawn on the tabletop below, revealing it to an observer for a split second, and then concealing it again. The observer calculates precisely how long the image was revealed and makes a record of what impression, if any, it made on the eye.

This is how 'tachistoscopes' worked in Germany in the 1850s.[1] At the time, they were used by physiologists researching human vision. Optical research examined various aspects of seeing, including light, depth perception, afterimages and how a pair of eyes constructed the image in three dimensions. The eye was to be probed and tested in search of different responses.

Today's equivalent of a tachistoscope can operate, relatively cheaply, via an ordinary computer webcam. The movement of the eye can be tracked, as can the dilation of the pupil. The length of time that the eye settles on a particular image, or part of an image, can be timed to the nearest millisecond. Private companies, with names like Affectiva and Realeyes, deliver commercial services to clients wanting to know how to win and keep the attention of their audiences. These techniques often operate within more extensive face-scanning programmes, which promise to unlock the secrets of our emotional states. Face-scanning technology is spreading into everyday situations, such as supermarkets and bus stops, to help tailor messages appropriately for individuals. Of course, these twenty-first-century tachistoscopes are not being employed for purely scientific purposes. More often than not, eye tracking of this sort is done in the service of market research and targeted advertising.

Since the late 1990s, market researchers have become increasingly fixated upon our eyes and faces for tell-tale signs of what we might buy. Underlying this has been a growing belief that consumption is driven primarily by emotions. A 1994 book by the Portuguese American neuroscientist Antonio Damasio, entitled *Descartes' Error*, exerted a profound influence across the advertising and market research industries. On the basis of brain scans, Damasio argued that rationality and emotion are not alternative or opposing functions of the brain, but on the contrary, that emotions are a condition of behaving in a rational way. For example, individuals who'd suffered brain damage hampering their emotional capacities were also discovered to be incapable of taking more calculated, rational decisions.

Damasio is now spoken of in hushed tones as the forefather of a mini-enlightenment in marketing theory and science. Gradually at first, but gaining momentum with the arrival of Malcolm Gladwell's 2005 book *Blink*, every leading advertising and market research guru has come to view the emotional aspects of the mind and brain as the target for their ad campaigns and research. This has yielded such dubious legacies as neuromarketing and scent logos. Psychologists such as Jonathan Haidt push this further, to analyse the emotional underpinnings of moral and political choices.[2]

In a way, this sounds a little surprising. We have long known that advertisers target our unconscious desires and insecurities in their efforts to get us to buy their products. It was in 1957 that *The Hidden Persuaders* first claimed to pull back the curtain and reveal the manipulations and tricks that the ad-men were practicing on us. Perhaps it's just that advertising theory is unusually fad-based, and emotions are back 'in' again right now but will soon be usurped by another concept. There is also the fact that advertisers have long resisted the portrayal of them as 'hidden persuaders', insisting that it is impossible to get someone to buy something he doesn't 'really' want. What's new?

To many market researchers, the dawn of neuroscience has fundamentally changed things. According to the more optimistic among them, scientists are close to discovering the brain's 'buy button', that specific area of mushy grey matter that triggers us to put an item in our shopping basket.[3] The neuroscience of emotions potentially means that advertisers are no longer faced with a choice between thinking creatively and thinking scientifically: they can identify what forms of image, sound and smell produce emotional attachments to specific brands. Add to this advances in the computerized coding of eye movement and facial muscles, and you have the apparatus to really know what people are feeling. Some are using hormonal testing, to add to the mix.

So much technological progress has led to a surge of scientific exuberance in the market research community. Discovering whether or not an advertisement actually works in targeting a specific emotion and, with it, the propensity to buy something, is now a real possibility. An objective, quantitative science of desire seems feasible.

Various new findings are emerging as a result. The South African advertising guru Erik du Plessis has convinced many businesses – most crucially, Facebook – that whether or not we 'like' something exerts the greatest emotional influence over what we will then do.[4] Another study has shown that fear is what drives people to buy products from big-name brands.[5] Brian Knutson, a Stanford neuroscientist, has discovered that most of the pleasure associated with buying something occurs during the anticipation of receiving it, and has advised companies to structure their sales practices accordingly.[6] Ways of reducing the 'pain' of the price tag – such as minimizing the number of syllables in the price when spoken – are also explored.[7] The psychological pain of spending money is reduced when the customer uses a credit card than when they pay with cash.[8]

Positive psychologists and happiness economists make a great play of the fact that money and material possessions don't lead to an increase in our mental well-being. But these experts are in a minority, compared to the vast assemblage of consumer psychologists, consumer neuroscientists and market researchers all dedicated to ensuring that we do achieve some degree of emotional satisfaction by spending money.

Less and less about our shopping habits is being left to chance. Advertisers will still swear that the 'hidden persuaders' image of them is inaccurate and unfair. After all, the emotions being targeted, generated and researched are not 'fake' in any way. This is not about lying to people. On the contrary, emotion has become the market research industry's preferred version of happiness or pleasure, as they existed for Bentham and his followers. It is the solid neural, chemical or psychological reality which underpins everything else that we experience or think is going on. Most importantly, it is what leads us to get our credit cards out of our pockets. But in a way that Jevons might have respected, we don't do so under the influence of lies or advertising ideology, but because we really will receive a quantity of positive feelings as a result. That, at least, is the claim.

As market research becomes increasingly swept up in this scientific exuberance, a number of questions are going unanswered. What precisely is an emotion anyway? It is all very well saying that it is a visible occurrence in the brain, but that doesn't help us understand what we mean by the term, or by specific words such as 'anxiety', 'joy', 'fear', 'happiness', 'hate', 'like' and so on. It is difficult to imagine how one would explain or describe these occurrences to someone who had never experienced them, no matter how good one's instruments of detection were.

Furthermore, it is deeply unclear within this new neuro-industrial complex where precisely agency lies. Are consumers considered to be sovereign, autonomous beings, whose emotions are constitutive of their free will and personality? Or are they passive vessels, who get emotionally buffeted by the images, sounds and smells that come before them? Marketers would hesitate to declare the latter, and yet their methods are scarcely compatible with the former view either. Maybe they don't really know. Accrediting decision-making to the brain is the preferred way of ducking this philosophical dilemma.

While the scanning technology that promises to unlock the secrets of our feelings is dazzlingly new, the philosophical and ethical questions that result from it are quite old. This points us to a recurring pattern within psychological research that dates back to those first optical tachistoscopes of the 1850s, and it concerns the mesmerizing lure of mind-reading technologies. With every wave of new methods and instruments for scanning the thought processes or sensations of others, so there occurs a resultant belief that hard science has ousted philosophy and ethics once and for all. At the same time, there is always the hope that it is possible to understand another human being without talking to them.

But on each occasion, there is still some residual vision of what freedom and consciousness really mean that escapes scientific validation. When psychologists, neuroscientists or market researchers claim to have liberated their discipline from moral or philosophical considerations once and for all, the question has to be posed – so where do you get your understanding of humanity from, including its various emotional states, drives and moods? From your own intuition? And what feeds that?

In the years since those first tachistoscopes were introduced, the answer has become increasingly plain. The residual notion of freedom that structures how this science progresses is the freedom to shop. If that is the case then contemporary neuro-marketing and facial coding might rightly be accused of being a circular venture. What they discover in the synapses of our brains and the flickering of our eyes is not raw data, to be injected afresh into advertising designs, but is unavoidably interpreted through a consumerist philosophy.

Therefore we need to examine the history of psychology and the history of consumerism as intertwined projects. Technology is absolutely integral to this entanglement. It is thanks to technical methods and instruments, from the tachistoscope onwards, that psychology can claim to be its own objective science in the first place. The seductive power of such instruments has allowed certain individuals to declare that philosophy and ethics are no longer needed. It is here that much of the Benthamite promise of a scientific politics has been channelled, a politics in which hard expertise over the feelings of others replaces the messiness and ambiguity of dialogue. But behind this version is not national government in pursuit of a public interest, rather a corporation in pursuit of a private one.

Between philosophy and the body

In 1879, a former physiologist and occasional philosopher named Wilhelm Wundt declared that a certain part of his office at Leipzig University had become off limits. Henceforth, it would be used for carrying out experiments, not unlike the ones he'd helped arrange when working as an assistant to the great German physicist Hermann von Helmholtz in Heidelberg during the 1860s. He'd also practised physiological experiments on human muscles while training to be a doctor. Wundt was never short of self-confidence, and at one point promised to reveal the truth of muscular reflex once and for all.

But Wundt also had philosophical ambitions, which he didn't intend to relinquish entirely for the sake of the natural sciences. He was convinced that, while mental processes could occur spontaneously, they also occurred at a certain 'speed', which could in principle be measured. The purpose of his new experimental space was to explore such philosophical questions, using techniques and instruments that he'd picked up from the physical sciences. Human subjects would be used, just as they had been when he was testing muscular responses.

That sealed-off area of Wundt's office is now recognized as the world's first-ever psychology laboratory. The physical delineation of the laboratory was highly symbolic, resulting in a disciplinary separation of psychology from the areas of theory and science on which it had previously been dependent. Forms of psychological research had been conducted across Europe since the early nineteenth century, often including elements of experimentation, as exemplified by Fechner's weight lifting. But these were conducted from within physiological and/or philosophical traditions of enquiry, and were typically carried out by researchers upon themselves, meaning they relied on introspection for their data. Wundt's achievement was to distinguish psychology as a discipline of its own, potentially separate from both physiology and philosophy.

In doing this, he made a statement with profound and far-reaching implications for how we understand ourselves and others. What Wundt effectively implied was that the psyche hovers in its own specific domain, between the realm of natural biology and that of philosophical ideas. Bentham had established a sharp binary opposition between the matters of 'reality' (for which read natural science) and those of nonsensical 'fiction' (for which read metaphysics). Wundt was adding a third option: a form of reality which we can acquire knowledge of but isn't reducible to the laws of nature. This includes the various categories that we recognize as 'psychological' today: 'mood', 'attitude', 'morale', 'personality', 'emotion', 'intelligence' and so on.

How could these apparently intangible, conceptual entities become an object of scientific investigation? Wundt was keen to avoid resorting to introspection of the sort that many English psychologists had used during the 1850s and 1860s. The purpose of the laboratory was to study mental processes in a more objective fashion than that. He and his assistants built various tools to test the response of experimental subjects to different stimuli. They also borrowed various instruments from physiology and physics labs to time neural reflexes. And they built their own version of a tachistoscope, which was used to time how long it took to get a person's attention. The eyes were a crucial area of study for the pioneering psychologists, but not merely in a physiological sense. Now they provided a glimpse of thinking itself.

Much of what went on in Wundt's lab would have appeared very similar to what was going on in physiological experiments on the body. Pulse rate and blood pressure were among the measurable indicators of inner emotional states. One of the key differences – which also distinguishes this early psychological research from what would come later – was that the subjects being experimented on were scholarly associates and students of Wundt. They were fully aware of what the experiments were seeking to test and contributed their own subjective insights to the findings.

The perspective of the experimental subject was important here, and there was no sense in which they were being manipulated. Conscious thought processes needed to be respected in their own right and not reduced to naturalistic questions of cause and effect. For instance, the speed of conscious reaction (when the subject became aware of something) could be compared to the speed of unconscious reaction (when the physical reflex occurred). Wundt's challenge was to avoid collapsing his research back into physiology, but also to avoid idle, untestable philosophical speculation. In truth, he was combining an element of both in the hope of achieving more than the sum of those two parts.

As the aesthetic theorist Jonathan Crary has argued, Wundt's focus upon the eyes and attention was indicative of a profound philosophical shift that was underway during the late nineteenth century.[9] The conditions of subjective experience, which had been matters of philosophical speculation since the seventeenth century, were gradually being rendered bodily, and therefore visible to the expert eye. Wundt did not dispense with the philosophical notion of 'consciousness', but he was happy to elide it with that of 'field of vision'. In doing so, the shift from a conceptual language to a scientific one was accelerated. The capacity to experience the outside world was no longer something God-given, lying invisibly within all human beings, but a function of the human body. As such, it could be seen, tested, known and influenced.

Despite the symbolic separation of the psychology lab from his office, Wundt himself never achieved an entirely clear delineation of psychological research. In Germany, psychology remained closely associated with philosophy right up until the First World War. In the early twentieth century, in the final years of his career, Wundt drifted back into philosophy, but also into the terrain of sociology. Zigzagging his way between methods he'd picked up from physical research, and metaphysical questions of consciousness, Wundt nevertheless produced some important psychological theories.

He identified three different measurable ways in which the emotions can vary: pleasure–displeasure, tension–composure, excitement–composure.[10] This may sound crude, but already the contrast between the mental insights of psychology and those of economics was becoming pronounced. According to Wundt, our instinctive emotional responses to things are critical in determining the choices we make. Human beings are far more complicated than mere calculators of pleasure, and the dawn of psychological experimentation revealed how.

In extending experimental instruments beyond the study of the human body and into terrain previously dominated by philosophers, Wundt's place in history was guaranteed. Many philosophers and economists merely fantasized about instruments capable of measuring thought, but Wundt actually built and used them. The path he carved between physiology and philosophy was only possible thanks to this new equipment and the authority he claimed for himself in applying it to the study of other minds. Today, neuroscience might appear to be bringing the Wundt project to a close: we no longer need to access the mind via the eyes or any other part of the body, but believe we can go direct to the brain. The very idea of the mind, as a knowable yet immaterial entity, is, as a result, in question.

Yet there is also an underlying intellectual honesty in Wundt's approach. He never claimed to be escaping profound philosophical dilemmas; the mind was not reducible to the body, but nor was it entirely separate from it either. Thinking and consciousness exert their own influence over how we act and the symptoms our bodies display. Our free will is not an illusion. For this reason, Wundt refused to purge psychology of philosophical language, much to the chagrin of one particular group of his students.

Migrating methods

Wundt's lab turned him into an academic celebrity. It made him an object of fascination for visitors to Leipzig and an appealing patron for ambitious young scholars. Numerous graduate students flocked to work with Wundt, and he oversaw the completion of an astonishing 187 doctoral research projects over the course of his career. Over the 1880s and 1890s, Leipzig was the focal point for anyone interested in the emerging discipline of experimental psychology.

These scientific developments in Germany coincided with the most transformative period in American history. Between 1860 and 1890, the population of the United States trebled, due to an influx of immigrants, largely into cities. The end of the Civil War saw a large population of African Americans migrate from the former slave states to the rapidly industrializing cities of the North-east and Midwest. Coinciding with this was an unprecedented wave of business mergers, leading to the creation of what we now recognize as the modern corporation. This in turn required that a new cadre of professional managers be produced to oversee these huge enterprises.

In a relatively short space of time, America went from being a largely agrarian economy of Anglo-Saxon small landowners (still romanticized by many conservatives today), to being an urban, industrial economy, driven by large, professionally managed businesses, which sucked in labour from impoverished parts of Europe at great speed. The identity crisis this caused in a society that had been founded on the basis of local, democratic participation among landowners and slave-owners was profound.

A further development during this period was the foundation of a number of new American universities, including Cornell, Chicago and Johns Hopkins. Right from the beginning, many of these institutions had close relationships with the business world, which became closer still as the century wore on, and the wealth and benefaction of corporations increased. To support the emerging managerial class, the world's first business school, Wharton Pennsylvania, was established in 1881. With the scale of domestic markets growing, thanks to the spread of railroads across the United States, businesses were increasingly hungry for knowledge they could use, especially regarding consumers.[11]

Some crude market research techniques were in existence by the 1860s, including newspaper straw polls and primitive survey techniques, plus a few advertising agencies had already been established. There were even some basic theories of consumer behaviour, borrowed largely from economics. But this was all clumsy stuff.

Who would teach in all of these new universities? Where would they acquire their expertise? German universities were also growing rapidly during this period and offered a crucial source of scientific training for a new generation of American scholars. Between the middle of the nineteenth century and the First World War, fifty thousand Americans travelled to Germany and Austria to undertake university degrees and research training to bring back to the United States.[12] This represents one of the biggest exports of intellectual capital in history, especially in areas such as chemistry, physiology and the new field of psychology.

Among this number was a collection of relatively junior American psychologists, eager to discover more about the celebrated goings-on in Wundt's laboratory. They included William James, the godfather of American psychology and brother of the novelist, Henry; Walter Dill Scott and Harlow Gale, the first psychological theorists of advertising; James McKeen Cattell, who went on to become an influential figure in New York's Madison Avenue advertising industry; and G. Stanley Hall, later founder of the *American Journal of Psychology*, who bequeathed us the term 'morale'.

The period spent by these Americans in Germany was not an altogether happy one. William James had initially struck up a long-distance relationship with Wundt, but on arrival in Leipzig became increasingly contemptuous of Wundt's continuing metaphysical language, which he deemed unscientific and mystical. Hall was even more horrified by all of the philosophical jargon and soon dropped out to return home. There is some indication that the low level animosity between the visitors and their host was mutual. Wundt complained that the Americans were basically economists, who assumed that human beings were slaves to external incentives, and not actually possessing free will at all. He described McKeen Cattell as 'typically American', which was not intended as a compliment.

What did impress James and his cohort, however, was the technology that Wundt had assembled. They looked in awe at the finely tuned tachistoscopes and other timing devices which Wundt put to work in his laboratory. They studied the physical layout of the lab itself and drew careful diagrams of its arrangement. Much of the intellectual narrative accompanying these instruments was left well alone, but the devices and space were an inspiration. Much of it was copied directly once the American visitors returned home; indeed the first psychology labs at Harvard, Cornell, Chicago, Clark, Berkeley and Stanford all clearly betrayed the influence of Wundt.[13] In addition to copying the floor plan and many of the instruments, they even tempted some of Wundt's students across the Atlantic: James persuaded Hugo Munsterberg to migrate to the United States, where he established the first psychology lab at Harvard and went on to become a prominent figure in the field of industrial psychology.

'What do they want, these English psychologists?' Friedrich Nietzsche had mused in his 1887 work, *The Genealogy of Morals*. The question was intended for the Benthamites and Darwinists of his day, such as Sully, Jevons and Edgeworth. *Why* were they so obsessed with understanding fluctuations in pleasure? If the same question had been put to their American contemporaries, as they feverishly hunted down new methods and designs to bring back from Germany, the answer would have been much easier to divine. Crudely put, they wanted to provide a set of tools for managers.

American psychology had no philosophical heritage. It was born into a world of big business and rapid social change, which risked spiralling out of control. If it couldn't offer to alleviate the problems that were afflicting American industry and society, then it had no reason to exist at all. That, at any rate, was the view expressed by leaders of the new league of universities, who were eager to please their corporate benefactors. In the early twentieth century, psychology made an explicit pitch to act as the 'master science' through which the American dream might yet be rescued.[14] If individual decision-making itself could be reduced to a hard science, with quasi-natural laws and statistics, then it might still be possible for a multinational, multi-ethnic, industrial, mass society to function, while still upholding the core Enlightenment principle of liberty on which the republic had been founded.

The journey time between the founding of American psychology and its application to business problems was extremely short. If we date modern psychology back to that moment in 1879, when Wundt drew a symbolic line around his laboratory, it was only another twenty years before the field of *consumer* psychology emerged. By 1900, James McKeen Cattell and Harlow Gale had returned from Leipzig and were carrying out their own experiments with tachistoscopes, specifically to understand how individuals responded to different advertisements. Using Wundt's tools, they hoped to understand not only consumer reactions to different advertisements, but also their emotions. Publishing in 1903 and 1908 respectively, Walter Dill Scott produced the first two classic works of advertising theory, *The Theory of Advertising* and *The Psychology of Advertising*. Cattell later established The Psychological Corporation, a business consultancy tailoring academic research for clients, after he was dismissed from Columbia University in 1917 due to his opposition to the draft.

None of this would have been possible without Wundt, but these former students were less than loyal to his legacy. With the entry of America into the First World War, anti-German sentiment saw many American psychologists attempt to scrub the Leipzig chapter from their history.[15] They believed that they had put Wundt and his metaphysics behind them, and the road ahead was purely scientific. It was never a coincidence that this was precisely what American business wanted to hear. Shortly before his death, William James expressed some regrets at quite how anti-philosophical American psychology had become. He worried that the mysteries and spontaneity of the mind risked being obscured by so much emphasis on observation and measurement, especially where it was in the service of business. But, by that standard, things were about to get a whole lot worse.

Is it possible to study and understand human beings, without allowing abstract concepts such as 'the will' or 'experience' to enter one's assessment? Can they be understood, without letting them speak for themselves? Clutching their various measurement devices and timing gauges, many of the first generation of American psychologists may have hoped that the answer to these questions was 'yes'. But some ambivalence remained. They may have moved well away from either philosophy or introspection, but the objects of their study, such as attention and emotion, were still somewhat abstract, and presumed something innately human. There was still a more radical option that they hadn't considered. What if psychologists were to try and forget that they were studying human beings altogether?

The invention of human behaviour

In 1913, an animal psychologist named John B. Watson gave a lecture at Columbia University, which would serve as a manifesto for one of the most influential scientific traditions of the twentieth century: behaviourism. Watson was making a clear pitch for its and his supremacy, not only within American psychology, but in the various areas of policy and management which it was seeking to shape.[16] 'If psychology would follow the plan I suggest, the educator, the physician, the jurist and the businessman could utilize our data in a practical way, as soon as we are able, experimentally, to obtain them'. A more explicit offer of scholarly complicity with power is harder to imagine.

Within two years of the Columbia address, Watson had become president of the American Psychological Association. The remarkable thing is that by this stage he had never even studied a single human being. If the purpose of American psychology was to take Wundt's methods and then get rid of all the metaphysical jargon, elevating a man whose only scientific experiments had been on white rats to the most prestigious position in the discipline was a stroke of genius.

In the early twenty-first century, the term 'behaviour' is everywhere. 'Behaviour change' preoccupies policy-makers, in their efforts to combat obesity, environmental degradation and civic disengagement. 'Health behaviours' regarding nutrition and exercise allegedly hold the key to controlling spiralling health-care budgets. 'Behavioural economics' and 'behavioural finance' indicate the ways in which people miscalculate the optimal use of their time and money, as popularized in the best-selling *Nudge*, whose two authors advise presidents around the world. We are encouraged to learn tricks to alter our own 'behaviour' (or 'nudge ourselves', as some experts put it), to help us pursue more active, resilient lifestyles.[17]

In 2010, the British government opened a 'Behavioural Insights Unit' to bring such findings into policy-making. This unit has been so successful that in 2013 it was part-privatized to enable it to offer commercial consultancy to governments around the world. In 2014, a $17 million gift from the Pershing Square family philanthropic trust led to the launch of the Harvard Foundations of Human Behavior Initiative, aimed at pushing the science of behaviour to the next level. Brain sciences occupy the current frontier for the investigation of what *really* leads us to behave as we do.

Contained within each of these policy projects is a single ideal: that individual activity might be diverted towards goals selected by elite powers, but without either naked coercion or democratic deliberation. Behaviourism stretches Bentham's dream of a scientific politics to its limit, imagining that beneath the illusion of individual freedom lie the cold mechanics of cause and effect, observable only to the expert eye. When we put our faith in 'behavioural' solutions, we withdraw it from democratic ones to an equal and opposite extent.

Until the 1920s, however, the term 'behaviour' would have been scarcely associated with people at all. It would have made perfect sense to talk of the behaviour of a plant or an animal. Doctors might have used the term to refer to the behaviour of a particular body part or organ.[18] This tells us something important about contemporary appeals to 'behavioural science'. When this category is being invoked, there is no specific recognition that the behaviour in question is displayed by a person, as opposed to anything else that reacts to stimuli. The behaviourist believes that observation can tell us everything we need to know, while interpretation or understanding of actions or choices can be sidestepped altogether.

This was exactly why Watson believed the concept held such huge promise for psychology, if it was serious about becoming a science. In 1917 (by which point he had finally made the switch to the study of human subjects) he made his position brutally clear:

The reader will find no discussion of consciousness and no reference to such terms as sensation, perception, attention, will, image and the like. These terms are in good repute, but I have found that I can get along without them both in carrying out investigations and in presenting psychology as a system to my students. I frankly do not know what they mean.[19]

This was not merely anti-philosophical. It was virtually anti-psychological, at least in the sense that we typically understand psychology. His rubbishing of abstract mental concepts – 'sensation, perception . . .' – has strong echoes of Bentham. But Bentham didn't have a psychology lab and couldn't progress without a little speculation regarding the nature of human motives. Watson was calling his colleagues' bluff: if you really want to be a proper science, cleansed of metaphysics, then you have to give up everything that can't be observed scientifically. The search for hard, objective *reality* of the psyche would now be the exclusive preserve of specialists, with specialist equipment.

Watson revelled in provocation. He declared that 'thinking' was no less observable an activity than baseball, scoffing at the privilege that philosophers attached to subjective experience. He famously proclaimed that, since there was no such thing as 'personality' or 'innate' ability, he could take a child from any background and turn him into a successful businessman or sportsman, purely through conditioning. Humans were like white rats, which responded to their environment and whatever stimuli came their way. Our actions could not be scientifically attributed to us, as free-thinking, autonomous persons; rather they could only be explained in terms of other aspects of our environment or previous environmental factors that have trained us to behave that way.

There is something subtly seductive about this vision, which may account for its enduring popularity in spite of its technocratic ideal. 'Nudging' has been criticized on grounds of 'paternalism', but of course paternalism can also be comforting. The sense that someone else is taking the important decisions, that we have been relieved of full responsibility for our actions, can come as a relief. To learn that I'm 'hard-wired' or conditioned to take certain decisions may represent a welcome break from the constant modern demand to exercise free will. If our actions are shaped by our environment, nature or upbringing, at least we're part of some larger collective, even if it is only visible to experts. The problem is that we often have little idea what those experts want.

Watson's appearance on the academic stage prefigured a bonfire of metaphysical language. The science of behaviour would either dominate all rival areas of scholarly expertise (such as sociology, management, public policy) or simply destroy them altogether (the fate intended for philosophy). Was this really intellectual progress of any sort? Only if the natural sciences are viewed as the sole model for sensible and honest debate. And implicit in Watson's agenda was an even greater reverence for the capabilities of technology than even his forbears had displayed, following their return from Leipzig.

What he was effectively promising was this: using exceptional powers of experimentation, the psychological observer will reveal *everything* that can be known about human beings, and all other claims (such as those made by the person being studied) are entirely irrelevant. In that sense, behaviourism was only possible if the practice of psychology was re-founded on a fundamental power imbalance, between the status of the psychologist and that of the ordinary layperson.

In Watson's hands, psychology would become a tool of expert manipulation. Wundt had assumed that it was more revealing to experiment on subjects who understood what was being tested. This was why he conducted experiments on his own students and associates: they could contribute informed insights to the research. Watson assumed the opposite. To discover how the human animal responded to different stimuli, and might be re-programmed to respond differently, it was far more revealing to use subjects who were entirely ignorant of what was being tested and how. This would also ensure that psychology could deliver on its promise of practical utility, in the hands of marketers, policy-makers and managers. If psychology were to help keep the sprawling, complex mass of American society under some sort of control, it was no use acquiring insights from studies that were only valid in relation to the behaviour of other psychologists.

For these reasons, behaviourism runs inevitably into problems of research ethics. It is not just that behavioural experiments seek to manipulate; they also work through a modicum of deception. Even where informed consent is used, the subjects must remain partly ignorant of exactly what is being tested, or else there is the fear that they might adjust their behaviour accordingly. The goal is to minimize conscious understanding of what is going on.

Nevertheless – if one can still be bothered to think this way – a familiar philosophical contradiction arises once more. Is the autonomous, critical, conscious mind *really* eliminated from this psychological science? Within the behaviourist worldview, the general public are not unlike white rats, whose inner thought processes are effectively non-existent, until they become observable in some way. But the thoughts of the psychologist are far from irrelevant and are communicated via academic articles, lectures, books, policy reports and conversations. Behaviourism only succeeds in eliminating all forms of 'theory' or interpretation, to the extent that it privileges the perspective of one single scientific discipline and profession, and trashes all others. In that respect, the eradication of metaphysics can only succeed as a tangible, political project, in which the vast majority of people have no legitimate view (be it scientific or otherwise) to be taken into account.

The buying animal

Behaviourism was ready-made for clients in the government and private sector. It didn't take much to help it spread to Madison Avenue and beyond, although the journey was accelerated by an event of professional disgrace. In the period after World War One, Watson was a highly celebrated academic at Johns Hopkins University, winning large research grants and pay rises. But in

1920, it emerged that he'd been having an affair with a young graduate student and assistant, Rosalie Rayner.[20] Unfortunately for him, the Rayners were a revered Maryland family, who had made generous donations to Johns Hopkins. News of the affair spread fast, making national newspapers, which even published a letter between Watson and Rayner.

Given the somewhat nihilistic view of human nature that underpinned Watson's research agenda, some observers could not help but make a connection. His colleague, Adolf Meyer, who would later exert a powerful influence over the American psychiatric profession, was of this view:

> I cannot help seeing in the whole matter a practical illustration of the lack of responsibility to have a definite philosophy, the implications of not recognising meanings, the emphasis on the emancipation of science from ethics.[21]

Watson, evidently, had failed to avoid 'responding' to the physical 'stimulus' represented by Rosalie Rayner, but behaviourism did not cut it as a defence. Johns Hopkins forced him out, and he left Baltimore for New York.

By 1920, the advertising industry was fully alert to the potential riches offered by psychology. At the forefront of this movement was the Madison Avenue firm J. Walter Thompson (JWT), whose president at the time, Stanley Resor, pledged to turn his business into a 'university of advertising'. 'Scientific advertising' was all the rage. Resor was especially bullish about the emerging possibilities. 'Advertising', he argued, 'is educational work, mass education'. The great advertising campaigns of the future would send messages directly to their passive recipients, who would respond accordingly in their shopping habits.

What this new 'university' needed were the scientists to provide them with the data on how to do this.

Resor was specifically seeking someone who could advise them on the psychology of 'appeal', believing that successful ads triggered that particular emotional response. Perhaps recognizing that he needed a scholar of flexible morals, he initially contacted another recently disgraced academic, William I. Thomas, who had been kicked out of the University of Chicago sociology department for his own extramarital affair. Thomas viewed Madison Avenue as too grubby a business, so he passed them on to Watson, a personal friend of his. Resor had found his man.

That same year, Watson joined JWT as an account executive, on a salary four times what he was earning at Johns Hopkins. As part of the new position, he had to undergo some training, including travelling the backwaters of Tennessee, trying to sell coffee, and working several months behind the counter at Macy's in New York. With that out of the way, he was free to start applying his behaviourist doctrines to the design of advertising campaigns, and advising his JWT colleagues on how to trigger the right responses.

The most crucial thing for advertisers to remember, Watson implored his colleagues, was that they are not selling a product at all, but seeking to produce a psychological response. The product is simply a vehicle with which to do this, along with the advertising campaign. Consumers can be conditioned to do anything if the environmental factors are designed in the right way. Don't appeal to the consumer's existing emotions and desires, Watson urged, but *trigger new ones*. As part of a contract with Johnson & Johnson, he explored ways of marketing washing powder in terms of the emotions experienced by mothers, such as anxiety, fear and the desire for purity. He is also credited with identifying celebrity endorsements as an effective route to achieving consumer attachments to brands.

These were exactly the sort of messages and methods that Resor was hoping to receive. In 1924, Watson was made a vice president of JWT. Looking down on Lexington Avenue, from his office high up in JWT's headquarters near Grand Central Station, he had far outstripped the fame and fortune of any psychologist who had remained in the academy.

But Watson's hubris was problematic. Business had bought into the notion that psychology could reveal everything that managers needed to know in order to sell their products effectively. Watson was content to stoke up this optimism further. 'Love, fear, and rage are the same in Italy, Abyssinia and Canada,' he bragged. He was confident that he knew how to trigger any emotion in any situation, purely through designing the 'stimulus' in the right way. From the perspective of the advertiser and the marketer, this was a hugely seductive way of understanding their task. But it was all one-way traffic: psychological stimuli would be chucked at the public, and they would respond accordingly in the supermarket aisles. What if they didn't? What if Watson's own understanding of 'love, fear and rage' wasn't the same as other people's? How would businesses find out?

To complete the science of advertising, it was necessary that some form of feedback was also built into the system that would bring information back to the marketer. This could also be understood in behavioural terms, that is, whether a given ad directly prompted a certain response. For instance, discount coupons could be included in newspaper advertisements, to be cut out and used to purchase the product in question. This feedback mechanism would allow the marketer to discover which ads stimulated the best response. Seventy years later, the rise of online advertising and e-commerce would make such behavioural analysis of marketing effectiveness far more widespread: the response of the person viewing an ad is that much easier to assess, in terms of click-throughs and purchases.

In the 1920s, the risk of Resor and Watson's scientific exuberance was that they overlooked what members of the public actually thought and felt, so confident were they that they could dictate emotional responses from scratch. Corporate America could not depend on this leap of faith alone. Behaviourism's radically scientific view of the mind suggested there was nothing to fear here. There was nothing lurking, hidden, in the dark recesses of the mind that actually existed beyond what could be observed by psychologists. In fact, the very idea of the 'mind' was just a philosophical distraction.

The worry this generates is that a brand (or, for that matter, a politician or ideology or policy) might have become unappealing in ways that are apparent to the public but not yet to scientists and elites. The science of desire also required discovering what people wanted, finding out what they hoped for, in addition to trying to shape it. Doing this required an unusual psychological technique that Watson had hoped to abandon: speaking to people.

Glimpsing democracy

Watson could not help but notice that humans have a tendency to speak. He referred to this as 'verbal behaviour'. He was even prepared to accept that it could play a role in psychological research, though a deeply regrettable one. He ruefully reflected that:

We suffer in psychology today greatly because methods for observing what goes on in another individual's internal mechanisms in general are lacking. This is the reason we have to depend in part at least upon his own report of what is taking place. We are gradually breaking away from this inexact method; we shall break away very rapidly when the need is more generally recognized.[22]

What Bentham called the 'tyranny of sounds' frustrates the behaviourist as much as the utilitarian. Today, the facial-coders, neuromarketers and eye-trackers are living Watson's dream of 'breaking away' from subjective reports of experience, and finding supposedly more objective routes to our internal states.

Before behavioural psychology or market research achieved this 'break-away' feat, they found themselves in some quite unusual alliances. In the process, business came to understand people not only as passive recipients of corporate 'education' or 'stimuli', but as active, tentatively political actors with judgements about the world around them. If the task was to find out what people felt, wanted or thought, going out and asking them risked revealing some far more radical responses than JWT or Watson would have been prepared to countenance. What if they were sick of mass-produced goods? What if they didn't want lots more advertising? What if, above all, they wanted a say?

As the craze for psychological analysis swept American business over the course of the 1920s, large foundations such as Rockefeller and Carnegie looked to fund cutting-edge forms of market research. Statisticians had just invented randomized sampling methods, which greatly improved the authority of surveys as representations of large populations.[23] Before sampling methods became available, surveys were very much skewed in terms of who happened to respond to them. They gave a flavour of opinion, but this couldn't claim to be typical. The foundations offered to fund researchers who would put the new sampling techniques to work in the service of better market intelligence on the part of US corporations. But they were frustrated to discover that most of the individuals or organizations capable of delivering this type of knowledge were political activists, socialists and sociologists.[24]

Since social surveys had first been conducted in Europe in the 1880s, they had tended to be carried out in pursuit of progressive political agendas. Charles Booth in East London, or W. E. B. Du Bois in Philadelphia, set the stage for quantitative sociological research, which would go out and find how ordinary people lived, by seeing them in their domestic environments and asking them questions. The techniques for doing this work became increasingly professionalized with the establishment of progressive institutions such as the London School of Economics and the Brookings Institute in Washington, DC.

As the statistical techniques of social research developed, they became a matter of public fascination in their own right. One of the studies funded by Rockefeller became a national obsession, debated across the mainstream media. Conducted by a socialist husband and wife, Robert and Helen Lynd, from 1924 onwards, the 'Middletown Studies' produced a series of best-selling publications. The research purported to hold up a mirror to American society, revealing banal yet fascinating details of the minutiae of how people went about their day-to-day lives. The researchers were hopeful that people would read these studies and challenge the culture of consumerism that was engulfing them.

The Rockefeller Foundation believed that they were helping to identify new ways of connecting social values to corporate agendas. The Lynds believed they were helping to raise class-consciousness. At the intersection of the market and democratic socialism, the new survey techniques could serve either and both goals at the same time. Following a sequel 1937 study, 'Middletown in Transition', one sales journal announced that 'the only two books that are absolutely necessary for an advertising man are the Bible and Middletown!'[25] A new form of shared national self-consciousness had occurred, and its political implications were entirely open-ended.

These sorts of unlikely ideological alliances became a feature of how psychological surveys would advance over the course of the 1930s. The same techniques of enquiry moved seamlessly among market research departments, sociology, socialist campaigns and the media. In one of the more extreme ideological balancing acts, the émigré Frankfurt School Marxist Theodor Adorno was hired to work on another Rockefeller-funded research project, to study CBS radio audiences, along with the psychologists Hadley Cantril, Paul Lazarsfeld and a future president of CBS, Frank Stanton. Adorno had no immediate objection to the use of survey methods, which he saw as potentially emancipatory. He recognized that surveys had the capacity to challenge the dominance of the market, as a form of collective expression. But he was quickly appalled by the more simplistic aspect of the research, in which individuals were invited to push buttons marked 'like' and 'dislike' when played different types of music. He left the project, which was soon redesigned to serve the needs of the CBS marketing department more closely.

In Britain, market research was pioneered by a number of left-wing intellectuals and campaigners, including the philanthropist Joseph Rowntree and the Labour Party advisor Mark Abrams.[26] Like the Lynds, figures such as Abrams were openly critical of advertising and consumer culture, yet never gave up on the idea that market research could be used in a more noble fashion. With more objective knowledge of how people really lived, perhaps business might focus on serving real desires and needs, and not manufacturing new ones. A British equivalent of the Middletown studies, The Mass Observation Project, was launched in 1937.

In defiance of the behaviourist prejudice that humans are automatons to be programmed, these survey specialists had come to view individuals as the bearers of their own personal 'attitudes', towards anything from Coca-Cola, to the Catholic Church, to the government. These attitudes were psychological phenomena that were amenable to quantification. As someone with an 'attitude', I am able to tell you how much I like a given product or institution on a scale of -5 to +5. But crucially, in ways that defy the behaviourist prejudice, I alone am best placed to know what that attitude is, and any scientist who wishes to know will have to ask me. Button-pressing machines for the capturing of attitudes (like the 'worm' that reveals how the audience feels during a presidential debate, or the Facebook 'like' button) cut out the use of speech from attitudinal research, but not the judgement of the attitude-holder. This was the crypto-democratic underbelly of how market research developed as the Great Depression took hold, and elites grew increasingly concerned as to what the masses had in mind.

Understanding the attitudes of radio audiences, newspaper readers and the voting public became big business over the course of the 1930s. It also became big politics. In 1929 and 1931, President Herbert Hoover commissioned surveys on social trends and consumer habits, partly in the hope of understanding what level of political unrest might be brewing. This variety of political knowledge soon became commercially available, with the establishment of George Gallup's opinion-polling company in 1935. When Gallup predicted the outcome of the 1936 presidential election with uncanny accuracy, the prestige of his techniques soared. President Franklin Roosevelt was a compulsive commissioner of polls from then on, and hired Hadley Cantril (formerly of the CBS radio research project) as his in-house pollster.

Anti-capitalism for sale

Once the judgement and voice of the ordinary person is admitted into market research, things can start to shift in a democratic direction. This is an unpredictable and – from the perspective of a corporation, government or advertising account executive – worrying situation. It contains the possibility that drove the Lynds to conduct the Middletown studies, or Abrams's market research activities, namely that people may report a negative attitude towards consumerism, or even towards capitalism itself.

On the other hand, it is precisely the capacity to detect such threats that made these techniques indispensable for corporations and governments. Roosevelt may have conducted endless polls on how the public perceived his policies, but he never once altered a policy in response. Cantril revealed that every commission for a new attitudinal study also included the requirement for advice on 'how the attitude might be corrected', for which read 'propaganda'.[27]

Combine an effective survey technique with a ruthless behaviourist approach to advertising and you have a complete information loop. Messages go out to the public, individuals respond via behaviour and surveys, and information then returns to the message-sender. Each element of this has changed dramatically since the 1930s. The emphasis on mass society and the attitude of the general public came to appear dated in the post-war period, as smaller consumer niches started to appear and multiply. In place of the mass survey, another crypto-democratic form of consultation came to the fore, namely the 'focus group'. The rise of digital 'data analytics' represents the latest phase in this evolution. Meanwhile, the current neuromarketing frontiers of behaviourism make John B. Watson look positively innocent by comparison.

What has remained constant, however, is the interplay and tension between behaviourist technique and quasi-democratic forms of consumer voice. The behaviourist does not want to hear what people feel, want or demand; he wants to discover ways of producing feelings, wants or demands, as objective entities which can be seen. This way, he believes he can eliminate the subject from psychology altogether, producing an entirely scientific basis for business practices such as advertising. The problem is that he ends up reliant on his own presupposition about what these feelings mean, drawing on his own experiences and ideals about what rational behaviour might look like. No amount of data can explain what 'happiness' or 'fear' means to someone who has never experienced them himself. If the researcher happens to be located in an advertising agency or a business school, terms like 'choice', 'desire', 'emotion' and 'rationality' take on an unavoidably consumerist hue. Behaviourism and the advertising industry are necessarily parasitic on pre-existing spaces and techniques of deliberation, or else they have no way of escaping their own presuppositions or discovering what other people's emotions and desires actually mean.

The advertiser who does listen, on the other hand, may be

somewhat disturbed by what she hears. She may discover that people want a form of 'authenticity' or 'community' or sheer 'reality' that no product or advert can deliver. The challenge then becomes one of how to package up critical, political, democratic ideals in ways that can be safely delivered via products or public policies, without disrupting the status quo. Elements of anti-capitalist politics, which promise an uncommodified, more honest existence, have long been a fixture of advertising copy. As far back as the 1930s, advertisements contained images of pre-industrial, communal and family life, which seemed to be imperilled by the chaos of the industrial American city.[28] By the 1960s, counter-cultural imagery was featuring in commercials, even before the counter-culture had fully emerged.[29] Under the influence of market research, political ideals are quietly converted into economic desire. The cold mechanics of marketing and the critique of capitalism are locked into a constant feedback loop, such that there is no remaining idea of what freedom might look like, beyond that of consumption.

In utilitarian terms, the trick of marketing is to maintain a careful balance between happiness and unhappiness, pleasure and pain. The market must be designed as a space in which desires can be pursued but never fully satisfied, or else the hunger for consumption will dwindle. Marketers speak of various emotions today, including 'liking' and 'happiness', but these positive ones can never be the end of the matter. 'Anxiety' and 'fear' are also important parts of the mix, or else the shopper may find a degree of peace and comfort which requires no further satisfaction.

In the twenty-first century, popular psychologists and neuroscientists are doing a roaring trade, as consultants and authors, in promising to reveal the 'truth' of how we take decisions, how influence works, and what will deliver the target emotions and moods. The need to ask people what they want tends to diminish somewhat during these upturns in behaviourist excitement, as it did during Watson's day. The Benthamite distrust of language as an indicator of our feelings is manifest in how the neuromarketers claim to bypass what we say we feel, directly to the feeling itself.

The plausibility of this project is built on various strategic acts of forgetting or not seeing, of both history and political possibility. History falls by the wayside, or else somebody might notice that the waves of scientific marketing exuberance tend to resemble each other, yet never quite deliver on what they originally promised to. The dream of rendering people completely predictable and controllable is always dashed, and that rather low-tech alternative form of engagement – dialogue – is reintroduced in some form or other. And politics disappears, to the extent that, whenever dialogue does come back in, it does so within safely administered routines and spaces, where political desire can appear but not translate into political transformation.

The power of human speech is, ultimately, necessary for consumer culture to be sustained. A science built on the study of white rats, combined with clever tools for peering at our eyes and other body parts, is not, in the final instance, adequate for selling products. Less still is it adequate for the management of human beings in workplaces. For this latter purpose, yet another set of techniques, instruments and measuring devices is required, of which 'happiness' evaluations are the latest instalment.

4

The Psychosomatic Worker

The end of capitalism has often been imagined as a crisis of epic proportions. Perhaps a financial crisis will occur that is so vast not even government finances can rescue the system. Maybe the rising anger of exploited individuals will gradually congeal into a political movement, leading to revolution. Might some single ecological disaster bring the system to a halt? Most optimistically, capitalism might be so innovative that it will eventually produce its own superior successor, through technological invention.

But in the years that have followed the demise of state socialism in the early 1990s, a more lacklustre possibility has arisen. What if the greatest threat to capitalism, at least in the liberal West, is simply lack of enthusiasm and activity? What if, rather than inciting violence or explicit refusal, contemporary capitalism is just met with a yawn? From a political point of view, this would be somewhat disappointing. Yet it is no less of an obstacle for the longer-term viability of capitalism. Without a certain level of commitment on the part of employees, businesses run into some very tangible problems, which soon show up in their profits.

This fear has gripped the imaginations of managers and policy-makers in recent years, and not without reason. Various studies of 'employee engagement' have highlighted the economic costs of allowing workers to become mentally withdrawn from their jobs. Gallup conducts frequent and wide-ranging studies in this area and has found that only 13 per cent of the global workforce is properly 'engaged', while around 20 per cent of employees in North America and Europe are 'actively disengaged'.[1] They estimate that active disengagement costs the US economy as much as $550 billion a year.[2] Disengagement is believed to manifest itself in absenteeism, sickness and – sometimes more problematic – presenteeism, in which employees come into the office purely to be physically present.[3] A Canadian study suggests over a quarter of workplace absence is due to general burn-out, rather than sickness.[4]

Few private sector managers are required to negotiate with unions any longer, but nearly all of them confront a much trickier challenge, of dealing with employees who are regularly absent, unmotivated or suffering from persistent, low-level mental health problems. Resistance to work no longer manifests itself in organized voice or outright refusal, but in diffuse forms of apathy and chronic health problems. The border separating general ennui from clinical mental health problems is especially challenging to managers in twenty-first-century workplaces, seeing as it requires them to ask personal questions on matters that they are largely unqualified to deal with.

Lack of engagement from the workforce also registers as a problem for governments, inasmuch as it bites into economic output, and in doing so hits tax receipts. In societies with socialized health insurance and unemployment insurance, the problem is far more serious. There is a growing economic problem of individuals dropping out of work due to some often ill-defined personal and intangible problem, then gradually sinking into a more generalized inactivity. These people may show up at the doctor's surgery on a regular basis, making complaints about undiagnosable pains and problems. This is often because they have nobody else to speak to and are lonely. Unemployment undermines their sense of self-worth, and inactivity brings various other psychosomatic problems with it. A general deflation of psychological and physical capacity is the end result, which in many societies produces costs for the state to pick up.

Nor is the economic threat posed by declining mental health confined only to the periphery of labour markets. The World Health Organization caused a stir in 2001 by predicting that mental health disorders would have become the world's largest cause of disability and death by 2020. Already, some estimates suggest that over a third of European and American adults are suffering from some form of mental health problem, even if many are going undiagnosed.[5] The economic costs this imposes are vast. Mental health disorders are estimated to cost 3–4 per cent of GDP in Europe and North America. In Britain, the overall cost of this to the economy (including various factors, such as workplace absence, reduced productivity, medical costs) is put at £110 billion per year.[6] This is already far more than the economic cost of crime, yet it is a figure that is expected to double in real terms over the next twenty years, unless the current trend is diverted in some way.[7]

The causes of mental health problems are obviously complex and do not lie simply in the economy any more than they do in brain chemistry. But it is the way in which these problems manifest themselves in the workplace, threatening productivity as they do so, that has placed them amongst the greatest problems confronting capitalism today. It is the principal reason that the World Economic Forum is now so concerned about our health and happiness.[8] The murky grey area separating workplace dis-affection from a clinical disorder has required managers, and the human resources profession especially, to equip themselves with various new ways of intervening in the minds, bodies and behaviours of their workforce. The term most commonly used to describe the goal of these new interventions is 'well-being', which encompasses the happiness and health experienced by employees.

There is a clear economic incentive for managers to consider the positive attitude of employees. Endless studies have shown that workers are more productive when they feel happy, possibly by as much as an additional 12 per cent of output.[9] And in workplaces where they feel respected, listened to, consulted and involved, they are more likely to work harder, and less likely to take sick leave. Where employees have no say in how their work is organized, this is known to generate some of the psychological problems that now concern businesses, up to and including mental health problems.[10] By emphasizing well-being, managers hope to turn a vicious circle of disengagement and ill-health into a virtuous one of active, fulfilling commitment.

It is tempting to be cynical about some of this: the manager is after all still attempting to extract effort from the worker. But why not also recognize the opportunity contained in this current business anxiety? If capitalism is being ground down by the chronic, unspecifiable alienation of those it depends on, then surely solving that problem may also open up possibilities for political reform? The hard economic costs that ennui now places upon employers and governments means that human misery has shown up as a chronic problem that elites cannot simply shove aside. The question of what type of work, and what type of workplace organization, might generate a real sense of commitment and enthusiasm on the part of workers should not be abandoned altogether.

The difficulty is that the enthusiasm managers are seeking to promote is no less slippery than the psychosomatic problems they are seeking to avoid. A report commissioned by the UK government on the importance of employee engagement found it impossible to say exactly what this gaseous entity consists of. Expert insights that 'you sort of smell it' and 'know it when you see it' confirmed a shortage of objectivity on this particular issue.[11] Managers and policy-makers yearn for a hard science of workplace happiness. But it is with that sort of hard science that many of our problems begin.

Happiness boot camps

Confronted by other people's problems which are both ambiguous and personal, senior decision-makers have a tried and tested coping method: bring in the external contractors and consultants. There is copious political and market demand for experts willing to pronounce and act upon the well-being of others, on the basis of some presumed scientific authority. These sit on a spectrum between qualified medical practitioner and ill-informed bully. When handling painful issues of other people's health and happiness, outsiders have the great advantage of being able to duck full moral accountability and, if necessary, withdraw from the job altogether. Bentham's vision of a 'National Charity Company', a corporation established by the state to put people to work, foreshadowed today's murky world of workfare that lies in the unaccountable gaps between market and state.

In its bid to push people off reliance on the welfare state and into the labour market, the UK government appointed the public service outsourcing company Atos to conduct individual 'work capability assessments' of individuals. As this agenda was ramped up by the Conservative-led government from 2010 onwards, it led to a number of tragedies and acts of cruelty. These included the suicide of a 53-year-old blind and agoraphobic man, Tim Salter, only weeks after his benefits were stopped in 2013, following an assessment by Atos that he was able to work.[12] Atos also found individuals suffering brain damage and terminal cancer to be 'fit for work'. In 2011, Britain's General Medical Council investigated twelve doctors working for Atos as disability assessors, due to allegations that they were not performing their duty of care towards patients.[13] Between January and November 2011, 10,600 sick and disabled people died within six weeks of their benefits being stopped.[14] In one darkly comic computer malfunction, Atos confirmed that a disability benefit claimant was fit to work, even after they'd died of their illness.

When it comes to then motivating people to seek work, once again, the government also stands back, letting its contractors perform the most controversial psychological interventions. Those being forced to seek work are assessed, in terms of their attitude and optimism, and then have their motivation reactivated. The companies who carry out this task in the British context are A4e and Ingeus, who hold contracts with the government to get unemployed people into jobs. Around a third of the people who come through their doors report some sort of mental health problem, although the companies suspect that the rate is really twice that. Questionnaires are used to try and spot what the behavioural and mental obstacles are towards working (lack of jobs not being viewed as an adequate excuse).

In the eyes of these contractors, unemployment is really a

'symptom' of some broader personal malaise, which manifests itself in inactivity. The solution consists of a range of coaching programmes, combined with 'behavioural activation' courses, aimed at restoring the unemployed individual's self-belief and optimism with ruthless efficiency. As one participant in an A4e course reported, they were shouted at by a self-help guru to 'talk, breathe, eat, shit belief in yourself' and that 'you are the product – you either believe it or you don't'.[15]

Wherever the economics of mental health become more explicit, the gap between care and punishment tends to shrink. In 2007, the economist Richard Layard laid out the 'business case' for cognitive behavioural therapy (CBT), demonstrating that it could save the UK government money, given the treatment's brevity and apparent success rate in keeping people in work.[16] This was instrumental in the creation of the Increasing Access to Psychological Therapies programme, which involved a dramatic rise in the number of cognitive behavioural therapists trained and employed by the National Health Service.

But with the dawning of austerity, this sympathy for talking cures started to look somewhat different. In 2014, the government announced that disability benefit claimants could have their payments stopped if they refused to attend sessions of CBT. People would effectively be forced to receive a talking cure. Quite how therapy could be expected to 'work', when it was only being undergone under the threat of losing £85 a week, was not explained.

To close down every route for the avoidance of work, doctors have had to be conscripted into this policy agenda too. A UK government report published in 2008 complained that 'the fallacy persists that illness is incompatible with being at work', which doctors were guilty of peddling.[17] A government campaign was launched to dissuade doctors of this, and their official 'sick notes' (which were once signed by doctors to declare that an individual *shouldn't* work) were replaced by 'fit notes', requiring doctors to describe the remaining ways in which an individual could still be employed, despite any illnesses or disabilities. Doctors were encouraged to sign a draft statement scripted by the state, agreeing that work is good for people.

At the opposite end of the labour market, things look a lot sunnier, but somehow no less brutal. While Atos, A4e and Ingeus grapple with the apparent sluggishness and pessimism of the poor, high-end wellness consultants make large sums of money by teaching corporate elites how to maintain themselves in a state of optimal psychosomatic fitness. Classes such as Dr Jim Loehr's 'Corporate Athlete Course' ($4,900 for two and a half days) introduce executives to elite 'energy investment' strategies, which will enable them to achieve a high performance level of physical and mental wellness. The American productivity guru Tim Ferriss sells advice on how senior managers should best employ their own brains over the course of the working day, following an earlier career selling dubious brain-enhancing nutritional supplements.

This consultancy circuit moves seamlessly among various apparently separate domains of expertise. The psychology of motivation blends into the physiology of health, drawing occasionally on insights from sports coaches and nutritionists, to which is added a cocktail of neuroscientific rumours and Buddhist meditation practices. Various notions of 'fitness', 'happiness', 'positivity' and 'success' bleed into one another, with little explanation of how or why. The idea which accompanies all of this is that there is one ideal form of human existence: hardworking, happy, healthy and, above all, rich. A science of elite perfectibility is built on the back of this heroic capitalist vision. The flip side of this, and the real driving force behind many executive wellness programmes, is a set of well-researched risks run by highly competitive businessmen, colloquially known as 'burn-out', which includes the higher chance of heart attacks, strokes and nervous breakdowns.

Of course, the majority of adults living in capitalist societies lie somewhere between the purview of Atos et al. and that of the executive wellness gurus. Is there no scope for a less individualized vision of well-being across the middle swathes of the labour market? Possibly there is. But here too are some brutally competitive injunctions offered to those managers worrying about worker disengagement and its impact upon productivity.

One of America's leading workplace happiness gurus, entrepreneur Tony Hsieh, argues that the most successful businesses are those which deliberately and strategically nurture happiness throughout their organizations. Businesses should employ chief happiness officers to ensure that nobody escapes workplace happiness. But if this sounds like the recipe for inclusive community, it isn't. Hsieh advises businesses to identify the 10 per cent of employees who are least enthusiastic towards the happiness agenda, and then lay them off.[18] Once this is done, the remaining 90 per cent will apparently become 'super-engaged', a finding which is open to more than one psychological interpretation.

As the science of happiness has moved closer to the front line of profit-maximizing business, something curious has happened to it. For Bentham, happiness was something which resulted from certain activities and choices. Neo-classical economists such as Jevons and behaviourist psychologists such as Watson assumed something similar, implying that individuals could be lured to make certain choices by dangling a pleasurable carrot in front of them. But in the context of business consultancy and individual coaching, happiness looks altogether different. Suddenly, it is represented as an input to certain strategies and projects, a resource to be drawn upon, which will yield more money in return. Bentham and Jevons's psychological premise, that money yields a proportionate quantity of happiness, is spun on its head, suggesting instead that a quantity of happiness will yield a certain amount of money.

One of a new generation of positive psychology management gurus, Shawn Achor, outlines a range of data in his book, *The Happiness Advantage*, suggesting that happier people achieve more in their careers.[19] They get promoted more, sell more (if they work in marketing) and enjoy better health. Happiness becomes a form of capital on which they can fall back amidst the turbulence of an uncertain economy. It is, as the title of his book suggests, a source of advantage in the battle to succeed. If this was the limit of his wisdom, Achor might sound like a fatalist: optimists are just luckier in all regards than pessimists.

The crucial supplement to the data is that we are all, supposedly, capable of influencing our own happiness levels. Happiness, Achor tells us, is a choice. We can either choose to be happy (and consequently successful) or choose to be unhappy (and suffer the consequences). Neuroscientist Paul Zak, another leading speaker and consultant on these issues, suggests that we view our happiness like a 'muscle', which needs exercising regularly in order to keep it in full working order, for when we need it. Lurking within this highly individualized agenda is the capacity to blame people for their own misery and failure, both of which are matters that they have evidently failed to act upon adequately.

What does 'happiness' even mean, once it is being conceived of in this way? It seems to imply a source of energy and resilience, but always directed towards goals other than being happy, such as status, power, employment and money. In the face of workplace ennui and psychological stagnation, the motivational gurus simply demand more willpower. By this account, the activities that might result in happiness, such as socializing or relaxing, are only valuable to the extent that they might restore brain and body to a level of fitness, from which they can then be propelled forwards to the next business challenge. This particular version of utilitarianism means expanding corporate rationality further into everyday life, such that there is now even an 'optimal' way of taking a break from work, and simply going for a walk can be viewed as a calculated act of productivity management.[20] What is going on? The misery of working people is a serious political issue. How did it become captured in this way?

The extraction of effort

The discovery of the 'conservation of energy' in the 1840s, which so excited physiologists and philosophers such as Fechner, also unleashed a wave of enthusiasm among industrialists and inventors. If quantities of energy remained the same, as they passed between man, matter, heat and motion, then mathematical analysis could yield ever-more productive technologies. The search for 'perpetual motion' machines was a manifestation of this optimism.

However, this enthusiasm was soon tempered by a more troubling discovery made by the physicist Rudolf Clausius in 1865. It transpired that energy did not remain a single quantity after all, as it changed from one state to another. In fact it was gradually diminished. This was the law of 'entropy', and it catalysed an outbreak of anxiety and pessimism regarding the very future of industrial capitalism. During the 1870s, as Jevons was converting economics into a form of psychological mathematics, physiologists – and industrialists – were growing increasingly concerned by the problem of physical human fatigue, especially in the factory. The Victorians had tended to view inactivity and unemployment as moral failings, associated with drink and bad 'character'. But by the 1880s, there was a creeping concern that industrial work was simply grinding people down. Human beings were running out of steam.

A fin-de-siècle neurosis developed. As capitalism's human resources were diminishing, the vitality on which Western civilization depended was in terminal decline. The syndrome of 'neurasthenia', a form of nervous exhaustion supposedly brought on by the strains of modern urban life, claimed thousands of victims among the European and American bourgeoisie. Progress just seemed like too much effort.

The science of work at the end of the nineteenth century was not entirely dissimilar to how it looks today. Fatigue was a preoccupation, just as general inactivity (for the poor) or burn-out (for the rich) is today. This was viewed as a matter of national economic priority: variations in national economic output were attributed to differences in the physiology and nutrition of rival national workforces.[21] As one study suggested, maybe Britain's economic advantage over Germany was that its workers ate more meat, whereas the latter's ate more potatoes. The science of ergonomics developed to study and photograph bodies in motion, in the attempt to spot precisely where energy was being wasted. The muscles, and even the blood, were examined, to try and understand how entropy afflicted the human body in the workplace.

This was the context into which the mechanical engineer Frederick Winslow Taylor launched his career as the world's first management consultant. Taylor was born into a prominent and wealthy Philadelphia family, with roots stretching back to Edward Winslow, one of the passengers on the Mayflower. This heritage was crucial. It was his eminent family name which granted him privileged access to the industrial firms of the city, in ways that would be decisive for his career. During the 1870s and 1880s, Taylor worked for a number of successful manufacturing and steel plants in the area, achieving automatic promotions to managerial positions, on account of his family connections.

Taylor was never an industrialist as such – he'd originally hoped to become a lawyer. Like every management consultant who would come after him, this put him in an ambivalent position, both an insider and an outsider. This granted him an unusual view of the shop floor of manufacturing plants, which he was able to look down on from a dispassionate white-collar position, with an air of objectivity. He had power within a business, but he also had scientific detachment. And much of what he saw, from this observational vantage point, looked deeply wasteful. There was no methodical, scientific analysis going into the design of work processes. Managers had a given quantity of resources, and a given quantity of hours in the day, but seemed bereft of any mathematical logic through which to exploit these for the greatest output.

Taylor never remained in the employment of a single company for very long, again setting a precedent for the consultancy industry that came after him. He kept moving from one Philadelphia manufacturer to the next, amassing insights into what was preventing more efficient modes of workplace organization. It was only in 1893 that he formally established himself as an independent consultant and began to sell his knowledge. His business card read, 'Consulting Engineer – Systematizing Shop Management and Manufacturing Costs a Specialty'.

In the late 1890s, Taylor was hired by Bethlehem Steel to study the manufacture of pig iron. This was the topic of his first quantitative, scientific analysis of 'time and motion' in the workplace, specifically looking at how to increase the amount of pig iron that labourers could load onto a wagon in a given day.[22] He not only looked at the process of labour itself, but also the physical conditions of work, and the physical condition of the individual labourers. He broke production down into individual tasks to be logged and rationalized. Even if economics had recently been converted into a utilitarian study of consumption, the problems of industrial management remained thoroughly physical, of how to extract as much produce from as few machines and human bodies as possible. He claimed to have increased the average output of pig-iron handlers from 12.5 to 47.5 tons per day, purely by rationalizing their time, motion and monetary incentives.

The Bethlehem study turned Taylor into a celebrity in business and academic circles. In 1908, Harvard Business School offered an MBA for the first time, but without much of a clue as to what would go in it. As the world's now pre-eminent scientist of management, Taylor was invited to lecture on the course and in 1911 published a synthesis of his various theories, *The Principles of Scientific Management*. Among businessmen, time and motion studies became all the rage, arriving in European factories in the years immediately prior to World War One.

While the immediate clients for Taylor's services were interested in maximizing their business revenue, the political appeal of scientific management was extremely broad. American progressives believed that with greater scientific insight, corporations could be harnessed for the common good. Socialists, including Lenin, saw in Taylorism a model for how society itself could be run in an efficient manner, without reliance on markets.

Taylor himself also attached a loftier social purpose to his new science, believing that scientific management would spell the end of industrial conflict, substituting 'hearty brotherly co-operation for contention and strife'. One of his professed advantages, when he entered firms as an outsider, was that he could avoid being dragged into industrial conflicts between management and labour and maintain a politically neutral position. In workplaces that had become conflict-riven, the consultant could have a tempering effect – though of course it was never labour that had invited the consultant to intervene in the first place.

The accident of Taylor's aristocratic roots created a template for how management consultants have behaved ever since. McKinsey & Co., Accenture, PwC presume a similar form of privilege, promising to sprinkle expertise upon organizations and workplaces, then very often exiting before the results become too apparent. That may be Taylor's most powerful legacy, because beyond that, the term 'Taylorism' has come to acquire some largely negative connotations. Even as companies continue to push surveillance and scientific analysis further into the lives of their workforce, now through digital data analytics and mobile devices, it has been deeply unfashionable for some time to hark back to the hard, scientific analysis of Frederick Taylor. The reason for this is simple: the brutalist approach to management is deemed to make people unhappy.

It would be perverse to defend Taylorism, but there was at least a transparency about its logic. Workplaces and managers existed to extract value, in the most efficient way possible. Workers were never expected to like this, which was a freedom of sorts. As Ian Curtis, the lead singer of Joy Division who hanged himself aged twenty-three, once said, 'I used to work in a factory and I was really happy because I could daydream all day'. Labourers in a Taylorist factory brought their physical capabilities into work, to be exploited for sure, but were never expected to give anything more personal or intangible. And this is exactly why managers soon turned their backs on Taylor's version of scientific management.

Psychology gets to work

In 1928, a researcher from Harvard Business School sat down with a young woman working in a telephone production plant in Cicero, Illinois, and asked her an unusual question: 'If given three wishes, what would they be?' The woman paused to reflect before listing her answers. 'Health, to take a trip home at Christmas time, and to take a wedding trip to Norway next spring.'

The reason the question was unusual was that the researcher was not, ultimately, interested in the woman's life or wish fulfilment. Like Taylor before him, he was interested in her productivity. The enthusiasm for Taylorism had waned considerably since its heyday in the years prior to World War One, but Taylor's basic scientific ambitions were still largely unquestioned among management theorists. Only in 1927 Harvard Business School had established a Fatigue Laboratory, containing rooms of various temperatures and state-of-the-art instruments to study the reactions of the human body to different types of work and recuperation. In an economy still dominated by manufacturing and physical labour, physiology and infrastructure seemed to hold the key for unleashing better workplace performance. Managers did not consider the Christmas or travel plans of their employees to be any of their business.

The man asking the questions in that telephone production plant was Elton Mayo, an Australian polymath of somewhat dubious scholarly provenance. He had dabbled in philosophy, medicine and psychoanalysis, and was seduced by many of the doom-laden cultural critiques published in the years following World War One, such as Oswald Spengler's *Decline of the West*. Mayo was convinced that civilization was heading for a fall, and that industrial conflict would be its trigger. Trade unions and socialists were thus a threat, not only to management and capital, but to world peace.

In some of Mayo's more outlandish theories, socialism was a symptom of physical fatigue and psychiatric illness. 'To any working psychologist', he asserted, 'it is at once evident that the general theories of Socialism, Guild Socialism, Anarchism and the like are very largely the phantasy constructions of the neurotic'.[23] He believed that the only solution lay in corporations coming to provide forms of psychoanalytic therapy to their employees, which would soothe them, bringing them closer into the arms of their employers. Employees who resisted the authority of their managers were in need of treatment.

Mayo emigrated to the United States in 1922, firstly to San Francisco, where he took a visiting lectureship at Berkeley. He soon discovered that the Rockefeller Foundation was a source of considerable funds for anyone seeking to pursue business-friendly research, and he won a series of lucrative grants over the next twenty years, which kept him in some personal luxury. These studies took him to the East Coast, where he had the chance to visit a number of factories and consider how his ideas might be applied. His psychosomatic theories assumed that psychiatric problems in the workplace would show up not only in terms of low productivity and industrial unrest, but high blood pressure. Between 1923 and 1925, he toured manufacturing plants in the Boston area in the company of a nurse and a blood pressure gauge, attempting to prove this link between the mental, the economic and the physical, which he was convinced existed quite regardless of the evidence.

The psychological study of work was an emerging field during the 1920s, led by some of the same scholars who had previously pioneered the psychological study of advertising a few years earlier. But Mayo had some much more far-reaching theories regarding the ways in which the insights of psychology might fundamentally reform and rescue capitalism. By focusing on the entire person in the workplace, including all of their personal concerns and mental well-being, work might provide the labourer with their deepest source of meaning, and offset the risk of industrial upheaval once and for all. In 1926, Mayo was hired by the Harvard Business School.

The research in Cicero, Illinois, known as the Hawthorne Studies, after the name of the manufacturing plant where they were carried out, quickly became a landmark of management science.[24] Mayo was one of the founders of the Fatigue Laboratory, but the impact of his work was to divert attention away from the working body and towards the mental happiness of employees. According to the mythology that now surrounds the Hawthorne Studies, Mayo's main discovery was accidental. The working women who were chosen to be observed and interviewed were taken off the regular shop floor and into a test room, where they were able to relax and interact in a more informal and convivial atmosphere. This seemed to correlate with improved performance, and Mayo had an inkling of why: the study itself, including the interview process, was what resulted in the productivity increases, because the women had developed a higher sense of group identity with one another. Their enthusiasm for work had grown, as their ability to form relationships with one another increased. The general phenomenon, whereby research subjects respond to being studied, is now known as the 'Hawthorne Effect' for this reason.

The lesson that Mayo drew from his repeated visits to the Hawthorne plant was that managers had to learn how to talk to their employees if they wanted to extract greater productivity from them. An unhappy worker was also an unproductive worker, and the unhappiness stemmed from a deep-set feeling of isolation. They also had to understand the unique psychological properties of social groups, which were not simply reducible to individual incentives, as Taylorism and neo-classical economics had supposed. A thriving and collaborative group identity could do far more for an employee's happiness, and hence for the manager's bottom line, than a pay rise.

There is some basis to doubt whether Mayo was really reporting on data acquired at Hawthorne or simply repackaging some theories that he'd long held about the future of capitalism. In fact, the productivity of the women did coincide with a pay increase in 1929, but Mayo was absent at the time and chose to ignore this in his analysis.[25] Regardless of the scientific validity of his work however, Mayo's impact on management thinking was profound and long lasting. Whenever we now hear that managers must focus on the 'whole person', and not just the 'employee', or that employee happiness is critical to the bottom line, or that we must 'love what we do' or bring an 'authentic' version of ourselves to work, we are witnessing Mayo's influence. When managers strive for more laughter in the work-place, as some consultants now insist they must, or seek to transform its smell so as to optimize our subjective feelings, they are practicing what Mayo first preached.[26]

Therapeutic management

Within the longer history of happiness expertise, what is inter-esting about Mayo's intervention is that he downplayed the more obvious material ways of tweaking the pleasures and pains of the mind. Neither money nor the physical body were deemed ade-quate for understanding or influencing levels of happiness, once the workplace came to be understood in terms of group psy-chology. Instead, talking to workers and facilitating their relations with one another became the main instruments for gauging and improving their happiness. Management, which originated as a technique for controlling slaves on plantations, and developed as a means of running heavy industrial corpora-tions, had become a 'soft', social and psychological skill.

While Mayo did not conceive of things in quite this way, this was a form of psychosomatic intervention, like a placebo. The aim of management in the 1930s was, after all, still the same as it was in Taylor's day: to increase output of physical produce. But now, rather than focusing on the physical and physiological work process, managers would focus on the social and psychological elements, in the expectation that this would yield behavioural, physical, economic improvements.

The term 'psychotherapy' today refers to a range of treat-ments, ranging from more psychoanalytic, long-term relation-ships, to the quick fixes such as CBT that are more akin to training or coaching. But the first known uses of the term referred to the 'talking cures' offered by medical doctors in the late nineteenth century, who came to recognize that their patients often responded as much to the manner in which they were spoken to, as they did to the medicinal treatment they received.

What Mayo was recommending was the industrial parallel to this. An open, conversational relationship could be conducted in such a way as to bring about a change in the worker's mentality, and a consequent change in their physical performance. Speech was instrumentalized, to make people feel better, and as a result, behave better. As a tonic to the harsh mechanics of Taylorism, this made perfect sense. It could even be taken in some more emancipatory directions, to investigate groups as autonomous entities, which might allow firms to be more democratically managed in future. Research on group psychology was put to various uses over the 1940s and 1950s, from the analysis of tank commandment during the war, to the analysis of consumers via focus groups.[27]

Mayo personally hoped to anaesthetize political sentiments. Therapeutic management would reduce unhappiness and, with it, resistance. Other avenues were possible, however. Once dialogue and co-operation become viewed as an essential element of economic production, one sees the glimmer of a more transformative economic democracy. Once the woman working on the shop floor is asked what her three wishes are, might the next step not be to invite her to have a say in how the business is managed? And might things not progress politically from there? Mayo would have scoffed at the idea. But the critique of management oligarchy cannot discount the emancipatory potential of social psychology altogether.

Yet the analogy to psychosomatic medical treatments would

gradually become more telling as the post-war period progressed, for a couple of coincidental reasons. Firstly, the nature
of work in the West became progressively less physical over the
second half of the twentieth century. By the 1980s, an employee's
customer care, service ethic and enthusiasm were not simply
mental resources, which existed to help churn out more products: they were the product. The importance of employee
happiness and psychological engagement becomes all the greater
once corporations are in the business of selling ideas, experiences
and services. Businesses speak of 'intangible assets' and 'human
capital' in the hope of capturing this amorphous workplace ethos,
but in practice it is nothing which resembles either an asset or
capital. Some other way of conceiving of work is required.

Secondly, the concept of health started to undergo some profound changes. In 1948, the newly founded World Health
Organization redefined health as 'a state of complete physical,
mental and social well-being' – an almost utopian proposition
that few of us ever attain for very long. Intangible aspects of
health and illness came to the fore. In particular, the notion of
'mental illness' emerged concurrently with the decline of mental
asylums, a category that could be applied liberally to people
living relatively ordinary lives in the community, not unlike sufferers from common bodily illnesses.

The awareness that mental processes were a crucial component of health exerted a profound influence across health policy
and medical practice, altering the nature of medical expertise as
they did. This was sometimes known as 'experience medicine',
as it brought the experience of the patient, and not just their
body, into the medical assessment for the first time. By the 1970s,
there was a range of quality of life measures that were used to
assess health outcomes, which took into account the subjective

perspective of the sufferer, and not simply their physical condition.[28] In place of binary analyses, between life and death, health and disease, new sliding scales of wellness were emerging. This is partly a symptom of medical progress: as medicine becomes better at preventing death, so attention turns to the question of how well it is able to support life.

What does any of this have to do with management or work? The problem confronting managers and policy-makers over the second half of the twentieth century was that everything seemed to be evaporating into thin air at the same time. Work was becoming intangible as manufacturing went into decline. Illness was becoming intangible as mental and behavioural problems increased. Money itself was becoming intangible as the financial system globalized from the late 1960s onwards. Problems of activity and enthusiasm moved elusively between the domains of medicine, psychiatry, workplace management and economics. The challenges of health care and those of business were becoming harder to disentangle, with the issue of mental health at the interface between the two. The job of management increasingly came to resemble psychotherapy in that original sense of 'talking cure', of propping up the well-being of individuals, in order to keep their enthusiasm for service-based jobs as high as possible.

And as the nature of work and management changes, so too does the nature of resistance. Opposition to management typically takes a form other than that preferred by the manager himself. The classical mode of opposition to Taylorism, which seeks to reduce human beings to physical capital, is for the worker to speak back or strike via a trade union. The manager, having ignored the feelings or desires of the worker, is told that they cannot do so any longer.

As Mayo's style of therapeutic management expanded over the post-war period, opposition to it began to take the opposite form. Gradually, as post-industrial workers were encouraged to be 'themselves', speaking 'openly' and 'honestly' to their manager, the sole remaining form of opposition was to return to the physical body once more. The only escape from a manager who wants to be your friend is to become physically ill. With the list of available diagnoses growing, and complete 'health' becoming idealized, sickness became one of the dominant ways in which refusal to work came to manifest itself, especially from the 1970s onwards. Evidently, management could not only focus on relationships and subjective feelings, any more than it could only focus on the productive body. What it needed, if it was to ensnare employees thoroughly, was a truly psychosomatic science that could treat the mind and the body as an integrated part of a single system to be optimized. This brings us to a final character in the story of psychosomatic management.

Holistic work and well-being

In 1925, a nineteen-year-old Austrian medical student at Prague University named Hans Selye noticed something so obvious that he almost didn't dare report it to his teacher. As his class was observing various patients with a range of different maladies, it dawned on Selye that all of the patients bore some resemblance to each other, regardless of their medical condition. They each reported aches and pains in the joints, loss of appetite and had a coated tongue. In short, all of them looked ill.

He later recalled this moment as follows:

Even now – after half a century – I still remember vividly the profound impression these considerations made upon me at the time. I could not understand why, ever since the dawn of medical history, physicians should have attempted to concentrate all their efforts upon the recognition of individual diseases and the discovery of specific remedies for them, without giving any attention to the much more obvious 'syndrome of just being sick'.[29]

When he did share the insight with his professor – namely that sick people look sick – he received the sarcastic reply that, indeed, 'if a man is fat, he looks fat'. But Selye refused to abandon his insight. As a child he had accompanied his father, one of a long line of doctors in the Selye family, on his visits to poor households in Vienna, and had a strong vocation towards a traditional, somewhat holistic, understanding of the healing process.[30] As the medical 'psychotherapists' had realized, the doctor's personal interaction with the patient was a crucial ingredient in how they responded to treatment.

The history of utilitarianism is littered with dashed hopes that there might be a single measure of human optimization which could serve as the instrument through which all public and private decisions might be taken. This ideal rests on the hope that the ambiguity and plurality of human culture might be overcome through knowledge of a single quantifiable entity. Whether it is via the idea of utility, energy, value or emotion, the project of monism always involves this form of simplification. In his apparently banal observation that ill people look ill, Selye had hit on another version of this. It took him another ten years before he had developed this into a scientific theory, which he termed 'General Adaptation Syndrome'.

The novelty of this idea, from the perspective of medicine, was that the syndrome Selye was describing was non-specific: it had a common set of symptoms, but these were not tied firmly to any particular causes or disorders. He explored this doing various experiments on animals, plunging them into cold water, cutting them, implanting poisons into them, to see how quite disparate forms of brutality could prompt the identical modes of biological response.

Like any biological system, an animal body experiences various external stimuli, intrusions and demands which it has to respond to. What Selye was interested in was the nature of this response, which could sometimes become a problem in its own right. Biological systems which are overstimulated start to shut down; the same also happens when they are under-stimulated. The health of any organism depends on an optimal level of activity, not too much, not too little. Humans were no different, as far as Selye was concerned. The patients who simply 'looked ill' in his medical class that day were all displaying a common form of physical reaction to a very diverse set of illnesses. A monistic theory of general wellness was emerging.

Until the 1940s, the term 'stress' was used principally in reference to metals and was virtually unknown outside the worlds of engineering and physics. An iron bar becomes 'stressed' when it is unable to cope with the demands that are placed on it. Selye recognized that what engineers saw as 'wear and tear' in, say, a bridge, was the same problem as what he had termed 'General Adaptation Syndrome' in the human body. General Adaptation Syndrome was effectively an indicator of the 'rate of wear and tear in the body'.[31] In the aftermath of World War Two, he re-christened the syndrome as 'stress'. By the 1950s, this was a distinctive new field of medical and biological research.

Like Mayo, Selye never saw himself as an academic only: he was on a mission. According to his holistic understanding of illness, entire societies and cultures could become sick if they lost the capacity to cope with external stimuli and demands. Equally, they could slump into passive inactivity if they were never stimulated sufficiently. As he grew older, Selye developed this idea into something approaching an ethical philosophy, though a frighteningly egocentric one. A healthy society, he argued, is built around 'egoistic altruism', in which every individual sets about doing his utmost to win the adoration of others. This produces a form of natural equilibrium, in which the egotist becomes integral to his own social system:

No one will make personal enemies if his egotism, his compulsive hoarding of valuables, manifest itself only by inciting live, goodwill, gratitude, respect, and all other positive feelings that render him useful and often indispensable to his neighbours.[32]

Despite his aspiration to offer a science capable of diagnosing every social problem, Selye stuck firmly to biology when it came to seeking explanations. His characteristically monistic assumption was that any society or organization was merely a larger, more complex biological system, whose behaviour could be reduced back to the actions of organisms and cells.

Away from Selye's own biological research, and his macho libertarian politics, the non-specific nature of stress represented an opportunity which would eventually permeate into the world of management. Stress, as Selye had argued, is simply a particular type of reaction to any excessive demand. This was equally amenable to psychological or organizational forms of exploration. In fact, without using the term 'stress', the US military had become aware of the same syndrome during World War Two, in the common forms of psychological collapse experienced by soldiers who had spent too long in battle. The stressful demands placed on a human being are not merely physical, but social and psychological too. What went on between the demand and the response was open to a range of different scientific explanations beyond merely biological ones. The study of stress became an expressly interdisciplinary field.

As the study of how humans cope with physical and mental demands, it also lent itself perfectly to the study of work. By definition, stress is something we encounter without having chosen to, but cannot avoid. It often occurs when we are trapped in a certain situation, simply forced to react to it. The field of occupational health emerged during the 1960s to understand precisely how work impacts upon us, physically and mentally. Studying how different types of job demand produce different hormonal and emotional responses yielded a number of potentially transformative findings. It wasn't simply that excessive demands were bad for people; insufficient workplace demands – or boredom – could also be unhealthy, as Selye had recognized. Our current concern with unemployment as a potential health risk is one manifestation of the latter anxiety.

Just as Mayo's emphasis on dialogue created an opening for a more thoroughly egalitarian critique of business hierarchy, the study of stress in the workplace achieved something similar for a while. Work carried out by the psychologist Robert Kahn and his colleagues at the University of Michigan during the early 1960s highlighted the various ways in which power structures and work design impact upon the health of employees.[33] Badly designed jobs and lack of proper recognition in the workplace were clear contributors to physical and mental ill-health. Lack of any influence over where and when one carries out a task is a stress factor, which takes its toll on both mind and body. A number of clear routes, between the injustices of hierarchical business and the vulnerabilities of the human body, were becoming apparent. One of the most important of these was the discovery that stress leads to the cortisol hormone being released into the bloodstream, hardening the arteries and increasing the risk of heart attack.[34] Despite the high-profile obsession with executive burn-out, this form of stress is far more common for those lacking power or status at work.

By the 1980s, the non-specific syndrome that Selye had first identified in his lecture hall in 1925 had become one of the most pressing problems confronting managers in the Western world. Workers were no longer reporting straight-forward physical fatigue of the sort that Frederick Taylor might have understood; nor were they simply unhappy in a way that Elton Mayo might have recognized. They were now exhibiting a generalized deflation of activity, a form of psychosomatic collapse that we have come to identify with the concept of stress. In the UK, stress overtook repetitive strain injury in 2012 as the leading cause of absence from work. This is not easily classified as either a physical illness or a mental illness. What prompts it may include work but may equally include other types of social, psychological or physical demands that the individual simply can't cope with.

The science of stress was of the utmost importance for managers worrying about the depletion of their workforce. It became one of the main preoccupations of the human resources profession, who sought out rudimentary wisdom on a wide panoply of 'bio-psycho-social' complaints. The sheer breadth of contributory factors to stress – some tangible, others intangible – made it extremely difficult to achieve any control over it. This is in addition to the graver psychosomatic risks faced by those in precarious jobs, who move in and out of work, without even managers to support them from one month to the next. One conclusion to draw from this would be, as per the occupational health studies of the 1960s, that the fundamental politics of work had grown dysfunctional and needed a more wholesale transformation, and not simply piecemeal medical treatment. But would this be the lesson that was learnt?

Taylor's revenge

When the young woman in the Hawthorne plant informed Elton Mayo in 1928 that she was hoping to visit Norway for a wedding, this would have represented an unusual level of intimacy, had Mayo been her boss. In the early twenty-first century, managers in large corporations pursue a very different form of intimacy with their employees.

Consider Unilever, the global manufacturer of food, beauty products and cleaning products. In 2001, its senior management demanded a programme to help them personally manage their own energy levels, as they feared the consequences of executive working lifestyles.[35] Being in the industry they were in, there was ample expertise to help them design this. The 'Lamplighter' health and well-being programme (named 'Ignite U' in Australia) was the result, tailor-made to help senior management keep up their performance levels and offset the risk of stress. The business benefits for Lamplighter quickly became clear, with evaluations suggesting that every £1 spent on the programme yielded £3.73 in return. It was quickly rolled out across dozens of Unilever offices around the world before being extended to cover the rest of the workforce.

Programmes such as Lamplighter are becoming more and more common. They seek to identify a wide range of health and well-being risks in their workforce, including the sporting activities of employees and their 'mental resilience'. Lamplighter requires Unilever employees to be formally (albeit, confidentially) assessed in terms of a range of 'behaviours', relating to nutrition, smoking and drinking, exercise and personal stress. The state-of-the-art workplace of today has taken on features of the doctor's surgery, just as the doctor has been required to take on skills of the motivational manager. What are referred to as 'Health 2.0' technologies for the digital monitoring of well-being are often indistinguishable from productivity enhancements. The iPhone 6's Health app, launched in September 2014, was celebrated as another example of Apple's reimagining of our everyday lives, without much pause to think who it had really been designed for. Needless to say, employers, health insurers and wellness service providers are amongst the main enthusiasts for the phone's constant measurement of bodily behaviour.

Many 'best practice' employers now offer free gym membership to their most valued staff, and even free counselling. Business services, such as Virgin Pulse (a telling name, seeing as pulse rate represents life in its most quantifiable form), offer an integrated suite of psychosomatic programmes aimed at optimizing their physical energy, their attention span and their 'true motivations', through extensive digital surveillance and coaching. As the physical and the psychological character of work – and of illness – start to blend into each other, notions of 'health', 'happiness' and 'productivity' become ever harder to distinguish from each other. Employers end up treating all three things as a single entity, to be maximized via a range of stimuli and instruments. This is the monistic philosophy of the twenty-first century manager: each worker can become better, in body, mind and output.

The political hope that perhaps the human benefits of dialogue and workplace empowerment might be more thoroughly recognized turns into disappointment, as performance management and health care are fused into a science of well-being optimization. And yet there are radical political economists for whom the de-materialization of contemporary work represents an opportunity for a whole new industrial model.[36] The shift towards a 'knowledge-based' economy, in which ideas and relationships are key sources of business value, could be the basis of entirely new workplace structures in which power is decentralized and decisions taken collaboratively. There are good reasons to suspect that such models might produce fewer psychosomatic stresses; in that sense, they may be more efficient than the status quo. If dialogue in the workplace is a necessary factor for productivity – as Mayo recognized – why not grant it some real influence over how decisions get made, right up to the highest level? Rather than ironic management speak, which twists words to manipulate emotions in the expectation that this will yield greater output, a more honest reflection on the problems of occupational ill-health would question the hoarding of status and reward by a small number of senior managers. Instead, traditional forms of management and hierarchy are rescued by the new ubiquity of digital surveillance, which allows informal behaviour and communication to be tracked, analysed and managed.

Rather than the rise of alternative corporate forms, we are now witnessing the discreet return of the 'scientific management' style of Frederick Winslow Taylor, only now with even greater scientific scrutiny of bodies, movement and performance. The front line in worker performance evaluation has shifted into bodily-monitoring devices, heart-rate monitoring, and sharing of real-time health data, for analysis of stress risks. Strange to say, the notion of what represents a 'good' worker has gone full circle since the 1870s, from the origins of ergonomic fatigue studies, through psychology, psychosomatic medicine and back to the body once more. Perhaps the managerial cult of optimization just needs something tangible to cling onto.

5

The Crisis of Authority

In recent years, Britain's Conservative Party has viewed its annual conference as a PR disaster waiting to happen. These meetings, traditionally held in seaside towns such as Brighton and Blackpool, see thousands of delegates from local Conservative clubs congregate in search of leaders finally willing to throw off the scourge of political correctness and modern values. Whether it be low-level racism emanating from the conference platform, the bland male greyness of the figures in the spotlight or the sight of elderly supporters expressing their disgust with same-sex relationships, potential embarrassment lurks around every corner.

But in 1977, two years into Margaret Thatcher's leadership of the party, a dose of youthful and unexpected colour was injected into proceedings. A sixteen-year-old schoolboy with a thick Northern accent, William Hague, took the platform and elicited hoots of approval from the otherwise staid conference, including from the woman who would go on to be prime minister for eleven years.

In between tearing into the 'socialist state' of the Labour government of the day, the teenager gently ribbed his audience: 'It's alright for most of you – half of you won't be here in thirty or forty years' time'. He proceeded to identify the nub of the socialist threat. 'There is at least one school in London', he announced, 'where the pupils are allowed to win just one race each, for fear that to win more would make the other pupils seem inferior. That is a classic illustration of the socialist state, which draws nearer with every Labour government.'

Twenty years later, Hague was the new leader of his party. He never got to taste the electoral victory as leader that his heroine had over the course of the 1980s. But he would no doubt have been delighted with how British society had developed in the meantime. After twenty years of Thatcherite policy-making, the 'socialist state' was scarcely discernable anywhere, least of all in Tony Blair's recently elected Labour government. A pro-business, free-market creed had taken hold across the Western world. And in keeping with the teenage Hague's vision, the political appeal of competitive sport had never been higher.

During the long economic boom that lasted from the early 1990s up until the banking meltdowns of 2007–08, sport was the great unquestionable virtue for political leaders everywhere. Attracting international sporting contests, such as the FIFA World Cup and Olympics, to particular cities became a cause célèbre for political elites who hoped to bask in the reflected glory of successful professional athletes. As prime minister, Tony Blair took to the sofa of the BBC's flagship football programme to chat informally about the skills of his favourite midfielder. His successor, Gordon Brown, tried to get in on the act, using his first day in 10 Downing Street to give a speech citing his school rugby team as his abiding inspiration. And when his authority was tottering in the summer of 2008, Brown returned to Hague's original theme, throwing his weight behind more competitive school sport. 'That is the spirit we want to encourage in our schools,' he declared, 'not the medals for all culture we have seen in previous years, but more competition'.

Meanwhile, there was little sporting metaphors couldn't apparently justify. Every further inflation of executive pay was explained in terms of maintaining a 'level playing field' in a 'war for talent'. When pressed by an interviewer in 2005 about the rising inequality that his government had overseen, Tony Blair responded that 'it's not a burning ambition for me to make sure that David Beckham earns less money', despite the fact that football had nothing to do with the question.[1]

Even after the epic failure of the neoliberal model of 2008, Britain's political class has returned to this rhetoric, announcing that the 'global *race*' requires that welfare is slashed and labour markets further deregulated. The need to entrench 'competitiveness' as the defining culture of businesses, cities, schools and entire nations, so as to out-do international rivals, is the mantra of the post-Thatcher era. A science of winning, be it in business, sport or just in life, now brings together former sportsmen, business gurus and statisticians to extend lessons from sport into politics, from warfare into business strategy, and from life coaching into schools.

But as the teenage Hague imagined the future thirty or forty years hence, there was one defining trend of the new era that neither he nor anybody else could foresee. It transpires that competition and competitive culture, including that of sport, is intimately related to a disorder that was scarcely discussed in 1977 but which had become a major policy concern by the end of the century. As the 1970s drew to a close, Western capitalist countries stood on the cusp of a whole new era of psychological management. The disorder at the heart of this was depression.

One way of observing the relationship between depression and competitiveness is in statistical correlations between rates of diagnosis and levels of economic inequality across society. After all, the function of any competition is to produce an unequal outcome. More equal societies, such as Scandinavian nations, record lower levels of depression and higher levels of well-being overall, while depression is most common in highly unequal societies such as the United States and United Kingdom.[2] The statistics also confirm that relative poverty – being poor in comparison to others – can cause as much misery as absolute poverty, suggesting that it is the sense of inferiority and status anxiety that triggers depression, in addition to the stress of worrying about money. For this reason, the effect of inequality on depression is felt much of the way up the income scale.

Yet there is more to this than just a statistical correlation. Behind the numbers, there is troubling evidence that depression can be triggered by the competitive ethos itself, afflicting not only the 'losers' but also the 'winners'. What Hague identified as the socialist fear, that competition makes many people 'seem inferior', has been proved far more valid than even left-wing 1970s schoolteachers could have imagined; it also tells them that they *are* inferior. In recent years, there has been a flurry of professional sportspersons confessing their battles with depression. In April 2014, a group of prominent ex-sportsmen in the UK penned an open letter urging 'sporting directors, coaches, and leaders of development programmes, to attend to the development of "inner fitness" alongside "athletic fitness"', to protect professional sportsmen from this epidemic.[3]

A study conducted at Georgetown University found that college footballers are twice as likely to experience depression as non-footballers. Another study discovered that professional female athletes display similar personality traits as those with eating disorders, both being linked to obsessive perfectionism.[4]

And a series of experiments and surveys conducted by the American psychologist Tim Kasser has revealed that 'aspirational' values, oriented around money, status and power, are linked to higher risk of depression and a lower sense of 'self-actualization'.[5] Wherever we measure our self-worth relative to others, as all competitions force us to, we risk losing our sense of self-worth altogether. One of the sad ironies here is that the effect of this is to dissuade people, including schoolchildren, from engaging in physical exercise altogether.[6]

Perhaps it is no surprise, then, that a society such as America's, which privileges a competitive individual mindset at every moment in life, has been so thoroughly permeated by depressive disorders and demand for antidepressants. Today, around a third of adults in the United States and close to half in the UK believe that they occasionally suffer from depression, although the diagnosis rates are far lower than that. Psychologists have shown that individuals tend to be happiest if they credit themselves for their successes, but not for their failures. This might sound like a symptom of delusion, but it is arguably no more delusional than a competitive, depressive culture which attributes every success *and every failure* to individual ability and effort.

Hasn't America always been a competitive society? Isn't that the original dream of the settlers, the Founding Fathers and the entrepreneurs who built American capitalism? This myth of society-as-competitive-sport surely dates back far earlier than the late 1970s; and yet it was only in the late 1970s that the epidemic of depression first took hold. It seems extraordinary now to consider that, in 1972, British psychiatrists were diagnosing depression at five times the rate of their US counterparts. And as recently as 1980, Americans still consumed tranquilizers at more than twice the rate of antidepressants. What changed?

From 'better' to 'more'

The sixteen-year-old Hague had taken the conference platform at a turning point in the history of economic policy-making in the Western world. According to the most respected measure of income inequality, Britain has never been more equal than it was in 1977.[7] But at the same time, the case for market deregulation was becoming increasingly credible, urged on by corporations that felt that they had become victimized by regulators, unions and consumer pressure groups.[8] Persistently high inflation had led a number of governments, including Britain's, to experiment in 'monetarism', an attempt to control the amount of money in circulation but which also threatened economic growth and jobs. Thatcher and Ronald Reagan were waiting in the wings to usher in the era that would become known as 'neoliberalism'.

One way of understanding neoliberalism is to examine how things progressed from there: the spiralling executive pay, the unprecedented levels of unemployment, the growing dominance of the financial sector over the rest of the economy and society, the expansion of private sector management techniques into all other walks of life. Analysing these trends is important. But it is also important to understand how and why they were possible, and that involves turning in the opposite direction, to the twenty-year period which preceded young Hague's call to arms. It is during those two decades that many of the critical ingredients of neoliberalism would shift from the outer margins of intellectual and political respectability to becoming the orthodoxies of a new era. Among these were a renewed reverence for *both* competitiveness *and* the management of happiness.

At the heart of the cultural and political battles of the 1960s was an acute relativism which attacked the roots of moral, intellectual, cultural and even scientific authority. The right to declare some behaviours as 'normal', certain claims as 'true', particular outcomes as 'just', or one culture as 'superior' was thrown into question. When the traditional sources of authority over these things attempted to defend their claims, they were accused of offering just one partial perspective, and of using their own parochial language to do so. In place of some values being 'better' or 'truer' than others, there was simply conformity on the one hand and difference on the other.

The core political and philosophical questions posed by the 1960s were these. How to take *any* publicly legitimate decisions, once there are no commonly recognized hierarchies or shared values any longer? What *will* provide the common language of politics, once language itself has become politicized? How *will* the world and society be represented, once even representation is considered to be a biased and political act? The problem, from a governmental point of view, was that the reach of democracy was extending too far.

Jeremy Bentham's vision of a scientific, utilitarian politics was initially motivated by an urge to cleanse legal process and punishment of the abstract nonsense that he believed still polluted the language of judges and politicians. In that sense, he hoped it would rescue politics from philosophy. But viewed differently, it could also serve a different function. The recourse to mathematical measurement could also rescue politics from excessive democracy and cultural pluralism. The Benthamite emphasis on a robust and scientific measure of psychological welfare reappeared in the wake of the 1960s, in various guises, some of which were associated with the counter-culture, others of which were ostensibly being peddled by conservatives. But they succeeded politically to the extent that they could claim to sit outside the fray. What they shared was an attempt to use numbers as a means of recreating a common public language.

In a world where we cannot agree what counts as 'good' and what counts as 'bad', because it's all a matter of personal or cultural perspective, measurement offers a solution. Instead of indicating quality, it indicates quantity. Instead of representing how good things are, it represents how much they are. Instead of a hierarchy of values, from the worst up to the best, it simply offers a scale, from the least up to the most. Numbers are able to settle disputes when nothing else looks likely to.

At its most primitive, the legacy of the 1960s is that *more* is necessarily preferable to *less*. To grow is to progress. Regardless of what one wants, desires, or believes, it is best that one gets as much of it as possible. This belief in growth as a good-in-itself was made explicit by some subcultures and psychological movements. Humanistic psychology, as advanced by Abraham Maslow and Carl Rogers, attempted to reorient psychology – and society at large – away from principles of normalization and towards the quest for ever greater fulfilment.[9] Individuals were perceived to be hemmed in by the dull conformity of 1950s culture, which blocked their capacity to grow. To assume that there was a 'natural' or 'moral' limit to personal growth was to fall back into repressive traditions. It wasn't long before corporations were making the identical argument about the malign impact of market regulation on profit growth.

The first-ever attempt to compare the happiness levels of entire nations was conducted in 1965, by the former pollster to President Roosevelt, Hadley Cantril.[10] In collaboration with the Gallup polling company, Cantril surveyed members of the public around the world in an entirely new way, which he termed the 'self-anchoring striving scale'. Pollsters had historically been

interested in how individuals felt towards specific products, policies, leaders or institutions. Cantril's innovation was to ask them
how they felt about their lives, relative to their own aspirations.
Attitudinal research had invited people to look outwards upon
the world and express their opinion as a number. Cantril asked
them to look inwards upon themselves and do the same. This
was a landmark in the development of contemporary happiness
studies. But in the notion of 'self-anchored striving', it also hinted
at the loneliness and aimlessness of a society with nothing but
private fulfilment as its overarching principle.

The problem is that even a society of self-actualization and
growth still needs some form of government and recognized
authority. Who will provide it? Where will the expertise come
from, to write the ground rules of this new growth-obsessed, relativist society?

What we witness, in the period from the late 1950s to the late
1970s, is the rise of a new breed of expert, capable of recon-
structing authority for this new cultural landscape. Unlike the
scientific and political authorities that they – often deliberately
– displaced, their authority was devoid of the traditional moral
baggage of professionalism, and rooted instead in a dispassionate
ability to measure, rank, compare, categorize and diagnose,
apparently uncluttered by moral, philosophical or social concerns. The old experts carried around notions such as the 'public
interest', 'justice' and 'truth'. As Bentham might have put it,
they were victims of the 'tyranny of sounds' that theory exerts
over the mind. The new experts were simply technicians,
applying tools and measures which they were proud to declare
were 'theory neutral'.

At a time when political disputes were raging to the point of
violence and beyond, dispassionate scientists, who were simply

qualified to measure and to classify, were an attractive new source of authority. Crucially, this ethos was both counter-cultural and conservative at the same time: counter-cultural, because it knocked the old establishment authorities off their perch, and conservative because it lacked any vision of political progress of its own. In that respect, these experts offered an exit route from the 'culture wars'. In the biographies of a handful of scholars who moved from the periphery of American academia circa 1960 to becoming the architects of a new competitive-depressive society by 1980, we can see the seeds of neoliberalism being sown.

Bentham in Chicago

There is something a little eerie about Chicago's Hyde Park neighbourhood. Its tree-lined streets of late-nineteenth-century houses feel typical of many traditional upper-middle-class American suburbs. At its heart sits the great University of Chicago, mimicking the gothic style of an Oxford college, complete with mediaeval turrets and stain-glassed windows. Wandering around the leafier parts of Hyde Park, where ivy creeps up walls and lawns are groomed immaculately, the visitor could be forgiven for forgetting where they actually were. A reminder comes in the form of the emergency phones, located in white posts on every corner in and around the university, with a blue light on top. Hyde Park is a sanctuary of peace and scholarship, but it is located in Chicago's South Side, and visitors are advised against straying too far in any single direction on foot.

This cocoon in which the university sits was a significant

factor in the development of the 'Chicago School' of economics, which was instrumental in the design and implementation of the neoliberal policy revolution. Chicago itself is 700 miles from Washington, DC, and 850 miles from Cambridge, Massachusetts, the homes of Harvard and MIT, the original bastions of American economics. Not only were Chicago School economists tightly congregated in Hyde Park, they were also several hundred miles from the core of the political and academic establishments. They had little choice but to seek debate with one another, and for three decades after the end of World War Two, they engaged in this with a rare fury.

The scholars who became known as the Chicago School began to cluster around the leadership of economists Jacob Viner and Frank Knight during the 1930s. By the late 1950s, they had grown into a tight-knit family. In one case, the family ties were quite literal: Milton Friedman married Rose Director, sister of Aaron, who was the linchpin of the post-war Chicago School. Aside from a certain geographic isolation, these economists had a number of intellectual and cultural traits in common. Among these was the sensibility of the outcast.

Until cracks appeared in the previously dominant Keynesian policy programme during the early 1970s, Chicago was rarely taken entirely seriously as a centre of economics and was only grudgingly offered recognition by Harvard and MIT as the Reagan revolution unfolded. In time, however, the Chicago economists began a steady accumulation of Nobel Prizes. Friedman, who grew into the status of a conservative celebrity as the 1960s wore on, was the son of Jewish immigrants and boasted of his lack of establishment credentials. Gary Becker, another prominent member of the school, admitted that they all had a 'chip on their shoulder'.[11] Their sense of iconoclasm was fuelled by the sense that America was run by a northeastern elite of liberal intellectuals who simply *assumed* their right to rule.

Following from this was a shared suspicion of government. One way in which this was aired was via the application of economic analysis to the behaviour of law-makers and government bureaucrats, to demonstrate that they were equally self-interested as businesses or consumers in a marketplace. The work of George Stigler, known as 'Mr Micro' to Friedman's 'Mr Macro' (a joke on account of the microeconomist Stigler being over a foot taller than his macroeconomist friend), turned the spotlight of economic analysis away from markets and towards those in Washington who claimed to act in the public interest.

Suspicion of government is not necessarily the same thing as being anti-state, and so it proved. In the most controversial episode of a controversial career, Friedman visited Chile in spring 1975 to offer advice to the autarchic Pinochet regime. For a man who professed anarchist sympathies, this engagement with a military dictator appeared hypocritical to say the least. Friedman simply defended himself as someone who was in pursuit of scientific knowledge and willing to share it with whomever was interested. In any case, the Chicago School complaint against governments was not that they had too much power, but – à la Bentham – that they used it in an unscientific fashion. In short, policy-makers needed to listen to economists more closely, a view that reveals the most distinctive Chicagoan trait of all: the fundamental belief that economics is an objective science of human behaviour which can be cleanly separated from all moral or political considerations.

At the root of this science lay a simple model of psychology that can be traced back via Jevons to Bentham. According to this model, human beings are constantly making cost-benefit trade-offs in pursuit of their own interests. Jevons explained the movement of market prices in terms of such psychological rationality on the part of consumers, who are constantly seeking more bang for their buck (or less buck for their bang). What distinguished the Chicago School was that they extended this model of psychology beyond the limits of market consumption, to apply to *all forms* of human behaviour. Caring for children, socializing with friends, getting married, designing a welfare programme, giving to charity, taking drugs – all of these apparently social, ethical, ritualized or irrational activities were reconceived in Chicago as calculated strategies for the maximization of private psychological gain. They referred to this psychological model as 'price theory' and saw no limit to its application.

Nobody seized the implications of this more than Gary Becker. Today, Becker is known for having developed the notion of 'human capital', a concept that has helped shape and justify the privatization of higher education through demonstrating that individuals receive a monetary return from 'investment' in their skills.[12] More diffusely, Becker's influence has been felt in an approach that reduces all moral and legal questions to problems of cost-benefit analysis. Individuals are addicted to drugs? The price of the drugs is obviously too low, or perhaps the pleasure received from them is too high. Shoplifting is on the rise? The penalties (and risk of being caught) are obviously too low; but then again, maybe it makes more sense to endure the shoplifting than to invest money in closed-circuit television and security guards.

The economists who carried out this work were always fiercely resistant to the idea that they were ideologically motivated. All they were trying to do, they reasoned, was identify the facts, free from the moral and philosophical baggage that cluttered the minds of their liberal rivals in Harvard and MIT or the politicos in Washington. The behaviourist ghost of John B. Watson hovered in the background, insisting that human activity could be understood in its entirety, with sufficient scientific scrutiny by a detached observer.

Their analyses were tested in the infamous pressure-cooker environment of the economics department's 'workshop' system. In conventional academic seminars, a speaker reads a paper which the attendees are encountering for the first time. There is no time for an audience member to develop a very acute critique, even if she wanted to. But Chicago's 'workshop' system was different. Papers would be circulated in advance for reading and authors would have only a few minutes to defend what they'd written before the roomful of colleagues would dive upon them, seeking holes in their logic, pursuing errors in the argument like it was their prey. 'Where should I sit?' a nervous speaker once asked Stigler, who was organizing the workshop. 'In your case, under the desk', quipped Stigler grimly.

What if the psychological model or 'price theory' itself was faulty? What if people *don't* act like rational calculators of private gain, least of all in their domestic, social and political lives? What if economics *isn't* fully adequate to understanding why people behave as they do? In the seminar rooms of Chicago economics, these were the questions that could never be raised. All regimes of radical, sceptical, anti-philosophical empiricism require certain propositions which are exempted from scrutiny. In Chicago, that proposition is price theory, which, from the lectures of Viner during the 1930s through to the current pop-economics fad of *Freakonomics*, has been the central article of faith for an institution that proclaims to have no need for faith.

How to out-Chicago Chicago

> An Archimedes who suddenly has a marvelous idea and shouts 'Eureka!' is the hero of the rarest of events. I have spent all of my professional life in the company of first-class scholars but only once have I encountered something like the sudden Archimedian revelation—as an observer.

It was in these breathless tones that George Stigler recounted one particular workshop in 1960, which took place in Aaron Director's home in Hyde Park. Stigler would never forget that evening and later cursed Director for not having tape-recorded it.[13] It became a turning point for his career and for the Chicago School more generally. Arguably, it was a turning point for the project of neoliberalism.

The paper that was discussed that evening was the work of the British economist Ronald Coase, then of the University of Virginia. Coase always resisted the iconic status that Stigler and others were keen to bestow upon him. His career had progressed quietly and methodically, through asking simple scientific questions about why economic institutions are structured as they are. He claimed never to understand the excitement that his work had engendered. He collected his 1991 Nobel with the words 'What I have done has been determined by factors which were no part of my choosing', a sentiment that would have struck the chip-on-shoulder, competitive individualists of Chicago as akin to defeatism.

And yet, by accident or otherwise, this modest economist with a working class background in Kilburn, London, acquired the role of an 'Archimedes' for the intellectual bruisers from Hyde Park. In the process, he contributed to a new, more vicious understanding of how capitalism should be governed, and the form that competition should take. Coase's work ended up a crucial plank in a political worldview stating that there was no limit to how large and powerful a capitalist firm should be allowed to become, so long as it was acting in a 'competitive' fashion.

Coase has never been described as a 'neoliberal', less still a 'conservative'. He was, however, taught by two economists at the London School of Economics during the 1930s, Friedrich Hayek and Lionel Robbins, who were both instrumental in the emergence of neoliberal thought. Robbins and Hayek were seeking to muster a fight-back against the Keynesian and socialist thinking that thrived through the Depression, by highlighting the unique intelligence contained in the price system of competitive markets. Coase breathed this in. More importantly, he was exposed to Hayek's intense scepticism regarding what any social science, including economics, could be capable of knowing.

Armed with a radically sceptical eye, though nevertheless adhering to the basic tenets of 'price theory', Coase was able to ask a question that his more libertarian colleagues in Chicago had never properly considered: What exactly *is* the benefit of a market anyway? If it's to produce welfare, is it not possible that, under certain circumstances, this can be done even better through different types of organization, such as corporations? In their hostility to state intrusions in markets, Friedman and company had largely just assumed that free markets were intrinsically superior on principle. But paradoxically, this belief also committed them to certain types of state intervention, namely regulation and competition law, which would ensure that the market maintained its correct form.

Coase's brilliance was to spot within the Chicago School position a final remnant of metaphysical speculation that they themselves were not aware of. Up until this point, the Chicago School still assumed that markets needed to be open, competitive, run according to certain principles of fairness, or else they would become submerged under the weight of monopolies. Markets needed ground rules if they were to match up to the ideal of being a space of individual freedom. This meant that they still required authorities capable of intervening, once competitors ceased to play fair or grew too powerful, and the market started to 'fail'.

Ever the sceptic, Coase did not accept this style of reasoning. Nothing in real economic life was ever that simple. Markets were never *perfectly* competitive in actuality, so the categorical distinction between a market that 'works' and one that 'fails' was an illusion generated by economic theory. The question economists should be asking, Coase argued, is whether there is good evidence that a specific regulatory intervention will make everyone better off overall. And by 'everyone', this shouldn't just mean consumers or small businesses, but the party being regulated as well. This argument was straight out of Bentham: he was advocating that policy be led purely by statistical data on aggregate human welfare, and abandon all sense of 'right' and 'wrong' altogether. If there isn't sufficient data to justify government intervention – and such evidence is hard to assemble – then regulators would be better off leaving the economy alone altogether.

One of the most far-reaching implications of Coase's argument was that monopolies are not nearly as bad as economists tend to assume. Compared to a perfectly competitive, perfectly efficient market, then yes, monopolies are undesirable. But this was what Coase disparagingly called 'blackboard economics'. If economists opened their eyes and looked at capitalism as it actually existed, they might discover that regulatory efforts to produce efficient markets were often counter-productive. Meanwhile, leaving firms alone to work things out for themselves (using private contracts and compensation where necessary) could actually produce the best available outcome overall – not a perfect outcome, just the best one available. The function of economics was to carefully calculate what should be done, on a case-by-case basis, not to offer utopian visions of perfect scenarios.

Coase's scepticism towards regulation first appeared in a 1959 paper on the telecoms market. This made a stir. While the Chicago School were no friends of government, they had at least assumed that markets needed to be kept in check to some extent, if they were not to become dominated by vast corporations making excessive profits. On the other hand, they were intrigued by Coase's critical style of reasoning, and the radicalism of his conclusions. Director invited the Englishman to give a paper defending his position, a paper which was later published as 'The Problem of Social Cost', becoming one of the most cited articles in the history of economics.

Scenting blood, twenty-one leading figures from the Chicago economics department arrived. All had read Coase's paper, and a vote taken at the beginning of the evening suggested that all twenty-one of them disagreed with it. In the timeworn style of the Chicago workshop, Coase was introduced by Director, then given five minutes to explain and justify his argument, before he would be torn apart by force of economic logic. As ever on these occasions, when it came to the latter part, Milton Friedman led the way. But on this occasion, something unusual happened – Friedmanite logic did not appear to be working. Here's George Stigler again:

Ronald didn't persuade us. But he refused to yield to all our erroneous arguments. Milton would hit him from one side, then from another, then from another. Then to our horror, Milton missed him and hit us. At the end of that evening the vote had changed. There were twenty-one votes for Ronald and no votes [against].[14]

As one of his students later put it, 'He had out-Chicagoed Chicago'.[15] Coase had no ideological axe to grind against government. He was not possessed of any particular love of unregulated, dog-eat-dog capitalism, which was more than could be said of Friedman.

What he *did* have, which the Chicago economists found irresistible, was a desire to question every assumption about how the economy ought to be governed, every assumption about what 'good' and 'bad' competition looked like, and to challenge the assumptions of policy-makers that they could necessarily tell the difference between the two. Through his scepticism towards the very possibility of a perfect market, he was even more doubtful of the state's authority than Friedman et al. Scientific economic analysis alone could determine whether a regulatory intervention was needed.

Sympathy for the capitalist

Stigler believed that an entire paradigm had shifted before his eyes. The theoretical case that underpinned government regulation of markets had evaporated, right there in Aaron Director's living room. It turned out that, up until 1960, *even the Chicago School* had been labouring under some metaphysical moral presumption that certain situations were essentially in need of government intervention and others weren't. 'Coase's Theorem', as Stigler later christened it, stated that this wasn't the case, and there was no basis on which to believe that regulation could automatically improve on situations that arose spontaneously between competing actors.

Except that this wasn't quite what Coase had argued. The paper he had defended in Director's home that evening in 1960 said that there were no grounds *on principle* to assume that market regulation was ever necessary. There were no grounds *on principle* to assume that one competitor exploiting another was necessarily a bad thing. But nor were there any grounds on principle to believe that regulatory intervention was a bad thing either. Coase was simply making a plea for robust economic analysis of the data available, as an alternative to the utopian propositions of 'blackboard economics'. To maintain authority amidst various conflicting perspectives on the rights and wrongs of a competitive situation, regulators needed to be staffed by economists who would simply represent the facts.

Stigler and his colleagues had little interest in such even-handedness. What they now possessed was a devastating critique of the moral authority of regulators and legislators, who purported to act in the 'public interest' but were typically just acting either in their own interests (to create more jobs for regulators) or out of political resentment towards large successful businesses. What regulators and left-wing liberals had singularly failed to recognize was that large, exploitative, monopolistic businesses also generate welfare. In fact, given a free rein, who knew how much welfare they might produce?

From the increasingly bullish Chicagoan perspective, the scale of giant corporations allowed them to work more efficiently, doing more good for consumers and society at large. The benefit they produced did not happen in spite of their aggressive competitive behaviour, but because of that behaviour. Let them grow as far as they can, as profitably as they can, and see what happens. Why worry about businesses getting 'too big'? Who is to say that they shouldn't be *even bigger*? By the end of the decade, Friedman was stating the pro-corporate argument even more nakedly. As he put it in a famous article published in *The New York Times Magazine* in 1970, the single moral duty of a corporation is to make as much money as it possibly can.[16]

The question that Coase posed that evening in 1960 was a radical one: regulators had long been striving to protect competitors from larger bullies, but *what about the welfare of the bully*? Didn't he deserve to be taken into account as well? And – as the Chicago School would later seek to explain – might consumers actually be better off being served by the same very large, efficient monopolists than constantly having to choose between various smaller, inefficient competitors? If the welfare of *everyone* were taken into account, including the welfare of aggressive corporate behemoths, then it was really not clear what benefit regulation was actually achieving.

Here was utilitarianism being reinvented in such a way as to include corporations in the state's calculus. Walmart, Microsoft and Apple didn't exist in 1960, but they could not have imagined a more sympathetic policy template than the one that was cooked up in Chicago on the back of Coase's work. Once Reagan was in the White House, these ideas spread quickly through the policy and regulatory establishments of Washington, DC, before permeating many international regulators over the 1990s.[17] In less than a decade, policy-makers went from viewing high profitability as a warning sign that a firm was growing too large to being a welcome indication that a firm was being managed in a highly 'competitive' fashion.

There is one deeply counter-intuitive lesson which emerges from this: American neoliberalism is not actually all that enamoured with competitive markets at all. That is to say, if we understand a market as a space in which there is a choice of people to transact with, and a degree of freedom as to whether to do so – think of eBay for example – the Chicago School was entirely comfortable with the notion of businesses restricting this choice, restricting this freedom, on grounds that it produces more utility overall.

What Stigler, Friedman, Director and their colleagues really admired was not the market as such, but the competitive psychology that was manifest in the entrepreneurs and corporations which sought to vanquish their rivals. They didn't want the market to be a place of fairness, where everyone had an equal chance; they wanted it to be a space for victors to achieve ever-greater glory and exploit the spoils. In their appeals to the limitless potential of capital, these Chicago conservatives were making a similar appeal to the logic of growth as the counter-culture and the humanistic psychologists were. With Gary Becker's metaphor of 'human capital', the distinction between corporate strategy and individual behaviour dissolved altogether: each person and each firm was playing a long-term game for supremacy, whether or not there was a market present.

In what sense is this winner-take-all economics still 'competition'? Perhaps the clue to the Chicagoan vision lay in their own combative intellectual culture. These professed outcasts, with a 'chip on their shoulder', believed that no game was ever really lost. Friedman made his career on the basis of arguing single-handedly against a global Keynesian orthodoxy for nearly four decades, until finally, by the late 1970s, he was perceived to have 'won'. Coase no doubt impressed his hosts partly by his willingness to stand up for his minority view, and willing them over. The elites of Harvard, MIT and the federal government were entitled to enjoy their period of dominance, but they should have taken these upstarts in Chicago a little more seriously from the start. Because when the neoliberals got to taste intellectual and political victory, they would fight just as hard to cling onto it. Chicago-style competition wasn't about co-existing with rivals; it was about destroying them. Inequality was not some moral injustice, but an accurate representation of differences in desire and power.

The Chicago School message to anyone complaining that today's market is dominated by corporate giants is a brutal one: go and start a future corporate giant yourself. What is stopping you? Do you not desire it enough? Do you not have the fight in you? If not, perhaps there is something wrong with you, not with society. This poses the question of what happens to the large number of people in a neoliberal society who are not possessed with the egoism, aggression and optimism of a Milton Friedman or a Steve Jobs. To deal with such people, a different science is needed altogether.

The science of deflation

The ability of individuals to 'strive' and 'grow' came under a somewhat different scientific spotlight between 1957 and 1958, due to accidental and coincidental discoveries made by two psychiatrists, Ronald Kuhn and Nathan Kline, working in the United States and Switzerland respectively. As with so many major scientific breakthroughs, it is impossible to specify who exactly got there first, for the simple reason that neither quite understood where exactly they had got *to*. The era of psychopharmacology was still very young, with the discovery of the first drug effective against schizophrenia in 1952 and the running of the first successful 'randomized control trials' (whereby a drug is tested alongside a placebo, with the recipients not knowing which one they've received) on Valium in 1954. These breakthroughs opened up a new neurochemical terrain for psychiatrists to explore.

Unlike the developers of those anti-anxiety and anti-schizo-phrenia drugs, Kline and Kuhn were not sure precisely what disorder they were seeking to target. Kline began experimenting with a drug called iproniazid, which had first been used against tuberculosis, while Kuhn was trialling imipramine in the hope that it might target psychosis. Had they both been certain of what effect they were looking for in advance, it's doubtful that they would have made any discovery at all. It was because they were not sure that they engaged in extremely careful observation of the drugs' recipients. Thanks to this, both psychiatrists noticed something that was both banal and revolutionary at the same time.

The drugs did not appear to have any particular effects that could be scientifically classified. There was no specific psychiatric symptom or disorder that they seemed to relieve. Given that psy-chiatrists of the 1950s still viewed their jobs principally in terms of healing those in asylums and hospitals, it wasn't clear that these drugs offered anything especially useful at all. As a result, drug companies initially showed little interest in the breakthrough. The drugs simply seemed to make people feel more truly themselves, restoring their optimism about life in general.

People felt *better* as a result of these pharmaceuticals, not in any specifically medical or psychiatric sense, but more in terms of their capacity for fulfilment and hope. As Kuhn observed, his new substance appeared to have 'antidepressant properties'. The extraordinary implication, which has since become our society's common sense, was that sadness and deflation, and hence their opposites, could be viewed in neurochemical terms.

For a while, psychiatrists struggled to know how to describe the new drugs. Kline chose to refer to his as a 'psychic energizer', which remains a decent description of many of the drugs currently marketed as 'antidepressants', but which are used to treat anything from eating disorders to premature ejaculation. The subtlety of their effects was perplexing, but this very property – this *selectivity* – has since come to be the main promise of those who seek to transform and improve us via our neurochemistry. Unlike barbiturates, the new drugs did not alter physical metabolism or overall levels of psychic activity. They appeared to boost those parts of the patient that had been deflated or damaged but to leave mind and body otherwise unaffected. This wasn't just the discovery of a new drug, but of a whole new notion of personhood.[18]

In the decades since Kuhn and Kline first experimented with their new drugs, antidepressants have become celebrated for this alleged selectivity and their non-specificity. The supposed genius of the selective serotonin reuptake inhibitor (SSRI) is to seek out the precise part of the self that requires energizing and give it a boost. In the years following the launch of Prozac in 1988, enthusiasm for the potential of SSRIs reached unprecedented heights. Claims were made by psychiatrists such as Peter Kramer that Prozac didn't simply boost mood, but reconnected individuals with their real selves.[19] The notion of illness, not to mention that of sadness, has been transformed in the process.

It would take twenty-five years before Kuhn and Kline's new 'psychic energizers' would attain mass market appeal; indeed they were initially marketed as anti-schizophrenia drugs. But culturally, their discovery was perfectly timed. Psychiatrists and psychologists had shown virtually no interest in the notion of happiness or flourishing up until this time. The influence of psychoanalysis meant that psychiatric problems were typically viewed through the lens of neurosis, that is, as conflict with oneself and one's past. Depression was a recognized psychiatric disorder that could be treated with electric shock therapy if severe enough, but it received comparatively little attention from the psychiatry profession, let alone the medical profession. The Freudian category of 'melancholia', as the inability to accept some past loss, continued to shape how chronic unhappiness was understood within much of the psychiatry profession.

But these psychoanalytic ideas were relatively useless when it came to dealing with a more diffuse form of depression, manifest as a generalized deflation of desire and capability. It was this that psychiatrists and psychoanalysts were increasingly confronted by as the 1960s wore on, forcing them to question certain core aspects of their theoretical training.[20] Depressed individuals were not speaking in terms of shame or repressed desires any longer, but merely in terms of their own weakness and inadequacy. If anything, it was an *absence* of desire that afflicted them, more than a bottling up. Admittedly, drug companies were content to assist with the relinquishing of traditional psychoanalytic theory, as the pharmaceutical company Merck demonstrated in 1961 when it distributed fifty thousand copies of Frank Ayd's *Recognizing the Depressed Patient* to doctors around the United States, immediately after winning a patent battle over the antidepressant amitriptyline.[21]

But the drugs were entangled in a broader cultural and moral transformation.

The question of how to boost general energy and positivity was an entirely new one for psychologists at the close of the 1950s. But it was slowly emerging as a distinctive field of research in its own right, with a number of new questionnaires, surveys and psychiatric scales through which to compare individuals in terms of their positivity. The year 1958 saw the launch of the Jourard Self-Disclosure Scale and then in 1961 the Beck Depression Inventory, the work of Aaron Beck, the father of cognitive behavioural therapy. Mental health surveys conducted in the United States during the 1950s, aimed partly at assessing the psychological state of war veterans, discovered that generalized depression was a far more common complaint than psychiatrists had assumed. This psychic deflation was coming to appear as a risk that could afflict anyone at any time, whether or not there was psychoanalytic material to back that assessment up.

By the late 1960s, psychologists were studying depression far more closely, without the assumption that there must be an underlying neurosis. Martin Seligman's experiments on 'learned helplessness', in which he showed that if you electrocuted a dog enough it would eventually cease to resist, helped to map out a new understanding of depression. This sowed the seeds of the positive psychology movement, dedicated to the programmatic 'unlearning' of helplessness, of which Seligman is the figurehead.

A drug that is itself *selective* immediately weakens the responsibility of the physician or psychiatrist to identify precisely what is wrong with a patient. It can therefore be prescribed in a non-specific way, as if to say, 'Try this, and see if whatever is ailing you starts to fade'. Misery itself becomes the phenomenon to be dealt with, rather than any particular manifestation or symptom. In the early 1960s, this was an affront to the authority of psychiatrists and doctors, whose professional role involved specifying *exactly* what was causing a problem and offering a solution to it. The idea that individuals may be suffering from some general collapse of their psychic capabilities, manifest in any number of symptoms, challenged core notions of medical or psychiatric expertise.

Over half a century after the discovery of antidepressants, it remains the case that nobody has ever discovered precisely how or why they work, to the extent that they do.[22] Nor could anybody ever make this discovery, because what it means for an SSRI to 'work' will differ from one patient to the next. A great deal of attention has been paid to how SSRIs alter our understanding of unhappiness, relocating it in our brain neurons; but they also fundamentally alter the meaning of a medical diagnosis and the nature of medical and psychiatric authority.

A society organized around the boosting of personal satisfaction and fulfilment – 'self-anchored striving' – would need to reconceive the nature of authority, when it came to tending and treating the pleasures and pains of the mind. Either that authority would need to become more fluid, counter-cultural and relativist itself, accepting the lack of any clear truth in this arena, or it would need to acquire a new type of scientific expertise, more numerical and dispassionate, whose function is to *construct* classifications, diagnoses, hierarchies and distinctions, to suit the needs of governments, managers and risk profilers, whose job would otherwise be impossible.

Psychiatric authority reinvented

The Chicago School ultimately benefited from the ostracism that
it was long shown by the American economics and policy establishment. It offered a lengthy gestation period, during which
alternative ideas and policy proposals could mature and be ready
for application by the time the governing orthodoxy had been
engulfed in crisis. That crisis began brewing in 1968, as US productivity growth began to falter and the cost of the Vietnam War
ate into the government's finances. The crisis mounted from
1972 onwards, with sharp rises in oil prices and the breakdown of
the global monetary system that had been put in place after
World War Two.

The American psychiatry profession experienced its own
crisis, with an almost identical chronology. In 1968, the American
Psychiatric Association (APA) published the second edition of
its handbook, the *Diagnostic and Statistical Manual of Mental
Disorders* (DSM). Compared to later versions of the manual, this
publication initially elicited very little debate. Even psychiatrists
had little interest in the book's somewhat nerdish question of
how to attach names to different symptoms. But within five years,
this book was the focus of political controversies that threatened
to sink the APA altogether.

One problem with the DSM-II was that it seemed to fail in its
supposed goal. After all, what was the use of having an officially
recognized list of diagnostic classifications if it didn't appear to
constrain how psychiatrists and mental health professionals actually worked? The same year that the DSM-II was published, the
World Health Organization published a study showing that even
major psychiatric disorders, such as schizophrenia, were being
diagnosed at wildly different rates around the world. Psychiatrists

seemed to have a great deal of discretion available to them, being led by theories as to what was underlying the symptoms, which were rarely amenable to scientific testing in any strict sense. They shared a single terminology but lacked any strict rules for how it should be applied.

The 'anti-psychiatry movement', as it was known, included some who viewed the entire profession as a political project aimed at social control. But it also included others, such as Thomas Szasz, who believed that psychiatry's main problem was that it was incapable of making testable, scientific propositions.[23] In a famous experiment conducted in 1973, nineteen 'pseudo-patients' managed to get themselves admitted into psychiatric institutions, by turning up and falsely reporting that they were hearing a voice saying 'empty', 'hollow' and 'thud'. This was later written up in the journal *Science* under the title 'On Being Sane in Insane Places', adding fuel to the anti-psychiatry movement.[24]

Most controversially, the DSM-II included homosexuality in its list of disorders, provoking an outcry that gathered momentum from 1970 onwards, with the support of leading anti-psychiatry spokespersons. The APA was relatively untroubled by the problem of unreliable diagnoses, seeing as few of its members or governing body were especially interested in reliability in the first place. But the political storm generated by the homosexuality classification was far harder to ignore. Whereas the problem of diagnostic reliability was largely containable within the profession itself, the controversy over the DSM classification of homosexuality had spilled out into the public sphere.

Just as the Chicago School waited patiently in the cold until the economic policy crisis of the 1970s had run its course, there was one school of psychiatry which was blissfully untroubled by the turmoil sweeping the APA. This small group, based at Washington University in St Louis, had long felt alienated from the psychoanalytic style of American psychiatry. Far more indebted to the Swiss psychiatrist Emil Kraepelin than to Freud (or to Adolf Meyer, whose adaptation of Freud's ideas dominated much APA thinking through the 1950s and '60s), they treated classification of psychiatric symptoms as of the foremost importance. Mental illness was to be viewed in the identical way as physiological illness, an event in the body – more specifically, the brain – which required objective scientific observation and minimal social interpretation.

Through the 1950s and 1960s, the St Louis group, led by Eli Robins, Samuel Guze and George Winokur, was left to operate in its own intellectual and social bubble. They were repeatedly refused funding by the National Institute of Mental Health, who preferred instead to fund studies within the Meyerian tradition, which focused on the relationship between mental illness and the social environment. The St Louis school were outcasts from the establishment, relying on networks with European sympathizers and throwing some rollicking parties among themselves, but peripheral to American psychiatry.

For these 'neo-Kraepelinians', psychiatry's claims to the status of science depended on diagnostic reliability: two different psychiatrists, faced with the same set of symptoms, had to be capable of reaching the same diagnostic conclusion independently from one another. Whether a psychiatrist truly understood what was troubling someone, what had caused it, or how to relieve it, was of secondary importance to whether they could confidently identify the syndrome by name. The job of the psychiatrist, by this scientific standard, was simply to observe, classify and name, not to interpret or explain. Within this vision, the moral and political vocation of psychiatry, which in its more utopian traditions had aimed at healing civilization at large, was drastically shrunk. In its place was a set of tools for categorizing maladies as they happened to present themselves. To many psychiatrists of the 1960s, this seemed like a banally academic preoccupation. But it was about to become a lot more than that.

While they were rejected by the psychiatry profession itself, the St Louis school were not the only voices arguing for greater diagnostic reliability at the time. Health insurance companies in the United States were growing alarmed by the escalating rates of mental health problems, with diagnoses doubling between 1952 and 1967.[25] Meanwhile, the pharmaceutical industry had a clear interest in tightening up diagnostic practices in psychiatry, thanks to a landmark piece of government regulation. There was an increasingly powerful business case for establishing a new consensus on the names that were attached to symptoms.

In 1962, Senator Estes Kerfauver of Tennessee and Representative Oren Harris from Arkansas had tabled an amendment to the 1938 Federal Drug, Food and Cosmetic Act, aimed at significantly tightening the rules surrounding regulatory approval of pharmaceuticals. This was a direct response to the thalidomide tragedy, which led to around ten thousand children around the world being born with physical deformities between 1960 and 1962 as a result of a new anti-anxiety drug that had begun to be prescribed for morning sickness. The United States was relatively unaffected, due to the prudence (later viewed as heroism) of one FDA official who blocked the drug on grounds that it wasn't adequately tested.

One feature of the Kerfauver-Harris amendment was that drugs had to be marketed with a clear identification of the syndrome that they offered to alleviate. Again, this made clarity around psychiatric classification imperative, although in this case for business reasons. If a drug seemed to have 'antidepressant properties', for example, this wasn't enough to clear the Kerfauver–Harris regulatory hurdle. It needed a clearly defined disease to target – which in that case would need to be called 'depression'. As the British psychiatrist David Healy has argued, this legal amendment is arguably the critical moment in the shaping of our contemporary idea of depression as a disease.[26] Thanks to Kerfauver–Harris, we've come to believe that we can draw clear lines around 'depression', and between varieties of it – lines that magically correspond to pharmaceutical products.

By 1973, the APA was facing charges of pseudoscience, homophobia and the peddling of regressive 1950s moral standards of normality. No less critically, they also represented a threat to the long-term profitability of big pharma. Both cultural and economic forces were pitted against the profession, throwing the very purpose of psychiatry into question. Ultimately, the St Louis approach to psychiatry would be the winner in this crisis, and the strict, anti-theoretical diagnostic approach would soon move from the status of nerdish irrelevance to orthodoxy. But it would take a particularly restless figure within the higher ranks of the APA to bring this volte-face about.

Robert Spitzer came from a traditional psychiatric background, joining the New York State Psychiatric Institute in 1966. He fell in with the authors of the DSM-II after hanging out with them at the Columbia University canteen in the late '60s, but was growing somewhat bored of the psychoanalytic theories peddled by his colleagues.[27] Spitzer was someone who enjoyed a fight. He'd grown up in a family of New York Jewish communists and spent his youth engaged in lengthy political and intellectual arguments with his father, not least over the latter's Stalinist sympathies. Today, he is commonly recognized as the most influential American psychiatrist of the late twentieth century. But as much as anything, this was down to his entrepreneurial zeal and imagination as it was to his ideas. What Spitzer had in spades, and which professional associations tended to lack, was an appetite for radical change.

In the late 1960s, Spitzer had a growing interest in diagnostic classification, spotting an alternative to the status quo. But his status within the APA was marginal, until he was given the task of defusing the homosexuality controversy. To achieve this, he mounted an aggressive campaign within the APA, offering an alternative description of the syndrome concerned – 'sexual orientation disturbance' – which highlighted that *suffering* must be involved before any diagnosis of sexuality disorder could be made. This was a subtle but telling distinction: Spitzer was implying that the relief of unhappiness should replace the pursuit of normality as the psychiatrist's abiding vocation. In 1973, he faced down opposition from senior colleagues within the APA on this issue and won. Thanks to Spitzer's advocacy, the question of sexual 'normality' was (not-so-quietly) replaced with one of classifiable misery, hinting at how the character of mental illness was changing more broadly.

The following year, Spitzer was given his next political challenge: to deal with the APA's diagnostic reliability. The DSM-II was already looking dated, and in any case needed rewriting to abide by the World Health Organization's own changing diagnostic criteria. Spitzer was appointed as chair of the Task Force on Nomenclature and Statistics, now with a clear mandate to deal with the problems of diagnostic reliability that had been brewing for over a decade. Crucially, he retained complete control over how the task force would be composed. He hand-picked its eight members with a clear intention to tear up the APA's existing theoretical principles and replace them with a set of methods which were straight out of St Louis.

Four of the eight appointees to Spitzer's task force were from St Louis, whom he described as 'kindred spirits'. The other four were judged to be sympathetic to the coup that Spitzer was about to stage. In appointing Spitzer, the APA – and certainly the health insurance industry – had hoped that stricter diagnostic categories would actually lead to a reduction in the levels of diagnosis overall. Greater rigor in the criteria attached to a diagnosis, it was assumed, would make it harder for syndromes to be diagnosed. What they hadn't calculated for was the exhaustiveness of the task force's approach to classification, which yielded a progressive multiplication in the varieties of recognized mental illness.

Every known psychiatric symptom was being listed, alongside a diagnosis. To do this, they drew heavily on a 1972 paper on diagnostic classification authored by the St Louis group, but adding further classifications and criteria.[28] Typing away in his office in Manhattan's West 168th Street, urging on his task force to recite symptoms and diagnoses like some endless psychiatric shopping list, Spitzer was unperturbed. 'I never saw a diagnosis that I didn't like', he was rumoured to have joked.[29] A new dictionary of mental and behavioural terminology was drafted.

Relatively unhappy

The resulting document that Spitzer and his team produced in 1978 provided the basis of the DSM-III, arguably the most revolutionary and controversial text in the history of American psychiatry. Finalized over the course of 1979 and published the following year, this handbook bore scarce resemblance to its 1968 predecessor. The DSM-II outlined 180 categories over 134 pages. The DSM-III contained 292 categories over 597 pages. The St Louis School's earlier diagnostic toolkit had specified (somewhat arbitrarily) that a symptom needed to be present for one month before a diagnosis was possible. Without any further justification, the DSM-III reduced this to two weeks.

Henceforth, a mental illness was something detectable by observation and classification, which didn't require any explanation of why it had arisen. Psychiatric insight into the recesses and conflicts of the human self was replaced by a dispassionate, scientific guide for naming symptoms. And in scrapping the possibility that a mental syndrome might be an understandable and proportionate response to a set of external circumstances, psychiatry lost the capacity to identify problems in the fabric of society or economy.[30] Proponents described the new position as 'theory neutral'. Critics saw it as an abandoning of the deeper vocation of psychiatry to heal, listen and understand. Even one of the task force members, Henry Pinsker (not from St Louis), started to get cold feet: 'I believe that what we now call disorders are really but symptoms'.[31]

The DSM-III came about because the APA had found itself on the wrong side of too many cultural and political arguments at once. The forms of truth that psychiatrists were seeking could not survive the turbulent atmosphere of 1968 and its aftermath: they were too metaphysical, too politically loaded and too difficult to prove. But amidst this is a story about how happiness – and its opposite – appeared as a preoccupation of mental health professionals, medical doctors, pharmaceutical companies and individuals themselves. To get to this point, the mainstream psychiatric establishment had to be virtually cut out of the loop. A landmark legal case in 1982, in which a psychiatrist was successfully sued for prescribing long-term psychodynamic therapy to a depressed patient, and not an antidepressant drug, offered a rousing demonstration of the new state of affairs.[32] Today, 80 per cent of the prescriptions that are written for antidepressants in the United States are by medical doctors and primary care practitioners, and not by psychiatrists at all.

In a post-1960s era of 'self-anchored striving', what can people possibly hold in common other than a desire for more happiness? And what higher purpose could a psychological expert pursue than the reduction of unhappiness? These simple, seemingly indisputable principles were what emerged from the cultural and political conflicts which came to a head in 1968. The growing problem of depression, experienced as a non-specific lack of energy and desire, combined with the emergence of a drug that seemed selectively to alleviate this, and the need of drug companies, regulators and health insurers to find clarity amidst such murkiness, meant that psychoanalytic expertise was heading for a fall.

A host of new techniques, measures and scales would be needed to track positive and negative moods in this new cultural and political landscape. Aaron Beck was well ahead of his time with his 1961 Beck Depression Inventory. In respect of physical pain, the influential McGill Pain Questionnaire was introduced in 1971. Various additional questionnaires and scales were introduced during the 1980s and 1990s to identify and quantify levels of depression, such as the Hospital Anxiety and Depression Scale (1983) and Depression Anxiety Stress Scales (1995). With the growing influence of positive psychology, which offered to mitigate the 'risk' of depression occurring, scales of 'positive affect' and 'flourishing' were added to these. Each of these represented a further manifestation of the Benthamite ambition to know how another person was feeling, through force of scientific measurement alone. Underlying them was the familiar monistic hope, that diverse forms of sadness, worry, frustration, neurosis and pain might be placed on simple scales, between the least up to the most.

The reconfigured DSM, together with the various newly designed scales, made it very clear what should be classified as depression and to what extent. A sufficient number of symptoms, such as loss of sleep, loss of appetite, loss of sexual appetite, in combination for two weeks or more could now be called 'depression'. But what it actually meant to be depressed, or what caused it, had disappeared from view, for many of the new league of psychological experts who emerged on the tails of Spitzer and the St Louis team. The voice of the sufferer was not quite silenced in the new diagnostic era, but it was regulated by the construction and imposition of strict questionnaires and indices. The neurosciences potentially now enable psychiatry to move away from even those restricted questions and answers.

So what really is this so-called disease that now afflicts around a third of people at some point in their lifetime, and around 8 per cent of American and European adults at any one time? It is often said that depression is the inability to construct a viable future for oneself. What goes wrong, when people suffer our contemporary form of depression, is not simply that they cease to experience pleasure or happiness, but that they lose the will or ability to seek pleasure or happiness. It is not that they become unhappy per se, but that they lose the mental – and often the physical – resources to pursue things that might make them happy. In becoming masters of their own lifestyles and values, they discover that they lack the energy to act upon them.

It is only in a society that makes generalized, personalized growth the ultimate virtue that a disorder of generalized, personalized collapse will become inevitable. And so a culture which values only optimism will produce pathologies of pessimism; an economy built around competitiveness will turn defeatism into a disease. Once the Benthamite project of psychic optimization loses any sense of agreed limits, promising only more and more, the troubling discovery is made that utilitarian measurement can go desperately negative as well as positive.

Depressive-competitive disorder

'Just do it'. 'Enjoy more'. Slogans such as these, belonging to Nike and McDonald's respectively, offer the ethical injunctions of the post-1960s neoliberal era. They are the last transcendent moral principles for a society which rejects moral authority. As Slavoj Žižek has argued, enjoyment has become an even greater duty than to obey the rules. Thanks to the influence of the Chicago School over government regulators, the same is true for corporate profitability.

The entanglement of psychic maximization and profit maximization has grown more explicit over the course of the neoliberal era. This is partly due to the infiltration of corporate interests into the APA. In the run up to the DSM-V, published in 2013, it was reported that the pharmaceutical industry was responsible for half of the APA's $50 million budget, and that eight of the eleven-strong committee which advised on diagnostic criteria had links to pharmaceutical firms.[33] The ways in which we describe ourselves and our mental afflictions are now shaped partly by the financial interests of big pharma.

One of the last remaining checks on the neurochemical understanding of depression was the exemption attached to people who were grieving: this, at the very least, was still considered a not unhealthy reason to be unhappy. But in the face of a new drug, Wellbutrin, promising to alleviate 'major depressive symptoms occurring shortly after the loss of a loved one', the APA caved in and removed this exemption from the DSM-V.[34] To be unhappy for more than two weeks after the death of another human being can now be considered a medical illness. Psychiatrists now study bereavement in terms of its possible mental health 'risks', without any psychoanalytic or common sense of *why* loss might be a painful experience.[35]

Corporations are also increasingly aware of the economic inefficiency of depression in an economy that trades on enthusiasm in the workplace and desire in the shopping mall.[36] Finding ways to lift people out of this illness, or reduce the risks of encountering it in the first place (through tailored diet, exercise or even brain scans to assess the risk early in children), is viewed as essential to the survival of corporate profitability. One report on the topic, sponsored by a number of UK corporations including Barclays Bank, stated with a peculiar absence of compassion, 'Today's brain-based economy puts a premium on cerebral skills, in which cognition is the ignition of productivity and innovation. Depression attacks that vital asset.'[37]

One way in which Bentham was shaped by the emancipatory social spirit of his age was in his assumption that the measurement and maximization of happiness were a collective venture. There was, in principle, a justification for one man's happiness to be impeded: for another man's benefit. Admittedly, the main arena in which he explored this was punishment: prison is justified to the extent that non-prisoners benefit from its existence. But nevertheless, the calculus of utility was one that took everyone into account. In economic policy, this could justify transfers of money from rich to poor, if it was clear that poverty was the cause of misery.

The depressive-competitive disorder of neoliberalism arises because the injunction to achieve a higher utility score – be that measured in money or physical symptoms – becomes privatized. Very rich, very successful, very healthy firms or people could, and *should*, become even more so. In the hands of the Chicago School of economics or the St Louis School of psychiatry, the logic that says we have a particular political or moral responsibility towards the weak, which may require us to impose restrictions on the strong, is broken. Authority consists simply in measuring, rating, comparing and contrasting the strong and the weak without judgement, showing the weak how much stronger they might be, and confirming to the strong that they are winning, at least for the time being.

Buried within the technocratic toolkits of neoliberal regulators and evaluators is a brutal political philosophy. This condemns most people to the status of failures, with only the faint hope of future victories to cling onto. That school in London 'where the pupils are allowed to win just one race each, for fear that to win more would make the other pupils seem inferior' was, in fact, a model of how to guard against a depressive-competitive disorder that few in 1977 could have seen coming. But that would also have required a different form of capitalism, which few policymakers today are prepared to warrant.

6

Social Optimization

Imagine walking into a coffee shop, ordering a cappuccino, and then, to your surprise, being informed that it has already been paid for. This sounds like a pleasant experience, one which might even make the coffee more pleasurable to drink. Where did this unexpected gift come from? It transpires that it was left by the previous customer. The only snag, if indeed it is a snag, is that you now have to do the same for the next customer to walk in.

This is known as a 'pay-it-forward' pricing scheme. It is something that has been practised by a number of small businesses in California, such as Berkeley's Karma Kitchen, and sometimes has been introduced spontaneously by customers themselves. On the face of it, it would seem to defy the logic of free market economics. After all, the basic premise of the price system, as it appeared to William Stanley Jevons and the neo-classical economists, is that I will exchange my money for a pleasure that I experience privately. Money for the shopkeeper is counter-balanced against satisfaction for me. Markets, surely, are places where we are allowed, even expected, to behave selfishly. With its hippy idealism, pay-it-forward would appear to defy the core tenets of economic calculation.

But there is more to it than this. Researchers based at UC

Berkeley's Decision Science Research Group have looked closely at pay-it-forward pricing and discovered something with profound implications for how markets and business work. It transpires that people will generally pay more for a good, under the pay-it-forward model, than under a conventional pricing system.[1] This is true even when the participants are complete strangers. As the study's lead author, Minah Jung, puts it, 'People don't want to look cheap. They want to be fair, but they also want to fit in with the social norms.' Contrary to what economists have long assumed, altruism can often exert a far stronger influence over our decision-making than calculation. If individuals can become seduced into relationships of reciprocity, rather than of selfish calculation, the capacity to influence them is that much greater. As Jung's research shows, so is the opportunity to charge them more money.

Similar research findings have been made in the workplace. The notion of 'performance-related pay' is a familiar one, suggesting, reasonably enough, that additional effort by an employee is rewarded by a commensurate increase in pay. But studies conducted by researchers at Harvard Business School have discovered that there is a more effective way of extracting greater effort from staff: represent pay increases as a 'gift'.[2] When money is offered in exchange for extra effort, the employee may be minded to view the extra money as their entitlement and carry on as before. But when the employer makes some apparently gratuitous act of altruism, the employee enters a more binding reciprocal relationship and works harder.

These findings are typical of the field of 'behavioural economics', which emerged in the late 1970s thanks to a reunion of psychology with economics, following their split at the end of the nineteenth century. Like regular economists, behavioural economists assume that individuals are usually motivated to maximize their own benefit – but not always. In certain circumstances, they are social and moral animals, even when this actually appears to undermine their economic interests. They follow the herd and act according to certain rules of thumb. They have some principles that they will not sacrifice for money at all. A number of much-hyped policy lessons follow from this, which have been referred to as 'nudges'.

For example, if some people are repeatedly creating a disturbance in their neighbourhood, how should they be dealt with? Jeremy Bentham would have supposed that the answer involved some sort of punishment: only if the behaviour were associated with pain would it become less appealing. An alternative answer, though with the same logic, is that they could be paid to behave better. But there is a third option, which Bentham might well have scoffed at. What if they sign a piece of paper, promising to change the way that they behave in future? Somewhat surprisingly, it transpires that this can often be the most effective strategy. Making an explicit moral commitment – even under duress – seems to bind people in certain ways that utilitarian penalties and incentives often do not.

It seems that this undermines the cynical, calculative, individualist theory of human psychology, which lies at the heart of Benthamism and orthodox economics. It transpires that we are as much motivated by moral principles as we are by our own selfish interests. Maybe the cold rationality of the market does not have quite the grip on our psychology as we have long feared. Could it be that we are decent, social creatures after all? A great deal of evidence from neuroscience, showing how sympathy and reciprocity are 'hard-wired' into the brain, confirms this. Perhaps this could be the basis for a new political hope, of a society in which sharing and gift-giving offer a serious challenge to the power of monetary accumulation and privatization.

But there is also a more disturbing possibility: that the critique of individualism and monetary calculation is now being incorporated into the armoury of utilitarian policy and management. The history of capitalism is littered with critiques of the dehumanizing, amoral world of money, markets, consumption and labour, offered by romantics, Marxists, anthropologists, sociologists and cultural critics among many. These critics have long argued that social bonds are more fundamental than market prices. The achievement of behavioural economics is to take this insight, but to then instrumentalize it in the interests of power. The very idea of the 'social' is being captured.[3]

John B. Watson had promised in 1917 that, in an age of behaviourist science, 'the educator, the physician, the jurist and the businessman could utilize our data in a practical way, as soon as we are able, experimentally, to obtain them.' Behavioural economics has been true to this mission statement. One of its key insights is that, if one wants to control other human beings, it is often far more effective to appeal to their sense of morality and social identity than to their self-interest. By framing notions such as 'fairness' and 'gift' in purely psychological and neurological terms, behavioural science converts them into instruments of social control.

Viewed from a more cynical perspective – as behavioural economists themselves do – activities such as pay-it-forward and random acts of managerial generosity have a pernicious element, which works through never being made explicit. In abandoning the psychology of pure self-interest, these projects shift to a far more invasive and constrictive alternative, namely the psychology of credit and debt. A psychological sense of social

184

obligation is first manufactured and then harnessed for particular purposes which remain concealed. If utilitarianism is, at its heart, a political logic in which every institution is to be judged in terms of its measured outcome, then the extension of this to encompass our basic moral sensibilities must represent that logic's final triumph.

The money-making 'social'

Generosity has become big business. In 2009, Chris Anderson, former editor of *Wired* magazine, published *Free: The Future of a Radical Price*. In this rallying cry, Anderson argued that there was now a strong business case for giving products and services away for free, so as to produce a better relationship with a customer. Of course money is not dispensed with altogether in this idyll of gift-giving. Giving things away for free becomes a means of holding an audience captive or building a reputation, which can then be exploited with future sales or advertising, this time commanding a price. Michael O'Leary, boss of Ryanair, Ireland's controversial budget airline, has even suggested that airline tickets might one day be priced at zero, with all costs recovered through additional charges for luggage, using the bathroom, skipping queues, and so on.

When it comes to the free market, all corporations dwell in a paradoxical position. They seek all of the freedoms that the market offers for their vested interests, but as few as possible for anybody else.[4] The trick is to maintain maximum autonomy for shareholders and executives while gaining maximum commitment from employees and customers. What Anderson was highlighting was simply the powerful potential of non-monetary

185

relationships in building closer bonds where they are useful in the service of profitmaking. To put it another way, the last thing a business wants from its customers (or their more valued staff) is for them to remember that they are in a market, with freedom of choice. Freebies are a useful way of disguising what's really taking place.

And just as corporate giving can be used as a way of boosting revenue, so can the magic words that are used in return. Marketing specialists now analyse the optimal way of saying the words 'thank you' to a customer, so as to deepen the 'social' relationship with them further. As one expert explains for the benefit of online retailers:

Thank you pages are much more than pieces of virtual real estate on which to display gratitude and order numbers. These pages are an integral part of an optimized conversion system that, when used properly, can continue to boost your revenue.[5]

The language of gratitude has infiltrated a number of high-profile advertising campaigns. Around Christmas 2013, a number of corporations – notably, those that had suffered serious reputational deficits in recent times – launched advertising campaigns offering general thanks to everyone around them. Naturally this included their customers, but it also extended to a general mood of gratitude for the gift of friendship.

Lloyds TSB, one of the British banks to be most embarrassed by the 2008 financial crisis, launched a campaign consisting entirely of cutesy images of childhood friends enjoying happy moments together, concluding with the words 'thank you' written in party balloons. There was no mention of money. More bizarrely, Tesco, a vast supermarket chain whose brand entered free fall in 2011, released a series of YouTube videos with men in Christmas jumpers singing 'thank you' to everyone from the person who cooks Christmas dinner, to those driving safely, to other companies such as Instagram and so on. Tesco, it was implied, sprays gratitude in all directions, regardless of its own private interests.

The strange spectacle of a corporation attempting to project feelings associated with friendship takes an even weirder turn when businesses seize the affordances of Twitter to grant them a quirky, conversational identity. Brands tweet at each other, in a coy, almost flirtatious fashion. Confronted by the phenomenon of the Denny's diner chain acting cool on Twitter, the writer Kate Losse observed how 'to become popular and "cool", brands have had to learn the very techniques we learned as resistant teens to deal with power: our sarcastic humor and our endlessly remixable memes'.[6] Corporations now want to be your friend.

There is, of course, a limit to how much of a social bond an individual can have with a PLC. Companies today are obsessed with being 'social', but what they typically mean by this is that they are able to permeate peer-to-peer social networks as effectively as possible. Brands hope to play a role in cementing friendships, as a guarantee that they will not be abandoned for more narrowly calculated reasons. So, for example, Coca-Cola has tried a number of somewhat twee marketing campaigns, such as putting individual names ('Sue', 'Tom', etc.) on their bottles as a way of inducing gift-giving, and even offered a 'twin pack', with the assumption that the drinks will be enjoyed by two people together. Managers hope that their employees will also act as 'brand ambassadors' in their everyday social lives and seek advice on how to influence them to do this. Meanwhile, neuromarketers have begun studying how successfully images and advertisements trigger common neural responses in groups, rather than in isolated individuals. This, it seems, is a far better indication of how larger populations will respond.[7]

The rise of the 'sharing economy', exemplified by Airbnb and Uber, and studies such as the pay-it-forward experiment, offer a simple lesson to big business. People will take more pleasure in buying things if the experience can be blended with something that feels like friendship and gift exchange. The role of money must be airbrushed out of the picture wherever possible. As marketers see it, payment is one of the unfortunate 'pain points' in any relationship with a customer, which requires anaesthetizing with some form of more 'social' experience. Shopping must be represented as something else entirely.

Yet the greatest catalyst for the new business interest in being 'social' is, unsurprisingly, the rise of social media. This offers a number of new opportunities and challenges from a marketing perspective. The story of marketing over the course of the twentieth century was one of a gradual disintegration of the mass media, mass market, broadcast model of advertising. From the 1960s onwards, brands were increasingly targeting niche groups and 'tribes' who had to be understood in a more subtle fashion, through careful observation and focus groups. Social media allows for an even finer grain of consumer insight, allowing researchers to spot how tastes, opinions and consumer habits travel through social networks. It allows advertising to be tailored to specific individuals, on the basis of who else they know, and what those other people liked and purchased. These practices, which are collectively referred to as 'social analytics', mean that tastes and behaviours can be traced in unprecedented detail.

The most valuable trick, from a marketing perspective, is how to induce individuals to share positive brand messages and adverts with each other, almost as if there were no public advertising campaign at all. The business practice known as 'friendvertising' involves creating images and video clips which social media users are likely to share with others, for no conscious commercial purpose of their own.[8] 'Sponsored conversations', in which individuals participate in online discussions and blogs with the commercial support of a business, are a slightly less-well-hidden attempt to achieve the same thing. The science of viral marketing, or the creation of 'buzz', has led marketers to seek lessons from social psychology, social anthropology and social network analysis.

At the same time that behavioural economics has been highlighting the various ways in which we are social, altruistic creatures, social media offers businesses an opportunity to analyse and target that social behaviour. The end goal is no different from what it was at the dawn of marketing and management in the late nineteenth century: making money. What's changed is that each one of us is now viewed as an available instrument through which to alter the attitudes and behaviours of our friends and contacts. Behaviours and ideas can be released like 'contagions', in the hope of 'infecting' much larger networks. While social media sites such as Facebook offer whole new possibilities for marketing, the analysis of email networks can do the same for human resource management in workplaces. The project initiated by Elton Mayo in the 1920s, of understanding the business value of informal relationships, can now be subjected to a far more rigorous and quantitative scientific analysis.[9]

One of the outcomes of this fine-grained level of social analysis is the discovery that different social relationships have very different levels of economic value. Once marketing campaigns are being mediated by individuals, in their informal social lives, it quickly becomes plain that certain individuals – well-connected influencers – are more useful instruments of communication than others. In the workplace, the socially connected employee will come to appear more valuable than the more isolated one. The business logic which emerges from this is to be highly generous towards a small minority of already well-connected people, and pay far less attention to everybody else. Celebrities have long had gifts lavished upon them by companies, hoping to have their brands boosted by association. The same process is beginning to apply to social networks: the people who are least in need of this corporate generosity are the most likely recipients of it, and vice versa.

The ideology of this new 'social' economy depends on painting the 'old' economy as horribly individualistic and materialistic. The assumption is that, prior to the World Wide Web and the Californian gurus that celebrate it, we lived atomized, private lives, with every relationship mediated by cash. Before it became 'social', business was a nasty, individualist affair, driven only by greed.

This picture is, of course, completely false. Corporations have been trying to produce, manage and influence social relationships (as an alternative to purely monetary transactions) since the birth of management in the mid-nineteenth century. Businesses have long worried about their public reputation and the commitment of their employees. And it goes without saying that informal social networks themselves are as old as humanity. What has changed is not the role of the 'social' in capitalism, but the capacity to subject it to a quantitative, economic analysis, thanks primarily to the digitization of social relationships. The ability to visualize and quantify social relations, then subject them to an economic audit, is growing all the time.

While the expert practitioners of 'social analytics' are best placed to do this, there is also a growing tendency and opportunity for individuals themselves to view their social lives in this mathematical, utilitarian sense. As this happens, the moral dimension of friendship and reciprocity starts to recede, and the more explicitly utilitarian dimension moves to the foreground. Something like pay-it-forward ceases to influence us because we want to fit in with social norms, and more because of the psychological kick we get out of it ourselves. People start to think of altruism in terms of incentives. Viewing social relations and giving in this tacitly economic way introduces an unpleasant question: what's in it for me? One of the most persuasive answers emerging is that friendship and altruism are healthy, for both mind and body.

The medical 'social'

In February 2010, I found myself sitting in a large hall, with a huge golden throne on my left, and the future leader of the UK Labour Party, Ed Miliband, to my right. We were watching images on a screen that reminded me of the fractal videos that used to be sold by the 'herbal remedy' salesmen in London's Camden Market in the early 1990s. Also present was a number of government policy advisors, all straining to appear as shambolically relaxed as possible, a status game which goes on in the corridors of power, played to indicate that one is at home there (the game was won under the subsequent government by David Cameron's closest confidant, Steve Hilton, who was notorious for wandering into meetings barefooted).

There were about ten of us in the room, one of the more

baroque offices in the government's Cabinet Office, and we were all staring at this screen, transfixed by the movement of individual lines and dots that were being displayed. Standing next to the screen, clearly enjoying the impact that his video was having on this influential audience, was the American medical sociologist Nicholas Christakis. Christakis was on a speaking tour, promoting his book *Connected*, and had been invited in to present some of his findings to British policy-makers during the dying days of Gordon Brown's government. As a sociologist with an interest in policy, I'd been invited along.

Christakis is an unusual sociologist. Not only is he far more mathematically adept than most, but he has also published a number of articles in high-ranking medical journals. The fractal-like images we were watching on the screen that day represented social networks in a Baltimore neighbourhood, within which particular 'behaviours' and medical symptoms were moving around. Christakis's message to the assembled policy-makers was a powerful one. Problems such as obesity, poverty and depression, which so often coincide, locking people into chronic conditions of inactivity, are contagious. They move around like viruses in social networks, creating risks to individuals purely by virtue of the people they happen to hang out with.

There was something mesmeric and seductive about the images. Could entrenched social problems really be represented by graphics of this sort? Christakis's technical prowess was certainly alluring. In the grand tradition of American GIs bringing chewing gum and nylon stockings to the British during World War Two, his high-tech social network analysis seemed novel and irresistible. The behaviourist promise, that policy might be grounded in hard science, will always get a hearing among senior decision-makers.

What I found slightly surreal that day, aside from the massive gold throne, was the freakish view of this particular inner-city American community that we were privy to. Like the social analytics companies, which try to spot consumer behaviour as it emerges and travels, here we were in London observing how the dietary habits and health problems of a few thousand relatively deprived Baltimore residents were moving around, like a disease. It felt as if we were viewing an ant colony from above. Indeed, the fact that these flickering images represented human beings, with relationships, histories and agendas, was almost incidental.

Of course the policy opportunities here are tremendously exciting, especially in an age of government austerity. If medical practitioners can change the behaviour of just a few influential people in a network for the better, potentially they can then spread a more positive 'contagion'. The question is whether policymakers could ever possibly hope to attain this kind of sociological data en masse, without some form of mass surveillance of social life. While we grow increasingly accustomed to the idea of a private company, such as Google, collecting detailed data on the everyday behaviour of millions, the notion that the government might do the same remains more chilling.

While marketers desperately seek to penetrate our social networks in order to alter our tastes and desires, policy-makers have come to view social networks as means of improving our health and well-being. One important aspect of this is the discovery that a deficit of social relations – or loneliness – is not only a cause of unhappiness, but a serious physiological health risk as well. The 'social neuroscience' pioneered by Chicago neuroscientist John Cacioppo suggests that the human brain has evolved in such a way as to depend on social relationships. Cacioppo's research suggests that loneliness is an even greater health risk than smoking.[10] Practices such as 'social prescribing', in which doctors recommend that individuals join a choir or voluntary organization, are aimed at combating isolation and its tendency to lead to depression and chronic illness.

The positive psychology movement, which has grown rapidly since the early 1990s, has done a great deal to highlight the psychosomatic benefits of reciprocal social relations. While positive psychologists like to speak in terms of 'flourishing' and 'optimism', lurking behind much of the rhetoric is the ongoing rise in diagnosis rates of depression. While the gurus of this movement may be all smiles, many of their readers and listeners are wrestling with a sense of pointlessness, loneliness and deflation, for which they are desperately seeking a remedy.

Once again, the logic of monetary market exchange is vigorously attacked in positive psychology. The words which recur over and over in positive psychology texts and speech are gratitude, giving and empathy. In a world that seems cold, calculating and careless, positive psychology invites its follower to adopt a more ethical stance, based around empathy and generosity. The fact that this stress upon social reciprocity is entirely in keeping with the current spirit of capitalism (clearly manifest in marketing) goes unremarked-upon. But what really leaps out from this new ethical orientation is the way in which it is ultimately justified: giving makes the giver feel happier. Equally, the mental habit of feeling grateful delivers positive mental benefits. The advice is to stop thinking so much of oneself – but the justification is ultimately a self-centred one.

As was clear from the Christakis seminar in the Cabinet Office throne-room, social networks are now recognized as tools of health policy. They are ways in which the pleasures and pains of our minds and bodies can be influenced. The utilitarian project has historically been dependent on some rather crude carrots and sticks – punishments to deliver pain, money and physical pleasures to deliver happiness. Now, thanks to the growing reach of medical research and policy, it is the people we socialize with who are becoming the latest instruments of psychophysical improvement. We now know that socially isolated people experience more physical pain following a hip operation than those who are more socially connected.[11] Adopting a positive outlook is known to aid recovery from medical illness and reduce the risk of it arising.

Driven particularly by neuroscience, the expert understanding of social life and morality is rapidly submerging into the study of the body. One social neuroscientist, Matt Lieberman, has shown how pains that we have traditionally treated as emotional (such as separating from a lover) involve the same neurochemical processes as those we typically view as physical (such as breaking an arm). Another prominent neuroscientist, Paul Zak (known in the media as Dr Love), has focused on a single neurochemical, oxytocin, which he argues is associated with many of our strongest social instincts, such as love and fairness. Scientists at the University of Zurich have discovered that they can trigger a sense of 'right and wrong' by stimulating a particular area of the brain.[12] Social science and physiology are converging into a new discipline, in which human bodies are studied for the ways they respond to one another physically.

It would seem a little perverse to suggest that policy-makers ignore this evidence of the impact of social networks and altruism on health. And if positive psychology can generate just a little more mutual concern, through self-help and cognitive tips, then why not? Yet there is still a danger lurking in this worldview, which is the same problem that afflicts all forms of social network analysis. In reducing the social world to a set of mechanisms and resources available to individuals, the question repeatedly arises as to whether social networks might be redesigned in ways to suit the already privileged. Networks have a tendency towards what are called 'power laws', whereby those with influence are able to harness that power to win even greater influence.

A combination of positive psychology with social media analytics has demonstrated that psychological moods and emotions travel through networks, much as Christakis found in relation to health behaviour. For example, through analysing the content of social media messages, researchers at Beihang University in China found that certain moods like anger tended to travel faster than others through networks.[13] A negative frame of mind, including depression itself, is known to be socially 'contagious'. Happy, healthy individuals can then tailor their social relationships in ways that protect them against the 'risk' of unhappiness. Guy Winch, an American psychologist who has studied this phenomenon, advises happy people to be on their guard. 'If you find yourself living with or around people with negative outlooks,' he writes, 'consider balancing out your friend roster'.[14] The impact of this friend-roster-rebalancing on those unfortunates with the 'negative outlooks' is all too easy to imagine.

There is something a little sad that the fabric of social life is now a problem which is addressed within the rubric of health policy. Loneliness now appears as an objective problem, but only because it shows up in the physical brain and body, with calculable costs for governments and health insurers. Generosity and gratitude are urged upon people, but mainly to alleviate their own mental health problems and private misery. And friendship ties within poor inner-city neighbourhoods have become a topic of government concern, but only to the extent that they mediate epidemics of bad nutrition and costly inactivity. This is all an attempt to grasp the social world without departing from mathematical, individualist psychology. While this may offer genuine medical aid to needy individuals, trying to understand society in purely psychological terms is also a recipe for narcissism. And the man who initiated it was nothing if not a narcissist.

Playing God

In 1893, a four-year-old boy sat on top of a rickety mountain of chairs that he and his friends had stacked on top of each other in the basement of his parent's house, on the outskirts of Bucharest near the Danube. The boy, Jacob Moreno, was seizing the opportunity of his parents' absence to play his favourite game. He was 'God', and the other children from his neighbourhood were his 'angels'. Perched on top of his chair stack, Moreno instructed his angels to start flapping their wings. They obeyed. 'Why don't you fly?' one of the angels then asked him. He agreed, launched himself into the air and within seconds found himself lying on the basement floor with a broken arm.

Moreno's desire to play God never really deserted him. The idea of humans as individual gods in their own social worlds, creators of themselves and creators of their relationships, animated his work as a psychoanalyst and social psychologist during his adulthood. His 1920 work, The Words of the Father, outlined a frightening humanistic philosophy, where individuals confront situations of infinite possibility, in which the only limiting factor upon their own powers of self-creation is that they exist in social groups. But social groups are also malleable and improvable. Every god needs its angels.

A fantasy of ultimate paternity was an abiding feature of Moreno's professional conduct, leading him to create some absurd myths surrounding his own originality. This included some outright lies, such as the claim he repeatedly advanced that he was born on board a ship in 1892, of unknown nationality, with an unknown father, when in fact he was born in Bucharest in 1889, the son of a struggling Jewish merchant with Turkish nationality. In later life, he exerted himself in claiming authorship over various concepts and techniques that were circulating in psychology and psychiatry at the time, with particular hostility aimed at the psychologist Kurt Lewin, who he believed was stealing his ideas. For one so interested in studying social relations, Moreno was unusually paranoid and egocentric.

His family moved to Vienna when he was a child, and it was there that he later enrolled to study medicine at university. This enabled him to attend the lectures of Sigmund Freud shortly before the First World War. Moreno was only marginally impressed by the celebrity psychoanalyst. As he left the lecture hall one day in 1914, he accosted him. 'Well, Dr. Freud, I start where you leave off,' he told him. 'You meet people in the artificial setting of your office. I meet them on the street and in their homes, in their natural surroundings.'[15] The onset of war provided him with his first opportunity to do just this.

His mixed nationality meant that he was unable to serve in the army, so he took a position as a doctor in refugee camps in Austria-Hungary between 1915 and 1918. Observing those who resided in these camps, Moreno began to consider ways in which their happiness could be influenced through altering their immediate social surroundings. Clearly their objective circumstances were a cause of considerable misery, but Moreno believed that careful observation to patterns of relationships might reveal ways in which psychological satisfaction could be improved, with relatively minor changes. In 1916, he laid down these thoughts in a letter to the Austro-Hungarian minister of the interior as follows:

The positive and negative feelings that emerge from every house, between houses, from every factory, and from national and political groups in the community can be explored by means of sociometric analysis. A new order by means of sociometric methods is herewith recommended.[16]

What was this 'sociometric' analysis he referred to? And how would it help? Though still undeveloped as a mathematical science, let alone a computational one, 'sociometry', as Moreno imagined it, laid the groundwork for what later became social network analysis and, consequently, social media. But before this could be developed as a scientific possibility, another part of Moreno's self-fantasy would have to be mobilized.

He claimed that he was always destined to live in the United States. Advancing the myth of his fatherless, nationless origins, he declared, 'I was born a citizen of the world, a sailor moving from sea to sea, from country to country, destined to land one day in New York harbor.' In 1922, he reported a dream in which he was standing on Fifth Avenue, Manhattan, in possession of a new device for recording and playing sound. Not content with giving birth to a whole new branch of psychology, the dream indicated to Moreno that he was also destined to invent the record player. With his collaborator, Franz Lornitzo, he set to work on such a device over the course of 1924, filing a patent on it in Vienna, resulting in an invitation to Ohio to develop the technology with the General Phonograph Manufacturing Company.

Moreno would be ultimately frustrated by the lack of recognition he would receive for this creation, characteristically refusing to acknowledge that there were multiple similar projects going on simultaneously. Nor were his hosts in Ohio as fawning towards this unlikely inventor as he had assumed they would be. But the invitation to Ohio did nevertheless allow him to realize his vision of himself as a self-parented, nationless *American*. Besides, New York City – the place that had occupied his dreams and fantasies for the previous decade – pointed towards a new model of society that seemed to chime with Moreno's assumption about sovereign selves existing in social groups of their own making.

As Moreno's curt remark to Freud indicated, his problem with psychoanalysis was that it studied individuals as separate from society, without the constraints offered by existing relationships. But what was the alternative? The danger was that the extreme individualism of Freudianism could flip directly into the equally extreme collectivism of Marxism, or else the form of statistical sociology pioneered by Émile Durkheim. In Moreno's eyes, this left Europeans with a bipolar choice, between the enforced collectivity of the socialist state and the unruly egoism of the unconscious self. New York, however, suggested that some sort of third way was possible. Here was a city where individuals lived on top of one another, cooperating in various subtle ways, but without having their individual freedom trammelled in the process. America, Moreno reasoned, was a nation built upon self-forming groups.

The mathematics of friendship

It was in New York that he got his first opportunities to develop the research techniques he had already conceived of as 'sociometry'. He was judicious enough to abandon the talk of individuals as their own personal gods, but other than that, Moreno was intent on building on the insights he'd acquired in the wartime refugee camps and the psychological theories in *The Words of the Father*. He described the project of sociometry as follows:

> It is important to know whether the construction of a community is possible in which each of its members is to the utmost degree a free agent in the making of the collectives of which he is a part and in which the different groups of which it consists are so organized and fitted to each other that an enduring and harmonious commonwealth is the result.[17]

Relationships are there to serve the individual. Spontaneity and creativity derive wholly from each of us individually, but our capacity to release them depends on being in the right social circumstances. The task of sociometry was to place the study of an individual's social relationships on a scientific footing, which would ultimately incorporate mathematics.

Moreno had toyed with various ways of doing this while still in Vienna. He had a hunch that visual diagrams might be the best way of representing complex webs of interaction. Having presented some of these ideas at a psychiatry conference in 1931, he was invited to try out this proposed mode of study on the inmates of Sing Sing prison, New York. Moreno devised a questionnaire to assess the prisoners according to thirty simple attributes, such as age, nationality, ethnicity and so on. In the age of the survey, there was nothing unusual about that; what he did next was ground-breaking.

Rather than analyse this data in terms of averages, aggregates and probabilities (as the market researchers and pollsters were beginning to do at this time), he compared each and every prisoner to each and every other prisoner, with a view to assessing how well matched they were to one another, individually. Here was the birth of a new form of sociology aimed at capturing the value of one-to-one relationships, in terms of how far they benefited the individuals who were party to them. He wasn't interested in what was normal or typical in general. What he wanted to know was how individuals were influenced by those people they happened to know.

Prior to the invention of computers, the mathematics of this research method was fearsome. To study every relationship in a group of four people involves looking at a maximum of six links. Increase the group size to ten people, and you're looking at forty-five possible connections. Increase it again to thirty people, and the potential number of relationships increases to 465. And so on. It was slow and laborious work. But men could not retain the status of gods in their own social worlds unless their individual autonomy was respected by the social research method.

The following year, Moreno got another chance to implement sociometry, at the New York Training School for Girls in Hudson. This time, he focused more explicitly on individual attitudes towards each other, asking them with whom they would like to share a room and whom they already knew. This study witnessed Moreno produce visual sociometric maps of the results for the first time, marking out webs of common links between girls in the school in hand-drawn red lines, later to be published in his 1934 work *Who Shall Survive?* The social world had just become visible in an entirely new way. This, arguably, was the means of visualization which would dominate twenty-first-century understandings of the 'social'.

The vision of social life that fuelled sociometry was undoubtedly a far more individualistic one than that which had inspired sociology up until then. Collective entities emerged only thanks to the spontaneous power of individual egos. They could just as easily be dispensed with again. As far as Moreno was concerned, American culture was founded on specifically this freedom to enter and exit groups. But creating a social science which recognized this individual freedom was far from straight-forward. Two problems in particular presented themselves.

Firstly, the rich, binding, comforting and sometimes suffocating nature of social life gets eliminated from view. The sorts of data that can be included in a sociometric study are necessarily very simplified. Just as social media sites offer users strict limits to how they can define themselves romantically ('single', 'in a relationship' or 'it's complicated') or in relation to each other ('friend' or 'unfriend', 'follow' or 'unfollow'), Moreno's sociometry would only succeed if nuance were stripped out. The price to be paid for exiting the restricted limits of the Freudian office was that the depths of the human psyche started to disappear from view. To carve a path between a science of society and a science of the isolated individual, sociometry necessarily had to simplify both substantially. Of course such simplification can also be attractive, as Nicholas Christakis's visualization demo in London that day testified. To act scientifically upon the social world, elites need to have nuance and culture removed.

Secondly, what to do with the reams of data that resulted from viewing society as a web of interpersonal relations? How to cope with it all or make sense of it? Moreno had no answer to this. The fact that social network analysis would not really take off until the 1960s wasn't for want of an adequate underlying theory, but for want of sufficient power to crunch the numbers. As we have seen, the mathematical challenge that Moreno laid down for the social sciences was onerous. Social network analysis developed slowly in the United States during the 1950s and 1960s, impeded by the problem of processing complex bodies of data. Algorithms were developed which could discover patterns in social data, but universities lacked the computing power to automate them.

It wasn't until the 1970s that a succession of software packages was developed for purposes of social network analysis.[18] Of course these still required academic researchers to go and collect data to feed into the computers. This was still a laborious way of analysing the social world, which – compared with statistics – had little hold over the public imagination. All it took was for a broad mass of individuals to become regular users of networked computers, and Moreno's methodology could become a dominant way of understanding the meaning of the term 'social'. At the beginning of the twenty-first century, this was the very situation which had arisen, the opportunities of which were seized by the 'Web 2.0' companies which emerged from 2003 onwards. The sociometric studies which Moreno had conducted through interviews with a few dozen people, producing hand-drawn diagrams, could now be carried out in Facebook HQ at the flick of a switch, with a billion participants.

But methods of social analysis are never as politically innocent as they appear. While social network analysis purports to be a simple, stripped-down mathematical study of the ties that bind us, it's worth reflecting on the philosophy that inspired its founder. As far as Moreno was concerned, other people are there to prop up and please individual egos. A friendship is valuable to the extent that it makes me feel better. Once the study of social life is converted into a branch of mathematical psychology, then this produces some worrying effects on how people start to relate to each other. The narcissism of the small boy playing God surrounded by his angels has become another model for how pleasure is now manufactured and measured.

Addicted to contact

The main charge that has been levelled against the DSM, since the introduction of the DSM-III in 1980, is that it converts everyday forms of sadness and personality quirks into illnesses. This has been particularly pronounced in the identification of ever more forms of addiction. Until the early 1970s, addiction would only have been understood as referring to syndromes which affect the metabolism, such as alcoholism, and even then its social and cultural dimensions would have been recognized. In the era of the DSM-III and since, new addictions have been identified and diagnosed in relation to all manner of hedonistic practices and experiences, from gambling to shopping to sex. Inevitably, the new diagnostic categories lend support to biological explanations that the behaviours are hard-wired into certain brains or genes.

The DSM-V, which was launched in early 2013, added a further item to the menu of dysfunctional compulsions: internet addiction. Many doctors and psychiatrists are confident that this latest syndrome qualifies as a true addiction, no less than addiction to drugs. Sufferers show all the hallmarks of addictive behaviour. Internet use can overwhelm their ability to maintain relationships or hold down a career. When internet addicts are cut off from the web as a form of 'cold turkey', they can develop physiological withdrawal symptoms. They lie to those they are close to in an effort to get their fix. Neuroscience shows that the pleasures associated with internet use can be chemically identical to those associated with cocaine use or other addictive pastimes.

If we can look beyond the neurochemistry for a moment, it is worth asking one simple question: what is the internet addict addicted to exactly? One of the psychiatrists who has explored this phenomenon most closely is Richard Graham, based at London's Tavistock Clinic. And the conclusion he has reached brings us squarely to the pathologies of the new concept of the 'social'.

In 2005, Graham was studying the ways in which video games impacted on the behaviour and attitudes of young people. It was thanks to this expertise that a teenage boy was referred to him with symptoms of depression, who was also a compulsive player of computer games, in particular a game called Halo. The boy played for four or five hours a day, obsessively trying to reach the next level of the game, cutting him off from his friends and family in the process. His parents were concerned about the amount of time he spent in his room. And yet the gaming in itself didn't strike Graham as a particular cause for concern.

But in 2006, the boy's situation became rapidly more serious. He switched to playing World of Warcraft, which coincided with a marked increase in his amount of gaming time, to as much as fifteen hours every day. His parents became increasingly concerned but felt powerless to do anything. The situation continued like this for another three years. Reaching breaking point on Mothering Sunday, 2009, they turned off his modem. The boy immediately became violent, to the point where they had to call the police. His relationship to the video game had become beyond his, or anyone else's, control.

The key difference between the two games is that World of Warcraft involves playing against other gamers in real time. It involves respect and recognition from real people. Unlike Halo, which the boy had played obsessively but not addictively, World of Warcraft is a social experience. Even while the boy remained alone in his room staring at moving graphics on a monitor, the knowledge that other players were present offered a form of psychological 'hit' that wasn't available from regular video games. Clearly, the boy was not simply addicted to technology but to a particular type of egocentric relationship which networked computers are particularly adept at providing.

Graham has since become a noted authority on the topic of social media addiction, especially among young people. What he noticed, in the case of the World of Warcraft addict, was simply an extreme case of an affliction that has become widespread in the age of Facebook and smartphones. Social media addiction may be classed as a particular subset of internet addiction, as far as the DSM is concerned, but it is the social logic of it which is so psychologically powerful. Not unlike the gamer, people who cannot put down their smartphones are not engaging with images or gadgetry for the sake of it: they are desperately seeking some form of human interaction, but of a kind that does nothing to limit their personal, private autonomy. In America today, it is estimated that 38 per cent of adults may suffer from some form of social media addiction.[19] Some psychiatrists have suggested that Facebook and Twitter are even more addictive than cigarettes and alcohol.[20]

The ubiquity of digital media has become a lightning rod for media hysteria. The internet or Facebook can be blamed for the fact that young people are increasingly narcissistic, unable to make commitments to one another, cannot concentrate on anything which isn't 'interactive'. This typically includes some latest discovery about what 'screen time' is doing to our brains. There is indeed some evidence to suggest that individuals who use social media compulsively are more egocentric, prone to 'exhibitionism' and 'grandiose behaviour'.[21] But rather than treat the technology as some virus that has corrupted people psychologically and neurologically, it is worth standing back and reflecting on the broader cultural logic at work here.

What we witness, in the case of a World of Warcraft addict, a social media addict or, for that matter, a sex addict, is only the more pathological element of a society that cannot conceive of relationships except in terms of the psychological pleasures that they produce. The person whose fingers twitch to check their Facebook page, when they're supposed to be listening to their friend over a meal, is the heir to Jacob Moreno's ethical philosophy, in which other people are only there to please, satisfy and affirm an individual ego from one moment to the next. This inevitably leads to vicious circles: once a social bond is stripped down to this impoverished psychological level, it becomes harder and harder to find the satisfaction that one desperately wants. Viewing other people as instruments for one's own pleasure represents a denial of core ethical and emotional truths of friendship, love and generosity.

One grave shortcoming of this egocentric idea of the 'social' is that none (or at least, vanishingly few) of us can ever constantly be the centre of attention, receiving praise. Nobody can be God the whole time; mostly they must be the angels who surround the deity. And so it also proves with Facebook. As an endless stream

Social Optimization

of grandiose spectacles, Facebook has been shown, on balance, to make individuals feel worse about themselves and their own lives.[22] The mathematics of networks means that most people will have fewer friends than average, while a small number of people will have far more than average.[23] The tonic to this sense of inferiority is to make grandiose spectacles of one's own, to seek the gaze of the other, thereby reinforcing a collective vicious circle. As the positive psychologists are keen to stress, this inability to listen or empathize is a significant contributor to depression.

A key category in social network analysis is 'centrality'. It refers to the extent to which a given 'node' (such as a person, but it could potentially be an organization) is integral to its own social world. In Moreno's terms, one might even say that it offers a measure of social 'godliness'. Again, where a network is larger than a few dozen people, this is something that is almost impossible to calculate without computing power. But throw in twenty-first-century processing power and the ubiquitous digitization of social networks, and the logic of centrality comes to divide and rule. It governs the Twitter user, who keeps anxious check on her ratio of followers to those followed. It underpins the depression and loneliness of the person who feels marginalized from a social world that he can observe but not participate in. The fetish of celebrity permeates our own social lives, now that we are able to gaze at the carefully curated images and utterances of people we are actually acquainted with.

If happiness resides in discovering relationships which are less ego-oriented, less purely hedonistic, than those which an individualistic society offers, then Facebook and similar forms of social media are rarely a recipe for happiness. It is true that there are specific uses of social media which lend themselves towards stronger, more fulfilling social relations. One study of Facebook use distinguishes between a type of 'broadcast-and-consume' model of usage (in which individuals are either on display, or watching others on display) which leads to greater feelings of isolation, and a more email-based usage, which can lead to cohesion through dialogue.[24] A group of positive psychologists has drawn on their own evidence of what types of social relations lead to greater happiness, to create a new social media platform, 'Happier', designed around expressions of gratitude and generosity, which are recognized to be critical ingredients of mental well-being.

What is left unquestioned by the science of happiness and any social media innovations that may spin off from it is the social logic in which relationships are there to be created, invested in and – potentially – abandoned, in pursuit of psychological optimization. The darker implication of strategically pursuing happiness via relationships is that the relationship is only as good as the psychic value or kick that it delivers. 'Friend rosters' may need to be 'balanced', if it turns out that one's friends aren't spreading enough pleasure or happiness. This logic undoubtedly has a hedonistic variant that may spiral into social addiction and narcissism, and a more Zen-like holistic version, which enjoys longer time horizons and fewer ups and downs. But the social serves an almost identical purpose in each case.

Neoliberal socialism

Our society is excessively individualistic. Markets reduce everything to a question of individual calculation and selfishness. We have become obsessed with money and acquisition at the

expense of our social relationships and our own human fulfilment. Capitalism spreads a plague of materialism, which
undermines our connectedness, leaving many of us isolated and
lonely. Unless we can rediscover the art of sharing, our society
will fragment altogether, making trust impossible. Unless we can
recover the values associated with friendship and altruism, we
will descend into a state of nihilistic ennui.

These types of claim have animated various critiques of capitalism and markets for centuries. They have often provided the
basis of arguments for political and economic reform, whether
moderate attempts to restrain the reach of markets, or more
wholesale demands to overhaul the capitalist system. Today, the
same types of lament can be heard, but from some very different
sources. Now, the gurus of marketing, self-help, behavioural
economics, social media and management are first in line to
attack the individualistic and materialist assumptions of the marketplace. But all they're offering instead is a marginally different
theory of individual psychology and behaviour.

The depressed and the lonely, who have entered the purview of
policy-making now that their problems have become visible to
doctors and neuroscientists, exhibit much that has gone wrong
under the neoliberal model of capitalism. Individuals want to
escape relentless self-reliance and self-reflection. On this, the positive psychologists have a very clear understanding of the malaise
of extreme individualism, which locks individuals into introverted,
anxious questioning of their own worth relative to others. Their
recommended therapy is for people to get out of themselves and
immerse themselves in relationships with others. But in reducing
the idea of society to the logic of psychology, the happiness gurus
follow the same logic as Jacob Moreno, behavioural economics
and Facebook. This means that the 'social' is an instrument for

one's own medical, emotional or monetary gain. The vicious circle of self-reflection and self-improvement continues.

How would one break out of this trap? In some ways, the example of 'social prescribing' is an enticing one. While it starts from a utilitarian premise, that individuals can improve their well-being through joining associations and working collaboratively, it also points towards the institutions to make this happen, and not simply more cognitive tips and nudges. If people have become locked in themselves, gazing enviously at others, this poses questions that need institutional, political, collective answers. It cannot be alleviated simply with psychological appeals to the social, which can exacerbate the very problems they aim to alleviate, once combined with digital media and the egocentric model of connectivity which those media facilitate. There is a crucial question of how businesses, markets, policies, laws, political participation might be designed differently to sustain meaningful social relationships, but it is virtually never confronted by the doyens of 'social' capitalism.

What we encounter in the current business, media and policy euphoria for being social is what might be called 'neoliberal socialism'. Sharing is preferable to selling, so long as it doesn't interfere with the financial interests of dominant corporations. Appealing to people's moral and altruistic sense becomes the best way of nudging them into line with agendas that they had no say over. Brands and behaviours can be unleashed as social contagions, without money ever changing hands. Empathy and relationships are celebrated, but only as particular habits that happy individuals have learnt to practise. Everything that was once external to economic logic, such as friendship, is quietly brought within it; what was once the enemy of utilitarian logic, namely moral principle, is instrumentalized for utilitarian ends.

The logic of neoliberalism, stating that 'winners' deserve whatever prizes they can grab, risks usurping the faint glimpse of social reform contained within this agenda. The 'social neuroscience' of Matt Lieberman, Paul Zak and others may prove most decisive here, because it offers a firm physiological basis on which to analyse social behaviour as a component of health, happiness and wealth. Focused resolutely on the individual brain and body, this science clearly offers as much – and probably more – to the powerful and rich as it does to the lonely and marginalized. Once social relationships can be viewed as medical and biological properties of the human body, they can become dragged into the limitless pursuit of self-optimization that counts for happiness in the age of neoliberalism.

It is not very long since the internet offered hope for different forms of organization altogether. As the cultural and political theorist Jeremy Gilbert has argued, we should remember that it was only a few years ago that Rupert Murdoch's media empire was completely defeated in its efforts to turn Myspace into a profitable entity.[25] The tension between the logic of the open network and the logic of private investment could not be resolved, and Murdoch lost half a billion dollars. Facebook has had to go to great lengths to ensure that the same mistakes are not made, in particular, anchoring online identities in 'real' offline identities, and tailoring its design around the interests of marketers and market researchers. Perhaps it is too early to say that it has succeeded. Resistance to Facebook's techniques of psychological control gave rise to Ello, a social media platform with no immediately apparent commercial logic, and which includes the right to anonymity. Even if Ello turned out to be a false dawn, it at least highlighted the extent of public dissatisfaction with social networks that are analysed and manipulated for the benefit of marketers.

The reduction of social life to psychology, as performed by Jacob Moreno and behavioural economists, or to physiology as achieved by social neuroscience, is not necessarily irreversible either. Karl Marx believed that by bringing workers together in the factory and forcing them to work together, capitalism was creating the very class formation that would eventually overwhelm it. This was despite the 'bourgeois ideology' which stressed the primacy of individuals transacting in a marketplace. Similarly, individuals today may be brought together for their own mental and physical health, or for their own private hedonistic kicks; but social congregations can develop their own logic, which is not reducible to that of individual well-being or pleasure. This is the hope that currently lies dormant in this new, neoliberal socialism.

7

Living in the Lab

Business ideas and practices do not simply spread of their own accord, not even when they appear to yield clear profits. They need pushing. Sometimes they need cultural and political barriers to be forcefully broken down before they are later adopted, until eventually they come to appear entirely natural. The idea of 'scientific advertising', pioneered in the 1920s by the firm James Walter Thompson (JWT), with support from John B. Watson, is a case in point.

JWT were the first of the large Madison Avenue firms to believe that advertising could target consumers scientifically thanks to psychological profiling techniques, such as surveys. They believed individuals could be influenced through such techniques to make purchases, even against their own better rationality. Today, the notion that advertising relies on detailed psychological insights into our intimate emotions and behaviours seems quite obvious. But its journey from Madison Avenue in the mid 1920s to the status of global common sense was not straight-forward.

JWT would not have succeeded in exporting scientific advertising around the world had it not been for the contract they won with General Motors (GM) in 1927.[1] By this time GM already had a powerful international presence, with production plants scattered across Europe. The deal that JWT struck with GM was that they would open an office in every country where GM was already located, so as to furnish the car giant with local marketing expertise. In return GM would grant JWT an exclusive account for all of its markets around the world. In 1927 alone, JWT opened offices in six European countries. Over the next four years, it would open further offices in India, South Africa, Australia, Canada and Japan. Thanks to the security offered by its corporate behemoth of a patron, JWT became an international player, and its particular style of marketing expertise went global. The capacity of US businesses to export to global markets, which surged after World War Two, was greatly aided by the fact that such networks of business intelligence had already permeated much of the capitalist world. Knowledge of foreign consumers was already on hand.

Following the acquisition of the GM contract, JWT set about accumulating consumer insight on an unprecedented scale. In less than eighteen months, over 44,000 interviews were done around the world, many in relation to cars, but also on topics such as food and toiletry consumption.[2] This was the most ambitious project of mass psychological profiling ever attempted. A detailed map of global consumer tastes was being built up from scratch. And yet this was not achieved without encountering some resistance.

JWT researchers quickly discovered that their techniques were not widely understood or appreciated beyond their home market. The level of consumer intimacy that they were seeking was often simply refused. In Britain, several researchers were arrested for conducting door-to-door surveys.[3] Another British interviewer found the job of consumer profiling so difficult that he was reduced to chasing people down the street shouting questions at them. A researcher conducting surveys in flats in Copenhagen in 1927 was met with such hostility that one resident threw him down a flight of stairs. And another, also in Copenhagen, was arrested for trying to get into people's homes by impersonating an inspection officer. The German Automobile Manufacturer's Association threatened to sue JWT for 'business espionage'.

The globalization of consumer intelligence required a combination of luck, guile and brute force. The challenge that JWT had set itself was deeply problematic. It wasn't simply to observe people in public or invite public opinions, as magazines had been doing for some time. It was to acquire a new level of intimacy with the consumer, which often meant observing the housewife in her home. Researchers didn't only want to know what these people thought or said about certain products, they also wanted to see the products in the home, watch how the consumer behaved. This knowledge could only be acquired through a degree of snooping around and asking somewhat personal questions.

The story of JWT's painful arrival in Europe points towards one of the gravest challenges that confronts the project of mass psychological measurement: how does one get ordinary people to cooperate? There is a political dimension to any social science, whereby the researcher must either negotiate with their research subjects in the hope of winning their consent, or else they must use some degree of force and privilege to oblige people to be studied and measured. Either that, or they operate in a more clandestine fashion.

When Wilhelm Wundt established his psychology laboratory in Leipzig, he used his own students and assistants as the focus of his experiments. Their full consent was deemed necessary for the type of science he was seeking to carry out. More commonly today, psychologists offer monetary incentives to their research subjects, who are typically hard-up students from other disciplines. For a counter-example, consider the history of statistics, which (as the word indicates) has always been intimately entangled with the violent power of states in order to ensure that the population is measured accurately and objectively. States are able to do what JWT initially struggled to do in observing people en masse. Similarly, Frederick Taylor was dependent on his aristocratic connections in order to peer inside numerous Philadelphia workplaces during the 1870s and 1880s.

The term 'data' derives from the Latin, *datum*, which literally means 'that which is given'. It is often an outrageous lie. The data gathered by surveys and psychological experiments is scarcely ever just given. It is either seized through force of surveillance, thanks to some power inequality, or it is given in exchange for something else, such as a monetary reward or a chance to win a free iPad. Often, it is collected in a clandestine way, like the one-way mirrors through which focus groups are observed. In social sciences such as anthropology, the terms on which data is gained (in that case, through prolonged observation and participation) are a matter of constant reflection. But in the behavioural sciences, the innocent term 'data' usefully conceals a huge apparatus of power through which people can be studied, watched, measured and traced, with or without their consent.

Evidently, this political dimension was still visible in the 1920s, when JWT were expanding oversees. In the years since, however, it has receded from view. Questions of what people think or feel, how they intend to vote, how they perceive certain brands, have become simple matters of fact. This is no less true of happiness. Gallup now surveys one thousand American adults on their happiness and well-being every single day, allowing them to trace public mood in great detail, from one day to the next. We are now so familiar with the idea that powerful institutions want to know what we're feeling and thinking that it no longer appears as a political issue. But possibilities for psychological and behavioural data are heavily shaped by the power structures which facilitate them. The current explosion in happiness and well-being data is really an effect of new technologies and practices of surveillance. In turn, these depend on pre-existing power inequalities.

Building the new laboratory

In 2012, Harvard Business Review declared that 'data scientist' would be the 'sexiest job of the twenty-first century'.[4] We live during a time of tremendous optimism regarding the possibilities for data collection and analysis that is refuelling the behaviourist and utilitarian ambition to manage society purely through careful scientific observation of mind, body and brain. Whenever a behavioural economist or happiness guru stands up and declares that finally we can access the secrets of human motivation and satisfaction, they are implicitly referring to a number of technological and cultural changes which have transformed opportunities for psychological surveillance. Three in particular are worth highlighting.

Firstly, there is the much-celebrated rise of 'big data'.[5] As our various everyday transactions with retailers, health-care providers, the urban environment, governments and each other become digitized, so they produce vast archival records that can be 'mined' with sufficient technological capability. Much of this data is viewed as a prized possession by the companies that acquire it, who believe that it holds untold riches for those wanting to predict how people will behave in future. Many, such as Facebook, are inclined to keep it private, such that they can conduct analysis of it for their own purposes, or sell it on to market research companies.

In other circumstances, this data is being 'opened up' on the basis that it is a public good. After all, we the public created it by swiping our smart cards, visiting websites, tweeting our thoughts, and so on. Big data should therefore be something available to all of us to analyse. What this more liberal approach tends to ignore is the fact that, even where data is being opened up, the tools to analyse it are not. As the 'smart cities' analyst Anthony Townsend has pointed out with regard to New York City's open data regulations, they judiciously leave out the algorithms which are used by e-government contractors to analyse the data.[6] While the liberal left continues to worry about the privatization of knowledge as enacted by intellectual property rights, a new problem of the privatization of theory has arisen, whereby algorithms which spot patterns and trends are shrouded in commercial secrecy. Entire businesses are now built on the capacity to interpret and make connections within big data.

The second development is one that can only be truly understood in cultural terms. To put it simply, the spread of narcissism has been harnessed as research opportunity. When JWT first sought to profile European consumers in the 1920s, this was experienced as an invasion of privacy, as indeed it was. More recently, tolerance for surveys has fallen all over again, though more out of impatience on the part of potential participants than anything else.[7] People simply cannot be bothered to share details of what they like, think or want with researchers holding clipboards any more. But when Facebook asks its one billion users that faux-innocent question 'What's on your mind?', we pour our thoughts, tastes, likes, desires and opinions into the company's massive databank without a further thought.

When obliged to report on their inner mental states for research purposes, people do so only grudgingly. But when doing so of their own volition, suddenly reporting on behaviour and moods becomes a fulfilling, satisfying activity in its own right. The 'quantified self' movement, in which individuals measure and report on various aspects of their private lives – from their diets, to their moods, to their sex lives – began as an experimental group of software developers and artists. But it unearthed a surprising enthusiasm for self-surveillance that market researchers and behavioural scientists have carefully noted. Companies such as Nike are now exploring ways in which health and fitness products can be sold alongside quantified self apps, which will allow individuals to make constant reports of their behaviour (such as jogging), generating new data sets for the company in the process.

There is a third development, the political and philosophical implications of which are potentially the most radical of all. This concerns the capability to 'teach' computers how to interpret human behaviour in terms of the emotions that are conveyed. For example, the field of 'sentiment analysis' involves the design of algorithms to interpret the sentiment that is expressed in a given sentence, for example, a single tweet. The MIT Affective Computing research centre is dedicated to exploring new ways in which computers might read people's moods through evaluating their facial expressions, or might carry out 'emotionally intelligent' conversations with people, to provide them with therapeutic support or friendship.

Ways of reading an individual's mood, through tracking his body, face and behaviour, are now expanding rapidly. Computer programmes designed to influence our feelings, once they have been gauged, are another way in which emotions and technology are becoming synched with each other. Already, computerized cognitive behavioural therapy is available thanks to software packages such as Beating the Blues and FearFighter. As affective computing advances, the capabilities of computers to judge and influence our feelings will grow.

Facial scanning technologies hold out great promise for marketers and advertisers wanting to acquire an 'objective' grasp of human emotion. These are beginning to move beyond the limited realms of computing or psychology labs and permeate day-to-day life. The supermarket chain Tesco has already trialled technologies which advertise different products at different individuals, depending on what moods their faces are communicating.[8] Cameras can be used to recognize the faces of unique consumers in the street and market products at them based on their previous shopping behaviours.[9] But this may be just the beginning. One of the leading developers of face-reading software has piloted the technology in classrooms, to identify whether a student is bored or focused.[10]

The combination of big data, the narcissistic sharing of private feelings and thoughts, and more emotionally intelligent computers opens up possibilities for psychological tracking that Bentham and Watson could never have dreamed of. Add in smartphones and you have an extraordinary apparatus of data gathering, the like of which was previously only plausible within university laboratories or particularly high-surveillance institutions such as prisons. The political, technological and cultural limits to psychological surveillance are dissolving. The great virtue of the market, for neoliberals such as the Chicago School, was that it acted as a constant survey of consumer preferences which extended across society. But mass digitization and data analytics now offer a rival mode of psychological audit that potentially extends even further, engulfing personal relations and feelings which markets do not ordinarily reach.

In moving beyond survey techniques, researchers believe that they can now circumvent the quasi-democratic, political aspect of finding out what people value, but without simply depending on the market either. By analysing tweets, online behaviour or facial expressions in a largely clandestine fashion, a degree of detached objectivity becomes possible which is not available to the researcher who actually has to confront people in order to collect data. Watson's dream of freeing psychology from its reliance on the 'verbal behaviour' of the subject looks to be nearly realized. The truth of our emotions will, allegedly, become plain, once researchers have decoded our brains, faces and unintentional sentiments.

As we move beyond the age of the survey, many of the same questions are being asked, but now with far more fine-grained answers. In place of opinion-polling, sentiment-tracking companies such as General Sentiment scrape data from 60 million sources every day, to produce interpretations of what the public thinks. In place of users' satisfaction surveys, public service providers and health-care providers are analysing social media sentiment for more conclusive evaluations.[11] And in place of traditional market research, data analytics apparently reveals our deepest tastes and desires.[12]

One interesting element of this is that our quasi-private

conversations with each other (for instance via Facebook) are viewed as good hard data to be analysed, whereas the reports we make to interviews or surveys are considered less reliable. Our conscious statements of opinion or critique are untrustworthy, whereas our unwitting 'verbal behaviour' is viewed as a source of inner psychological truth. This may make sense from the perspective of behavioural and emotional science, but it is disastrous from the point of view of democracy, which depends on the notion that people are capable of voicing their interests deliberately and consciously.

These developments have generated a new wave of optimism regarding what can be known about the individual mind, decision-making and happiness. Finally, the real facts of how to influence decision-making may come to light. At last, the truth of why people buy what they buy might come to light. Now, over two centuries after Bentham, we might be about to discover what actually causes a quantifiable increase in human happiness. And in the face of a depression epidemic, mass surveillance of mood and behaviour might unlock the secrets of this disease, so as to screen for it and offer tips and tools to avoid it.

The unspoken precondition of this utopian vision is that society becomes designed and governed as a vast laboratory, which we inhabit almost constantly in our day-to-day lives. This is a new type of power dynamic altogether, which is difficult to characterize purely in terms of surveillance and privacy. The accumulation of psychological data occurs unobtrusively in such a society, often thanks to the enthusiastic co-operation of individual consumers and social media users. Its rationale is typically to make life easier, healthier and happier for all. It offers environments, such as smart cities, which are constantly adapting around behaviour and real-time social trends, in ways that most people are scarcely aware of. And in keeping with Bentham's fear of the 'tyranny of sounds', it replaces dialogue with expert management. After all, not everybody can inhabit a laboratory, no matter how big. A powerful minority must play the role of the scientists.

We received a glimpse of this future in June 2014, when Facebook published a paper analysing 'emotional contagion' in social networks.[13] The public response was similar to that of JWT's survey subjects in Copenhagen and London in 1927: outrage. This one academic paper made headlines around the world, though not for the quality of its findings. Instead, the discovery that Facebook had deliberately manipulated the newsfeed of 700,000 users for one week in January 2012 seemed like an abuse of research ethics.[14] It turned out that this platform, on which friendships and public campaigns depended, was also being used as a laboratory to probe and test behaviour.

Will this sort of activity still prompt outrage in another ten or twenty years, or will we have grown used to it? More to the point, will Facebook still bother to publish their findings, or will they simply run experiments for their own private benefit? What is troubling about the situation today is that the power inequalities on which such forms of knowledge depend have become largely invisible or taken for granted. The fact that they combine 'benign' intentions (to improve our health and well-being) with those of profit and elite political strategy is central to how they function. The only way in which such blanket administration of our everyday lives can now be challenged is if we also challenge the automatic right of experts to deliver any form of emotion to us, be it positive or negative.

The truth of happiness?

How happy were you yesterday? How did you feel? Do you know? Can you remember? It's possible that, even if you don't, someone else could tell you. As the digital and neurological sciences of happiness progress, they are nearing the point where experts are more qualified to speak about your subjective state than you are. Or to put that another way, subjective states are no longer subjective matters.

Twitter is a case in point. Twitter's 250 million users produce 500 million tweets per day, producing a constant stream of data which can potentially be analysed for various purposes. This is one of the more dramatic examples of big data accumulation in recent years. Ten per cent of this stream is made freely available at no cost, opening up enticing opportunities for social researchers, both in business and universities. The rest of the stream, up to the complete fire-hose of every single tweet, is available for a range of fees.

The research challenge is how to make sense of so much data, which involves building algorithms capable of interpreting millions of tweets. At the University of Pittsburgh, a group of psychologists has built one such algorithm, aimed at capturing how much happiness is expressed in a single 140-character tweet. To do this, the researchers created a database of five thousand words, drawn from digital texts, and gave every word a 'happiness value' on a scale of 1–9. A tweet can then be automatically scored in terms of its expression of happiness.

The Pittsburgh project is designed to spot trends in happiness at an aggregate level, analysing 50 million tweets every day. It is not in itself interested in the happiness levels of individual users. Instead, it can identify some clear patterns in how happiness fluctuates across the population, both over time and over space. Happiness maps have been developed on the back of this data; the researchers now know that Tuesday is the least happy day of the week, and Saturday the most happy. This project might not actually report back on how happy you were last week. But a range of similar projects could, typically under the auspices that it would be for your own well-being, health or safety.

One such project is the 'Durkheim Project', developed by researchers at Dartmouth College, named after Émile Durkheim. Durkheim is known as one of the founders of sociology, and author of *Suicide*, an analysis of variations in national suicide rates in the nineteenth century. Durkheim was drawing on the new statistical data on death rates that had recently accrued over a number of decades in Europe at the time. The Durkheim Project aimed to go one better: drawing on analysis of social media data and mobile phone conversations, suicide would be predicted.

The targets of this analysis are former US military veterans, who are known to have a higher risk of suicide than the rest of the population. The question is how to identify those who need help before it is too late. With support from the Department of Veterans Affairs, who are able to access medical records as an additional source of data, the Durkheim Project aims to provide an early warning system that a certain individual is showing higher risk of suicide. This requires sophisticated forms of data analytics capable of extracting meaning from large quantities of data, again through learning what specific words are likely to mean. Sentences and grammatical constructions of suicidal people are studied and taught to computers. Without any intrusion into the individual's life, their feelings are being tracked. A similar project, at University of Warwick, UK, has used real suicide notes to teach computers how to spot suicidal thoughts within grammatical constructions.

If individuals can be co-opted into such psychological surveillance programmes, then the possibilities for measurement increase accordingly. The growth of mobile devices as tools for 'Health 2.0' policies, aimed at capturing the well-being of individuals on a moment-by-moment basis, means that the medical gaze can penetrate much further into everyday life, beyond the boundaries of the surgery, hospital or laboratory. 'Mood tracking' is now a particular wing of the larger quantified self movement, in which individuals seek to measure fluctuations in their own mood, either out of concern or just curiosity.[15] Apps such as Moodscope (based on a well-known psychiatric affect scale, PANAS) have been built to facilitate and standardize the tracking of one's own mood.

Smartphone apps such as Track Your Happiness developed at Harvard or Mappiness at London School of Economics, which prod people every few hours for details of their present mood (reported as a number) and present activity, enable economists and well-being specialists to accumulate knowledge which was impossible to imagine only a decade ago. It turns out that people are happiest while having 'intimate relations', though one wonders what reporting this via a phone does for the quality of that experience.[16]

When researchers first began trying to collect data on the happiness of entire societies during the 1960s, they encountered a problem. This is another of those technical problems which cut to the heart of utilitarianism: to what extent can you trust people's own reports of their happiness? The way people report happiness is likely to be skewed by a couple of things, though this of course assumes that there is something 'objective' about happiness to be reported in the first place. Firstly, they may forget how they actually experience their day-to-day lives and end up with a sunnier or gloomier overall take than is actually representative of their mood. We might consider this to be a form of delusion, although people are of course at liberty to narrate their lives however they see fit.

Secondly, they will be influenced by cultural norms regarding how to answer a survey question. If the question is, 'Overall how happy do you feel with your life?' or 'How happy were you yesterday?', some individuals may immediately react in certain ways, due to culture or upbringing, which lead them towards certain types of answer. They may feel that it is defeatist to complain and so exaggerate their happiness (a distinctly American problem), or conversely that it is vulgar to declare oneself happy and so under-report it (a more frequent phenomenon in France).

As happiness economics grew over the course of the 1990s, there emerged various strategies for getting around this problem. The goal was to access happiness as we actually experience it, rather than as we say we experience it. Obviously, this is as much a philosophical problem as a methodological one. What would it mean to access the 'truth' of happiness, without going via the individual's own conscious reflections on it? Unperturbed, psychologists and economists have developed various ways of doing just this. One technique is the day reconstruction method, in which individuals participate in a happiness study by sitting down at the end of every day and producing a diary of how happy they felt at various times and what they were doing. This has some obvious flaws in terms of the possibility of misremembered experiences. But it takes one step towards cutting out the conscious, reporting mind in pursuit of some ethereal quantity of happiness that rises and falls within the mind.

The new surveillance and self-surveillance opportunities offered by data analytics and smartphones promise to eradicate this problem. People don't need to report their happiness via a survey if their words can be interpreted en masse without them even knowing, or if they can offer real-time numerical feedback on it via a smartphone app. For two hundred years, the ambition to measure the ebbs and flows of mental life was restricted to the limits of institutions – prisons, university labs, hospitals, workplaces. The power hierarchies which facilitated this measurement were therefore visible, even if they were not challengeable. Today, as those institutional limits evaporate, they are neither of those things.

Yet this is not even the most extravagant possibility for utilitarian surveillance. At the outer reaches of the science of human happiness are research projects which strip away the experience or consciousness of it altogether. Happiness, by this account, is not so much a state of mind or consciousness, but a biological and physical state of being that can be known objectively regardless of the carrier's own judgement or reports of it.

What has always been so seductive about the science of happiness is its promise to unlock the secrets of subjective mood. But as that science becomes ever more advanced, eventually the subjective element of it starts to drop out of the picture altogether. Bentham's presumption, that pleasure and pain are the only real dimensions of psychology, is now leading squarely towards the philosophical riddle whereby a neuroscientist or data scientist can tell me that I am objectively wrong about my own mood. We are reaching the point where our bodies are more trusted communicators than our words.

If one way of 'seeing' happiness as a physiological event is via the face, the other way is to get even closer to its supposed locus:

the brain. Various types of mood and disorder are now considered visible, thanks to the affordances of EEG and fMRI scanners, including bipolar disorder and experiences of happiness.[17] The exaggerated claims that have been made for neuroscience are already legion, and the plausibility of ever entirely reducing mind (as studied by psychology) to brain (as studied by neuroscience) depends on fundamentally misunderstanding what the word 'mind' means in the first place. Nevertheless, it's possible that a new utilitarian epoch is opening up, the like of which Bentham could never have imagined, in which happiness science reaches the point where it can bypass not only traditional surveys and psychological tests, but all physical and verbal indicators of mood, to access the mood itself in its physical manifestation. The fundamental meaning of the word 'mood' is being transformed.

As familiar concepts of consciousness and emotion become increasingly marginalized by physical symptoms and neurological events, something rather strange is taking place. Moods and decisions, once attributable to the self, begin to migrate to other parts of our body. The cultural imperative to relocate depression in the body has reached the point where scientists now believe that it can be diagnosed through a blood test. What if the patient disagreed? Would they be wrong? More bizarrely, the term 'brain' is morphing into an abstract concept, that can refer to various body parts. The biologist Michael Gershon claims to have discovered a 'second brain' in the gut, which handles digestion, but which may experience its own moods and 'mental illnesses'.

Few of the new instruments of surveillance have been invented with the aim of manipulating us or invading our privacy for political purposes. They are largely motivated by an honest scientific or medical instinct that human welfare will be improved if the nature of well-being can be better understood, through tracking it across the population over time. For those walking in Bentham's footsteps, progress depends on the human sciences finding better ways of understanding the mind–body relationship, new means of linking emotive pleasures to physical things, and grappling with the endless riddle of what 'really' goes on inside our heads.

Where this is explicitly for our own health and well-being – which a great deal of it is developed for – it becomes difficult to mount resistance. On the contrary, many of the new digital apps and analytics tools aimed at uncovering the secrets of happiness and well-being require us to actively cooperate in the measurement of ourselves, and to share data on our mood enthusiastically. There must be obvious benefits available for doing so, or else these forms of measurement would largely cease to work.

The problem is that this is never the end of the matter. What begins as a scientific enquiry into the conditions and nature of human welfare can swiftly mutate into new strategies for behavioural control. Philosophically speaking, there is a gulf separating utilitarianism from behaviourism: the former privileges the inner experience of the mind as the barometer of all value, whereas the latter is only concerned with the various ways in which the observed human animal can be visibly influenced and manipulated. But in terms of methods, technologies and techniques, the tendency to slip from the former into the latter is all too easy. Inner subjective feelings are granted such a priority under utilitarianism that the appeal of machines capable of reading and predicting them in an objective, behaviourist fashion becomes all the greater.

Likewise, what often begins as a basis on which to understand human flourishing and progress – fundamental ideas of enlightenment and humanism – suddenly reappears as a route to sell people stuff they don't need, work harder for managers who don't respect them and conform to policy objectives over which they have no say. Quantifying relations among mind, body and world invariably becomes a basis for asserting control over people and rendering their decisions predictable.

The truth of decisions?

The Hudson Yards real estate project on the West Side of Manhattan is the largest development in New York City since the Rockefeller Center was built in the 1930s. When completed, it will be home to sixteen new skyscrapers, containing office space, around 5,000 apartments, retail space and a school. And thanks to a collaboration between city authorities and New York University (NYU), initially brokered by former mayor Michael Bloomberg, it will also be one vast psychology lab. Hudson Yards will be one of the most ambitious examples of what the NYU research team term a 'quantified community', in which the entire fabric of the development will be used to mine data to be analysed by academics and businesses. The behaviourist project initiated by Watson, of treating humans like white rats to be stimulated in search of a response, is now becoming integrated into the principles of urban planning.

One of the key ways in which the age of big data differs from that of the survey is that big data is collected by default, without any intention to analyse it. Surveys are costly to carry out and need to be carefully designed around specific research questions. By contrast, the main thing with transactional data is that researchers are in a position to collect as much of it as possible first and worry about their research questions second. The quantified community team are pretty sure they have an idea of what they're interested in: pedestrian flows, street traffic, air quality, energy use, social networks, waste disposal, recycling, and health and activity levels of workers and residents. But none of this really matters when it comes to the design of the project. The lead developer of Hudson Yards is enthusiastic and agnostic at the same time. 'I don't know what the applications will be', he says, 'but I do know that you can't do it without the data.'[18] Observe everything first. Ask questions later.

It is rare for academic researchers to be involved in projects of such a scale. But where it is feasible, the possibilities for behavioural analysis and experimentation are vast. Behavioural psychology is founded on a brutally simple question: how to render the behaviour of another person predictable and controllable? Experiments which manipulate the environment, purely to discover how people respond, always bring ethical dilemmas with them. But when these travel beyond the confines of the traditional psychology lab and permeate everyday life, the problem becomes more political. Society itself is used and prodded to serve the research projects of a scientific elite.

As always with behaviourism, it can only function scientifically on the basis that those participating in experiments do so naively, that is, they are not fully aware of what is going on or being tested. This can be disconcerting. In 2013, the British government was embarrassed when a blogger discovered that jobseekers were being asked to complete psychometric surveys whose results were completely bogus.[19] Regardless of how the user answered the questions, they got the same results, telling them what their main strengths are in the job market. It later transpired that this was an experiment being run by the government's 'Nudge Unit', to see if individual behaviour was altered by having this survey offer them these findings. Social reality had been manipulated to generate findings for those looking down from above.

This logic of experimentation allows for policies to be introduced which would otherwise seem entirely unreasonable, or even illegal. Behavioural experiments on criminal activity show that individuals are less psychologically prone to take drugs or engage in low-level crime if the resulting penalty is swift and certain. The association between the act and the result needs to be as firm as possible if punishment is to succeed as a deterrent. In that sense, due process becomes viewed as an inefficient blockage, standing in the way of behaviour change. The much-celebrated HOPE (Hawaii's Opportunity Probation with Enforcement) programme, which builds directly on this body of evidence, ensures that repeat offenders know they will be jailed immediately if found up to no good.

Projects such as the Hudson Yards quantified community, the Nudge Unit's fake survey and HOPE share a number of characteristics. Most obviously, they are fuelled by a high degree of scientific optimism that it may be possible to acquire hard objective knowledge regarding individual decision-making, and then to design public policy (or business practices) accordingly. This optimism is scarcely new; indeed it tends to recur ever few decades or so. The first wave occurred during the 1920s, inspired by Watson and Taylorist principles of 'scientific management'. A second occurred in the 1960s, with the rise of new statistical approaches to management, whose most high-profile proponent was US Defense Secretary Robert McNamara during the Vietnam War. The 2010s represent a third wave.

What really drives this behaviourist exuberance? The answer

in every case is the same: an anti-philosophical agnosticism, combined with an enthusiastic embrace of mass surveillance. These two things necessarily go together. What the behaviourist is really saying is this:

> I start with no theory about why people act as they do. I make no presumption as to whether the cause of their decisions is found in their brain, their relationships, their bodies, or their past experiences. I make no appeal to moral or political philosophy, for I am a scientist. I make no claims about human beings, beyond what I can see or measure.

But this radical agnosticism is only plausible on the basis that the agnostic in question is privy to huge surveillance capabilities. This is why new epochs of behaviourist optimism always coincide with new technologies of data collection and analysis. Only the scientist who can look down on us from above, scraping our data, watching our bodies, assessing our movements, measuring our inputs and outputs, has the privilege of making no presumptions regarding why human beings act as they do.

For the rest of us, talking to our neighbours or engaging in debate, we are constantly drawing on assumptions of what people intend, what they're thinking, why they have chosen the path they did, and what they actually meant when they said something. On a basic level, to understand what another person says is to draw on various cultural presuppositions about the words they've used and how they've used them. These presuppositions may not be theories in any strict sense, but more like rules of thumb, which help us to interpret the social world around us. The claim that it is possible to know how decisions are taken, purely on the basis of data, is one that only the observer in his watchtower can plausibly make. For him, 'theory' is simply that which hasn't yet become visible, and in the age of big data, fMRI and affective computing, he hopes to be able to abandon it altogether.

Look at how this works today. Firstly, the theoretical agnosticism. The dream that pushes 'data science' forwards is that we might one day be able to dispense with separate disciplines of economics, psychology, sociology, management and so on. Instead, a general science of choice will emerge, in which mathematicians and physicists study large data sets to discover general laws of behaviour. In place of a science of markets (economics), a science of workplaces (management), a science of consumer choice (market research) and a science of organization and association (sociology), there will be a single science which finally gets to the truth of why decisions are made as they are. The 'end of theory' means the end of parallel disciplines, and a dawning era in which neuroscience and big data analytics are synthesized into a set of hard laws of decision-making.

The fewer assumptions that are made about human beings, the more robust the scientific findings. For long periods of its history, behaviourism referred primarily to the study of animals, such as rats. What made Watson a revolutionary figure within American psychology was his adamant view that the identical techniques should be extended to the study of human beings. Today, the fact that it is 'quants' (mathematicians and physicists, equipped with algorithmic techniques to explore large data sets) who are rendering our behaviour predictable is deemed all the more promising, given these individuals are not burdened by any theory of what distinguishes human beings or societies from any other type of system.

Secondly, the surveillance. As examples such as Hudson Yards or the Nudge Unit indicate, the new era of behaviourist exuberance has emerged on the basis of new high-level alliances between political authorities and academic researchers. Without those alliances, social scientists continue to labour under the auspices of 'theory' and 'understanding', as indeed we all do when seeking to interpret what each other are up to in our day-to-day lives. Alternatively, there are companies such as Facebook, who are able to make hard, objective claims about how people are influenced by different tastes, moods or behaviours – thanks to their ability to observe and analyse the online activity of nearly a billion people.

Add mass behavioural surveillance to neuroscience, and you have a cottage industry of decision experts, ready to predict how an individual will behave under different circumstances. Popular psychologists such as Dan Ariely, author of *Predictably Irrational*, and Robert Cialdini, author of *Influence: The Psychology of Persuasion*, unveil secrets of why people really take the decisions that they do. It transpires, so we're told, that individuals are not in charge of their choices at all, that they can't really tell you why they do what they do. Whether it be the pursuit of workplace efficiency, the design of public policy or seeking a date, the general science of choice promises to introduce facts where previously there was only superstition. The fact that, no matter what the context, 'choice' always seems to refer to something which resembles shopping suggests that the decision scientists may not have thrown off the scourge of prejudice or theory as much as they may like.

And yet the apparent legitimacy of this data-led approach to understanding people is contributing to further expansions in surveillance capabilities. Human resource management is one of the latest fields to be swept up in data euphoria, with new techniques known as 'talent analytics' now available, which allow managers to evaluate their employees algorithmically, using data produced by workplace email traffic.[20] The Boston-based company Sociometric Solutions goes further, producing gadgets to be worn by employees, to make their movements, tone of voice and conversations traceable by management. 'Smart cities' and 'smart homes', which are constantly reacting to and seeking to alter their inhabitants' behaviour, are other areas where the new scientific utopia is being built. In an ironic twist in the history of consumerism, it has emerged that we could soon be relieved even of the responsibility for our purchasing decisions thanks to 'predictive shopping', in which companies mail products (such as books or groceries) directly to the consumer's home, without being asked to, purely on the basis of algorithmic analysis or smart-home monitoring.[21]

The rhetoric of the data merchants is one of enlightenment: of moving from an age of guesswork to one of objective science, echoing how Bentham understood the impact of utilitarianism on law and punishment. But this is to completely obscure the power relations and equipment necessary for this form of 'progress' to be achieved at all.

Perhaps there is nothing surprising about any of this. We all intuitively understand that making a digital transaction or sharing a piece of information with friends is to be a research subject in the new all-encompassing laboratory. Controversies surrounding smart cities and Facebook focus on the privacy threat that these types of platform involve. But for the most part, the science which the new laboratory produces is beyond reproach: we are seduced by the idea that, underneath the liberal myth of individual autonomy, every choice has some cause or objective driver, be that biological or economic. What is too often forgotten is that this idea makes no sense whatsoever, absent the apparatuses of observation, tracking, surveillance and audit. Either we can have theories and interpretations of human activity, and the possibility of some form of self-government; or we can have hard facts of behaviour, and reconstruct society as a laboratory. But we cannot have both.

The happiness utopia

In 2014, Russia's Alfa-Bank announced an unusual new type of consumer finance product called an Activity Savings Account.[22] Customers use one of several bodily-tracking devices, such as Fitbit, RunKeeper or Jawbone UP, which measure how many steps they take per day. Each step taken results in a small amount of money being transferred into the activity account, where it accrues higher interest than in the standard account. Alfa-Bank has found that the customers who use this account are saving twice as much as other customers and walking 1.5 times as far as the average Russian.

The previous year, an experiment was conducted in Moscow's Vystavochnaya subway station as part of the preparation for the 2014 Winter Olympics.[23] One of the ticket machines was replaced by a new one containing a sensory device. Passengers were given the option of either paying thirty rubles for their ticket or performing thirty squats in front of the machine in two minutes. If they failed to achieve this, they had to pay the thirty rubles instead.

Services such as the fitness-tracking ticket machine are currently still at the status of gimmicks. The activity bank account is more serious. Employee fitness-tracking programmes, which are sold in terms of their calculated productivity benefits, have nothing gimmicky about them at all. When Bentham confronted the question of how to measure subjective feelings, he expressed a vague hope that it might be done through either money or the measuring of pulse rate. In this, he anticipated the rudimentary tools of well-being experts entirely correctly.

The next stage for the happiness industry is to develop technologies whereby those two separate indicators of well-being can be unified. Monism, the belief that there is a single index of value through which any ethical or political outcome can be assessed, is always frustrated by the fact that no single ultimate indicator of this value can be found or built. Money is all very well, but it leaves out other psychological and physiological aspects of well-being. Measuring blood pressure or pulse rate is fine up to a point, but it cannot indicate how satisfied we are with our lives. fMRI scans can now visualize emotions in real time, but they miss broader notions of health and flourishing. Affect scales and questionnaires run up against cultural problems of how different words and symptoms are understood.

This is why the capacity to translate bodily and monetary measures into one another is potentially so important right now. It begins to dissolve the boundaries which separate otherwise discrete measures of well-being or pleasure, and to build an apparatus capable of calculating which decision, outcome or policy is *ultimately* best in every way. This is a utopian proposition (in the literal sense of utopia as 'no place'). There can be no single measure of happiness and well-being, for the good philosophical reason that there is not actually any single quantity of such things in the first place. Monism is useful rhetorically, and attractive from the perspective of the powerful who yearn for simple ways of working out what to do next. But does anyone actually *believe* that all pleasures and pains sit on a single index?

Sure, we might debate matters *as if* that were the case, using the metaphor of 'utility' or 'well-being' with which to do so. But take away its objective neural, facial, psychological, physiological, behavioural and monetary indicators, and the ghostly notion of happiness as a single quantity also vanishes into thin air.

In which case, why build such an apparatus of measurement? Why go to such lengths to ensure that the various separate bits of it are joined up, connecting our bank balances to our bodies, our facial expressions to our shopping habits, and so on? Under the auspices of scientific optimism, we are being governed by a philosophy that makes no real sense. It is unable to specify, finally, whether happiness is something physical or metaphysical. Every time it is asserted as the former, it slips away again. Yet the apparatus of measurement keeps on growing, creeping further into our personal and social lives.

The Copenhagen tenant who kicked the JWT researcher down the flight of stairs in 1927 saw this for what it is: a strategy of power. The surveillance, management and government of our feelings is successful to the extent that it neutralizes alternative ways of understanding human beings and alternative forms of political and economic representation. This project will never reach its destination. Despite claims by neuroscientists to be crossing 'final frontiers' regarding decision-making or emotions, the search for the 'objective' reality of our feelings will keep being dashed, and keep extending further. The main thing is that if unhappiness can be expressed via instruments of measurement, if success can be understood in terms of quantifiable outcomes, then critical and emancipatory projects are ensnared, and their energies are harnessed.

Utilitarianism can sanction virtually any type of policy solution in pursuit of mental optimization, including quasi-socialist forms of organization and production on a small scale, where they appear to make people feel better and healthier. It favours human 'flourishing' in an open-ended, humanistic sense, which may be achieved through friendship and altruism, as recommended by positive psychologists. But if a definition of optimization were offered which included control over one's circumstances and one's time, a voice that exerted power over decision-making, and a sense of autonomy that wasn't reducible to neural or psychological causality, this simply would not be computable. Such an idea of human fulfilment, in which each individual *speaks* her mind rather than reveals it unwittingly, where unhappiness is a basis for *critique and reform* rather than for treatment, and where mind–body problems are simply forgotten rather than targeted through relentless medical research, points towards a different form of politics altogether.

There are a number of critical psychologists over the years who have sought to point this out, by stressing how mental illness is entangled with disempowerment. There are plenty of inspiring ventures and experiments which seek to give people hope partly through restoring their say over their own lives. There are also businesses which do not rely on behavioural science to manage and sell to people. These scattered alternatives are all parts of some larger alternative, which correctly understood might even be a better recipe for happiness.

8

Critical Animals

It has long been understood that working outdoors has certain psychological and emotional benefits, especially when it involves tending nature. Gardening can prove helpful in alleviating depression, and there is evidence to suggest that the presence of foliage directly lifts an individual's mood. When the British Office for National Statistics produced its first official data on 'national well-being', it concluded that the happiest residents of the UK were those living in remote and beautiful parts of Scotland, while the happiest workers were those managing forests.[1] Some researchers have even suggested that the colour green has positive psychological effects.[2]

There is a long history of putting mentally troubled people to work on farms. The routines of milking, tilling and harvesting offer their own form of normality for those who cannot cope with the normality offered in society at large. People who can't seem to find coherence in their own lives, can't relate to a conventional job, or have suffered some brutal emotional rupture, discover that the presence of plants and animals has a calming influence. The harshness of agricultural life may sometimes be part of its value. Crops fail, weather turns bad, but the only plausible response is to laugh and collectively have another go. Neither individual glory nor individual blame are appropriate, in strong contrast to the ethos of twenty-first-century neoliberalism.

In the early 2000s, Beren Aldridge was looking to establish a farm of this sort in Cumbria, in Britain's Lake District. Aldridge had worked on a 'care farm' in America for a year and had experience working in mental health services in Cumbria. He identified farming as an obvious gap in the forms of mental health provision that were available and set about making the case to the regional development agency and various charitable trusts. Funding was agreed, and in 2004, Growing Well was established, a ten-acre farm producing vegetables that are sold locally. Volunteers can spend as little as half a day a week working on the farm, to help them recover from a variety of mental and emotional difficulties.

Judged from the perspective of funders, policy-makers and mental health experts, Growing Well has been a great success. Evaluations have shown that those who spend time working at the farm experience clear improvements in their conditions, which tend to be more sustainable than the improvements offered by medicalized forms of treatment. Initially, most of the people who came to Growing Well had been referred there by social services and social care practitioners. But with the emergence of 'social prescribing' as a recognized medical practice, Growing Well has also been able to forge relationships with doctor's practices around the north-west of England. By 2013, 130 volunteers had spent time working at the farm.

How should we make sense of the success of something like Growing Well? If one chooses to view the human mind or brain as some magically autonomous entity, with its own strange habits, tastes, fluctuations and dysfunctions, which we as human beings have to look after (with the assistance of managers, doctors and policy-makers), then the story is relatively obvious. People are occasionally victims of a spontaneous mental or neurological affliction which they are powerless to fix. Perhaps some neuron isn't firing properly. Perhaps a bad mix of hormones has been released into their blood, due to stress factors which they should have avoided. Maybe they haven't managed their happiness effectively enough, through diet, exercise and empathy towards others. The natural environment and physical activity offers a psychosomatic treatment for these sorts of ailment, not unlike a drug or a talking cure.

No doubt this is the sort of story that many of Growing Well's funders and NHS collaborators would tell. It is certainly the sort of story that has captured the imagination of policy-makers and managers today. And in the face of a constant drip-drip of neurological and behaviourist research findings into the mainstream media (or via self-help literature), it is the sort of story that individuals may now tell about their own lives. My brain has developed a dysfunction which requires a treatment. My mind has started playing up, like an errant dog. Spending time with plants becomes a medical fix. After all, as positive psychologists relentlessly remind us, well-being is a choice. Someone needs to take my mind or brain in hand.

But this is very different from how Beren Aldridge understands the project he founded. As far as he is concerned, Growing Well is a business, not some form of medical prescription in disguise. Prior to establishing the farm, Aldridge had done a master's degree in vocational rehabilitation, studying how work helps people recover from illnesses and painful life events. His dissertation looked at participatory management practices, exploring the benefits of democratic business structures, otherwise known as co-operatives. It struck him that including people in the running of businesses – be they social enterprises or not – was an obvious way of helping them rediscover a sense of purpose and agency in their own lives. Why not bring together the movement for 'care farming', which had traditionally been viewed as a service to mental health patients, with that of cooperatives, which offered a template for empowering people to organize and produce collectively?

Virtually all the scientific analysis of the psychological effects of spending time with plants completely ignores *why* a person might do so. Gardening and harvesting become merely therapeutic. The relationship between foliage and mood is represented as a simple one of cause and effect. The ethos of Growing Well is entirely different from this. Its organizing principle is that volunteers share the same purpose, of producing and selling good vegetables. The farm is established as an 'industrial and provident society', one of the legal forms available for the creation of co-operatives in the UK. Anyone who has an interest in Growing Well, be it as a customer, a volunteer or a visitor wanting to know more about farming, is encouraged to become a member, who is then able to participate in decision-making. Volunteers are offered the opportunity to engage in management of the business, at whatever level of seniority they would like. This isn't just about 'working with your hands'; it is also about expressing a view and taking some control.

The agencies funding Growing Well, and the doctors referring patients to volunteer there, have one theory as to what is going on. Aldridge and his colleagues have another one entirely. According to the former, the volunteers are medically ill and receiving a form of treatment. According to the latter, they are rediscovering their dignity, exercising judgement, and participating in a business which trades successfully in the local area. In the first theory, the volunteers are passive, without any medically relevant interpretation of their own of their situation. In the second theory, they are active and gaining opportunities to influence the world around them, through interpreting and debating it.

Could it not be that both views are correct? In a superficial sense, it could. People can maintain different ideas of what is going on, based on different types of evidence and scientific methodology. The more fundamental question is what it means for society, for politics or for personal life stories, to operate according to certain forms of psychological and neurological explanation. A troubling possibility is that it is precisely the behaviourist and medical view of the mind – as some sort of internal bodily organ or instrument which suffers silently – that locks us into the forms of passivity associated with depression and anxiety in the first place. A society designed to measure and manage fluctuations in pleasure and pain, as Bentham envisaged, may be set up for more instances of 'mental breakdown' than one designed to help people speak and participate.

Understanding unhappiness

Why do people become unhappy, and what should anyone do about it? These are questions which concern philosophers, psychologists, politicians, neuroscientists, managers, economists, activists and doctors alike. How one sets about answering such questions will depend heavily on what sorts of theories and interpretations one employs. A sociologist will offer different types of answers from a neuroscientist, who will offer different types of answers again from a psychoanalyst. The question of how we explain and respond to human unhappiness is ultimately an ethical and political one, of where we choose to focus our critique and, to be blunt about it, where we intend to level the blame.

Beren Aldridge's insight, on which the structure and ethos of Growing Well is based, is an important one. Treating the mind (or brain) as some form of decontextualized, independent entity that breaks down of its own accord, requiring monitoring and fixing by experts, is a symptom of the very culture that produces a great deal of unhappiness today. Disempowerment is an integral part of how depression, stress and anxiety arise. And despite the best efforts of positive psychologists, disempowerment occurs as an effect of social, political and economic institutions and strategies, not of neural or behavioural errors. To deny this is to exacerbate the problem for which happiness science claims to be the solution.

Beyond the various behaviourist and utilitarian disciplines that have been explored in this book, there are a number of research traditions which share this focus on disempowerment. The community psychology tradition, which emerged in the United States during the 1960s, insists that individuals can only be understood within their social contexts. Clinical psychologists have been among the most outspoken critics of the medicalization of distress, and the role of the pharmaceutical companies in encouraging it. Allied to a critique of capitalism, these psychologists — such as David Smail and Mark Rapley in the UK — have offered alternative interpretations of psychiatric symptoms, based on a more sociological and political understanding of unhappiness.[3] Social epidemiology, as practised by Carles Muntaner in Canada or Richard Wilkinson in the UK, tries to understand how mental disorders vary across different societies and different social classes, correlating with different socio-economic conditions.

At various points in history, these more sociological approaches even found their way into the thinking of business. As Chapter 3 explored, there was a period during the 1930s and 1940s when market research acquired a quasi-democratic dimension, seeking to discover what the public wanted from and thought about the world. Sociologists, statisticians and socialists became instrumental to how the attitudes of the public were represented. As Chapter 4 discussed, the emphasis which management came to put on teamwork, health and enthusiasm from the 1930s onwards has occasionally produced more radical analyses which highlight the importance of collective power and voice in the workplace as contributing factors to productivity and well-being. This potentially points towards whole new models of organization, and not simply new techniques of management.

At each point in the history of happiness measurement, from the Enlightenment through to the present, hopes for a different social and economic world flicker into view, as unhappiness becomes a basis to challenge the status quo. Understanding the strains and pains that work, hierarchy, financial pressures and inequality place upon human well-being is a first step to challenging those things. This emancipatory spirit flips swiftly into a conservative one, once the same body of evidence is used as a basis to judge the behaviour and mentality of people, rather than the structure of power. Hope is not so much dashed as ensnared. Critique is turned inwards. This is not necessarily how things have to be.

Once the critical eye is turned upon institutions, and away from the emotion or mood of the individual who inhabits them, things start to look very different indeed. Among wealthy nations, the rate of mental illness correlates very closely to the level of economic inequality across society as a whole, with the United States at the top.[4] The nature and availability of work plays a crucial role in influencing mental well-being, as do organizational structures and managerial practices. One of the most important findings in happiness economics is that unemployment exerts a far more negative effect on people psychologically than the mere loss of earnings would suggest.[5]

Meanwhile, types of work where individuals have no 'skill discretion' or 'decision authority' have been repeatedly found to trigger the release of cortisol into the blood, which leads to hardening of arteries and heightened risk of heart disease.[6] It is scarcely surprising that employee well-being is higher in employee-owned companies, where decision-making is more participatory and authority more distributed, than in regular, shareholder-owned firms.[7] In their extensive analysis of how recessions affect public health, David Stuckler and Sanjay Basu demonstrate the precise ways in which austerity policies have led to deteriorating mental and physical health, and unnecessary deaths.[8] They also indicate alternatives in which recessions can be an opportunity for improvements in public health. Which route is chosen is ultimately a political question.

While economists and policy-makers focus only on whether or not an individual has work or not, there is considerable evidence to suggest that the structure and purpose of an organization are crucial to its psychological and physiological effects on employees. For instance, people find work more fulfilling in not-for-profit organizations than in private businesses, leading to lower stress levels.[9] To view work as some contributor to well-being, as policy-makers now tend to do, without considering the purpose of work, is to fall into the behaviourist fallacy of viewing people as lab rats, just with slightly more developed 'verbal behaviour'.

Research on advertising and materialist aspiration offers an equally compelling critique. Led by the American psychologist Tim Kasser, a range of studies has looked at how materialist values correlate to happiness, and repeatedly tells the same troubling story. Business school students who have strongly internalized materialist values (that is, of measuring their own worth in terms of money) report lower levels of happiness and self-actualization than those who haven't.[10] Individuals who spend their money in obsessive ways – either too cautiously or too loosely – have been discovered to suffer from lower levels of well-being.[11] And materialism and social isolation have been shown to be mutually reinforcing: lonely people seek material goods more compulsively, while materialist individuals are more at risk of loneliness.[12]

Advertising and marketing play a crucial role in sustaining these negative spirals; indeed they (and their paymasters) have a clear economic interest in doing so. If consumption and materialism remain both cause and effect of individualistic, unhappy cultures, then the vicious circle is a profitable one for those involved in marketing. The precise role of advertising in the propagation of materialist values is disputed, although research does at the very least confirm that the two have risen in tandem with one another.[13]

None of the research cited here is especially surprising, and much of it has attracted a great deal of discussion in the mainstream media. What it all ultimately comes down to is the question of how power is distributed in society and in the economy. Where individuals feel buffeted by forces over which they have no influence – be that managerial discretion, financial insecurity, images of bodily perfection, relentless performance measures, the constant experiments of social media platforms, the diktats of well-being gurus – they will not only find it harder to achieve contentment in their lives, but they will also be at much greater risk of suffering some more drastic breakdown. As Muntaner's research has shown, those at the bottom of the income scale are most vulnerable in this respect. Trying to maintain a stable family while income is unpredictable and work is insecure is among the most stressful things a person can do. No politician should be permitted to stand up and talk about mental health or stress, without also clarifying where they stand on the issue of economic precariousness of the most vulnerable people in society.

If we know most of this, why does this critical discourse not achieve more political bite? If we want to live in a way that is socially and psychologically prosperous, and not simply highly competitive, lonely and materialistic, there is a great deal of evidence from clinical psychology, social epidemiology, occupational health, sociology and community psychology regarding what is currently obstructing this possibility. The problem is that, in the long history of scientifically analysing the relationship between subjective feelings and external circumstances, there is always the tendency to see the former as more easily changeable than the latter. As many positive psychologists now enthusiastically encourage people to do, if you can't change the cause of your distress, try and alter the way you react and feel instead. This is also how critical politics has been neutralized.

This is not to say that altering social and economic structures is easy. It is frustrating, unpredictable and often deeply disappointing. What is hard to deny, however, is that it becomes virtually impossible to do in any legitimate way once institutions and individuals themselves have become so preoccupied by measuring and manipulating individual feelings and choices. If there are to be social and political solutions to the problems which cause misery, then the first step must be to stop viewing those problems in purely psychological terms. And yet the utilitarian and behaviourist visions of an individual as predictable, malleable and controllable (so long as there is sufficient surveillance) have not triumphed merely due to the collapse of collectivist alternatives. It has been repeatedly pushed by specific elites, for specific political and economic purposes, and is experiencing another major political push right now.

Scientific tramlines

Since the 1980s, there has been a succession of 'decades of the brain'. George Bush Snr announced that the 1990s would be the 'decade of the brain'. The European Commission launched its own equivalent 'decade' in 1992. In 2013, the Obama administration announced a new decade-long programme of investment in neuroscience. Each of these has ratcheted up the amount of public investment in brain research to an ever-higher level. The Obama BRAIN Initiative, as it is known, is projected to cost $3 billion by the time it has run its course. The European Commission's 'FP7' research funding round saw nearly €2 billion invested in neuroscientific projects between 2007–13.

The 'military industrial complex', as President Eisenhower named it in 1961, has been the major driver of the neurosciences in the United States. The Pentagon sees new opportunities to influence enemy combatants and produce more 'resilient' US soldiers. The neuroscientist Paul Zak, whose work has focused

255

on the social and economic importance of oxytocin, includes the Pentagon among his various consultancy clients. In that case, the interest is in how US soldiers can behave in ways more likely to win trust from civilians in countries they've invaded. Zak offers advice on the neural underpinnings of moral engagement on the ground.

That industry is heavily invested in brain research is unsurprising. The pharmaceutical industry has some very obvious incentives to push the boundaries of science in this area, while neuromarketers maintain the hope that the brain's 'buy button' will eventually be identified once and for all. It is then only a question of working out how such a button might be pushed by advertising. The implications of neuroscience for anyone seeking to influence and control people – be they employees, delinquents, soldiers, 'problem families', addicts or whatever – are quite obvious, even if they are occasionally exaggerated. Crudely causal explanations of why an individual took decision x, as opposed to y, and how to alter this in future, have a lucrative market among the powerful.

The political focus upon the brain as an individual organ may only date back to the early 1990s, but it is in keeping with a much longer-standing tradition which has been producing alliances among university researchers, governments and businesses since the late nineteenth century. It is well known that a great deal of research investment in behavioural science and 'decision research' during the 1950s was driven by military imperatives of the Cold War.[14] The University of Michigan, which has been a leading centre of this research since World War Two, and occupies a central place in the evolution of behavioural economics, is a regular recipient of defence-related research contracts, to better understand teamwork and decision-making in combat situations.

The science of 'social contagion', to which the 2014 Facebook mood manipulation experiment contributed, also has links to US defence interests. The Pentagon's Minerva Research Initiative was launched in 2008 to gather social scientific knowledge on issues and regions of strategic importance to the United States.[15] This included a contract with Cornell University to investigate how civil unrest spreads as a social contagion. One of the recipients of Minerva funding at Cornell was communications professor Jeffrey Hancock, who was also one of the researchers on the Facebook study. This is not to imply 'guilt by association' but simply to point out that certain types of knowledge are useful to certain types of agency, with particular strategic interests.

Pop behaviourism, offering to reveal the secrets of social influence, has become a booming area of non-fiction publishing, making minor celebrities of psychologists such as Dan Ariely and Robert Cialdini and behavioural economists such as Richard Thaler. Speaking fees for these academics range between $50,000–$75,000 a day, giving an indication of the types of network that their knowledge is fed into.[16] The circuit of behavioural expertise feeds directly into the marketing and advertising industries, as it has done pretty much ever since the American visitors to Wilhem Wundt's laboratory returned home at the end of the nineteenth century.

Few of these examples are concerned with happiness or wellbeing as such, although neuroscientists now profess to 'see' emotions, affect, depression and happiness as embodied and behavioural phenomena. In that respect, happiness is being finally emptied of its subjective dimension once and for all, and becoming rendered an objective, behavioural event, to be inspected by experts. Whether or not the concern is explicitly Benthamite, in the sense of maximizing a positive emotion within the individual, what all of these traditions share is a certain political co-option of psychological science, in which human activities and feelings are studied so as to better understand how they might be predicted and controlled.

Utilitarian, biological and behaviourist representations of human life have acquired a near-monopoly on plausibility in the West today. But this is because the greatest sources of power and wealth in human history have been mobilized towards ensuring that this is the case. We might well describe this as 'ideology'. But to bracket it in this way is to risk ignoring the ways in which a certain vision of individual freedom is theorized, developed, sustained and enforced, thanks to extensive technological and institutional apparatuses. This does not occur simply in some ghostly way thanks to the market or capitalism or neoliberalism. It requires a lot of work, power and money in order to be as successful as it is.

The greatest successes of behavioural and happiness science occur when individuals come to interpret and narrate their own lives according to this body of expertise. As laypeople, we come to attribute our failures and sadness to our brains or our troublesome minds. Operating with constantly split personalities, we train our selves to be more suspicious of our thoughts, or more tolerant of our feelings, with the encouragement of cognitive behavioural therapy. In ways that will baffle cultural historians a century from now, we even engage in quantified self-monitoring of our own accord, volunteering information on our behaviours, nutrition and moods to databases, maybe out of sheer desperation to be part of something larger than just ourselves. Once we are split down the middle in this way, a relationship – perhaps a friendship? – with oneself becomes possible, which when taken too literally breeds loneliness and/or narcissism.

Mystical seductions

What would an escape from this hard psychological science look like? If politics and organization have been excessively psychologized, reducing every social and economic problem to one of incentives, behaviour, happiness and the brain, what would it take for them to be de-psychologized? One answer is a constant temptation, but we should be wary of it. This is to flip the harsh, rationalist objective science of the mind (and brain) into its opposite, namely a romantic, subjective revelling in the mysteries of consciousness, freedom and sensation.

Confronted by a social world that has been reduced to quasi-mechanical natural forces of cause and effect, the lure of mysticism grows all the greater. In the face of the radical objectivism of neuroscience and behaviourism, which purport to render every inner feeling visible to the outside world, there is a commensurate appeal in radical subjectivism, which claims that what really matters is entirely private to the individual concerned. The problem is that these two philosophies are entirely compatible with one another; there is no friction between them, let alone conflict. This is a case of what Gustav Fechner described as 'psychophysical parallelism'.

For evidence of this, see how the promotion of mindfulness (and many versions of positive psychology) slips seamlessly between offering scientific facts about what our brains or minds are 'doing' and quasi-Buddhist injunctions to simply sit, be and 'notice' events as they flow in and out of the consciousness. The limitation of the behavioural and neurosciences is that, while they purport to ignore subjective aspects of human freedom, they speak a language which is primarily meaningful to expert researchers in universities, governments and businesses. By focusing on whatever can be rendered 'objective', they leave a gap for a more 'subjective' and passive discourse. New age mysticism plugs this gap.

Many happiness advocates, such as Richard Layard, work on both fronts simultaneously. They analyse official statistics, draw on the lessons of neuroscience, mine data and trace behaviours to produce their own objective view of what makes people happy. And then they push for new 'secular religions', meditation practices and mindfulness, which will provide the narrative through which the non-scientist can master his own well-being. The result is that the powerful and the powerless are speaking different languages, with the latter's consequently incapable of troubling the former's. Nothing like a public denunciation or critique of the powerful is possible under these conditions.

The language and theories of expert elites are becoming more idiosyncratic and separate from those of the public. How 'they' narrate human life and how 'we' do so are pulling apart from each other, which undermines the very possibility of inclusive political deliberation. For example, positive psychology stresses that we should all stop comparing ourselves to each other and focus on feeling more grateful and empathetic instead. But isn't comparison precisely what happiness measurement is there to achieve? Doesn't giving one person a 'seven' and another person a 'six' work so as to render their differences comparable? The morality that is being offered by way of therapy is often entirely insulated from the logic of the science and technologies which underpin it.

This problem is exacerbated in the age of ubiquitous digital tracking and the big data that results. In his book *Infoglut*, the critical media theorist Mark Andrejevic looks at how the phenomenon of excessive information requires and facilitates new ways of navigating knowledge. But, as he shows, these have extreme forms of inequality built into them. There are those who possess the power of algorithmic analysis and data mining to navigate a world in which there are too many pieces of data to be studied individually. These include market research agencies, social media platforms and the security services. But for the rest of us, impulse and emotion have become how we orientate and simplify our decisions. Hence the importance of fMRI and sentiment analysis in the digital age: tools which visualize, measure and codify our feelings become the main conduit between an esoteric, expert discourse of mathematics and facts, and a layperson's discourse of mood, mystical belief and feeling. 'We' simply feel our way around, while 'they' observe and algorithmically analyse the results. Two separate languages are at work.

The terminal dystopia of Benthamism, as touched on in Chapter 7, is of a social world that has been rendered totally objective, to the point where the distinction between the objective and the subjective is overcome. Once happiness is understood completely, the scientist will know where and when it takes place, regardless of the person supposedly experiencing it. The need to learn from the 'verbal behaviour' of the person being studied will be eliminated once and for all by sophisticated forms of mind reading. Our faces, eyes, body movements and brains will communicate our pleasures and pains on our behalf, freeing decision-makers from the 'tyranny of sounds'. This may be an exaggeration of any feasible political society, but it represents an animating ideal for how particular traditions of psychological and political science progress. Mysticism may provide private philosophical succour in such a society, but also a final political quietism.

'I know how you feel'

Witnessing someone else's brain 'light up' is something that costs a lot of money. A state of the art fMRI scanner costs $1 million, with annual operating costs of between $100,000–$300,000. The insights that such technologies offer into mental illness, brain defects and injuries are considerable. Gradually, our everyday language of moods, choices and tastes is being translated into terms that correspond to different physical parts of our brains. Neuromarketers can now specify that one advertisement causes activity in a given part of the brain, while a different advertisement does not. This is believed to have significant commercial implications. But to what extent does so much technological progress aid us in a more fundamental problem of social life, that of understanding other people?

When Bentham wrote that 'nature has placed mankind under the governance of two sovereign masters, pain and pleasure', and declared that these entities were potentially measurable, he affirmed a certain philosophical approach in which the questions of psychology were not significantly different from those of the natural sciences. Indeed, psychology (and politics) would become truly scientific once it was grounded in matters as 'natural' and 'objective' as biology or chemistry. By the same token, human beings have nothing to distinguish them from other animals other than their particular biological features. All animals suffer, and humans are no different. In various ways, many of the characters explored over the course of this book have shared this philosophical prejudice. Our concepts have been shaped accordingly. Our notions of 'behaviour', 'stress' and 'learned helplessness' all originate with animal experiments using rats, pigeons and dogs.

262

But what if this philosophy is grounded in a mistake? And what if it is a mistake that we keep on making, no matter how advanced our brain-scanning, mind-measuring and facial-reading devices become? In fact, what if we actually become more liable to make this mistake as our technology grows more sophisticated? For Ludwig Wittgenstein, and those who have followed him, a statement such as Bentham's about our 'two sovereign masters' is based upon a fundamental misunderstanding of the nature of psychological language. To rediscover a different notion of politics, we might first have to excavate a different way of understanding the feelings and behaviours of others.

To understand what a word means, Wittgenstein argued, is to understand how it is used, meaning that the problem of understanding other people is first and foremost a social one. Equally, to understand what another person is doing is to understand what their actions mean, both for them and for others who are involved. If I ask the question, 'What is that person feeling?' I can answer by interpreting their behaviour, or by asking them. The answer is not inside their head or body, to be discovered, but lies in how the two of us interact. There is nothing stopping me from being broadly right about what they are feeling, so long as that is recognized as an interpretation of what they are doing and communicating, or what their behaviour means. I am not going to discover what they are feeling as some sort of fact, in the way that I can discover their body temperature. Nor would they be reporting a fact, should they tell me what they're thinking.

This points towards the unusual quality of psychological language. And neuroscientists and behaviourists repeatedly tie themselves in knots over precisely this.[17] To understand a psychological term such as 'happiness', 'mood' or 'motivation' is to understand it both in terms of how it appears in others (that is, as behaviour) and in terms of how it occurs in oneself (that is, as an experience). I know what 'happiness' means, because I know how to describe it in others, and to notice it in my own life. But this is an unusual type of language. If one ever believes that 'happiness' refers to an objective thing, be it inside you, or inside me, I have misunderstood the word.

'Psychological attributes', Wittgenstein argued, 'are attributes of the animal as a whole'. It is nonsense to say that 'my knee wants to go for a walk', because only a human being can want something. But due to the hubris of scientific psychology and neuroscience, it has become a commonplace to say, for example, 'Your mind wants you to buy this product' or 'My brain keeps forgetting things'. When we do this, we forget that wanting and forgetting are actions which only make any sense on the basis of an interpretation of human beings, embedded in social relations, with intentions and purposes. Behaviourism seeks to exclude all of that, but in the process does considerable violence to the language we use to understand other people.

Psychology is afflicted by the same error, time and time again, of being modelled on physiology or biology, either by force of metaphor or by a more literal reductionism. Of course, this attempt to either reduce psychology to the physical, or at least base it on mechanical or biological metaphors, is one of the main strategies of power and control offered by the various theorists explored over the course of this book. For Jevons, the mind was best understood as a mechanical balancing device; for Watson, it was nothing but observable behaviour; for Selye, it could be discovered in the body; for Moreno, it was manifest in measurable social networks; marketers now like to attribute our decisions and moods to our brains; and so on.

And yet we needn't (and mustn't) return to the dualism of Fechner or Wundt either. To assert the subjective, transcendent, intangible nature of the mind, in opposition to the physical body, is to keep flipping the same dualism on its head, like preaching a mindfulness doctrine that is one half neuroscience and the other half Buddhism. To return to a vision of the mental realm as entirely private and invisible to the outside world is to remain trapped in a state of affairs where we keep asking ourselves neurotic and paranoid questions, such as 'What am I really feeling?' or 'I wonder if he is truly happy'. It is in this sort of confused philosophical territory that the owner of the brain scanner can promise to resolve all moral and political questions, once and for all.[18]

At its most fundamental, the choice between Bentham and Wittgenstein is a question of what it means to be human. Bentham posited the human condition as one of mute physical pain, to be expertly relieved through carefully designed interventions. This is an ethic of empathy, which is extrapolated to a society of scientific surveillance. It also views the division between humans and animals as philosophically insignificant. For Wittgenstein, by contrast, there is nothing prior to language. Humans are animals which speak, and their language is one that other humans understand. Pleasure and pain lose their privileged position, and cannot treated as matters of scientific fact. 'You learned the concept "pain" when you learned language', but it is fruitless to search for some reality of consciousness outside of the words we have to express ourselves.[19] If people are qualified to speak for themselves, the constant need to anticipate – or to try and measure – how they are feeling suddenly disappears. So, potentially, does the need for ubiquitous psychosomatic surveillance technologies.

How else to know people?

Psychology and social science are perfectly possible under the sorts of conditions described by Wittgenstein; indeed they are much more straight-forward. Systematic efforts to understand other people, through their behaviour and speech, are entirely worthwhile. But they are not so different from the forms of understanding that we all make of one another in everyday life. As the social psychologist Rom Harré argues, we all face the occasional problem of not being sure what other people mean or intend but have ways of overcoming this. 'The only possible solution', he argues, 'is to use our understanding of ourselves as the basis for the understanding of others, and our understanding of others of our species to further our understanding of ourselves'.[20]

One implication of this, when it comes to acquiring psychological knowledge, is that we have to take what people say far more seriously. Not only that, but we have to assume that for the most part, they meant what they said, unless we can identify some reason why they didn't. Where behaviourism always attempts to get around people's 'reports' of what they're feeling, in search of the underlying emotional reality, an interpretative social psychology insists that feeling and speaking cannot be ultimately disentangled from each other. Part of what it means to understand the feelings of another is to hear and understand what they mean when they use the word 'feeling'.

Techniques such as surveys may have a valuable role to play in fostering mutual understanding across large and diverse societies. But again, there is too much misunderstanding as to what is going on when a survey takes place. Surveys can never be instruments which represent some set of quasi-natural, objective facts; rather they are useful and interesting ways of engaging with people, probing them for answers. As the critical psychologist John Cromby has argued with respect to happiness surveys:

> Happiness does not exert a determinate force that always makes all human participants tick the boxes on a . . . scale in a particular way. There is not the law-like relation between happiness and questionnaire response that exists between, say, the volume of a quantity of mercury and its temperature.[21]

This doesn't mean that a happiness survey doesn't communicate anything. But what it conveys cannot be disentangled from the social interaction between the surveyor and the surveyed. The ideal of discovering something more objective than this, through stripping out the self-awareness of the respondent (for instance, analysing Twitter sentiment instead) is a chimera. It also involves forms of trickery and manipulation which open up a breach between the researcher and everybody else.

Another way of understanding this argument is that psychology, clearly understood, is a door through which we pass on the way to political dialogue. This is in contrast to the Benthamite and behaviourist traditions explored in this book, which view psychology as a step towards physiology and/or economics, precisely so as to shut the door on politics. Unless something goes wrong, the core questions of psychology are relatively simple. 'What is that person doing?' 'What is that person feeling right now?' For the most part, the answers to these questions are relatively unproblematic, and the first and most important 'methodology' for answering them is one that we all use every day: just ask them.

That this methodology is not taken more seriously by

managerial elites is scarcely surprising. It requires processes of deliberation. It credits people with their own legitimate interpretations and critiques of their own circumstances. It also requires skills to listen, which become submerged in societies that have privileged the power to observe and visualize. Management and government are more secure with the notion of brains 'lighting up' or thinking being 'no less observable than baseball', than they are with the prospect of people intentionally expressing their emotions and judgements. For various reasons, making our minds visible seems safer than making them audible. Entire organizational structures would need to change if the behaviourist vision of an automated, silent mind were abandoned in favour of an intelligent, speaking one.

In a society organized around objective psychological measurement, the power to listen is a potentially iconoclastic one. There is something radical about privileging the sensory power of the ear in a political system designed around that of the eye. The clinical psychologist Richard Bentall argues that even quite severe forms of 'mental illness', which are routinely treated with drugs in the West today, can be alleviated through a patient, careful form of engagement with the sufferer and their life history. He suggests that:

If psychiatric services are to become more genuinely therapeutic, and if they are to help people rather than merely 'manage' their difficulties, it will be necessary to rediscover the art of relating to patients with warmth, kindness and empathy.[22]

Listening and talking will not 'cure' them, because they are not 'treatments' in the first place. But behind the symptoms of psychosis and schizophrenia there are stories and emotional injuries which only a good listener will discover.

The rediscovery of listening is a priority that permeates other fields of social science. The sociologist Les Back argues that 'listening to the world is not an automatic faculty but a skill that needs to be trained', noting it is this which gets lost in a society of 'abstracted and intrusive empiricism' of endless data, exposés, facts and figures.[23] To know others is to engage with their stories and how they tell them. In the past, critiques of 'ideology' have proposed that most people labour under a 'false consciousness', not knowing what their real interests are. There is a certain irony, in the age of 'nudges' and clandestine Facebook experiments, that it may now be more radical to highlight precisely the ways in which ordinary people *do* know what they're doing, *can* make sense of their lives, *are* clear about their interests. For this, researchers need to learn some humility.

Among all of this, one of the most important human capacities rediscovered by the sociological psychologist is the ability of the speaker to offer a critical judgement. To describe a critique or a complaint as a form of 'unhappiness' or 'displeasure' is to bluntly misunderstand what those terms mean, or what it means to experience and exercise them. 'Critique' will not show up in the brain, which is not to say that nothing happens at a neurological level when we exercise critical judgement. The attempt to drag all forms of negativity under a single neural or mental definition of unhappiness (often classed as depression) is perhaps the most pernicious of the political consequences of utilitarianism generally.

If we understand concepts such as 'critique' and 'complaint' properly, we will recognize that they involve a particular form of negative orientation towards the world, that both the critic herself and her audience are aware of. As Harré puts it, 'To complain verbally is a part of being discontented, because part of what is ascribed to a person who is described as "discontented" is a tendency to complain'.[24] Notions such as 'critique' and 'complaint' mean nothing without also appreciating that people have the unique power to interpret and narrate their own lives. Where the 'sentiment analyst', mining reams of Twitter data, is looking for evidence of psychological emotion which people have emitted *by accident*, to listen to someone explain the rights and wrongs of his own life is to grant him the human dignity of both understanding and articulation.

Recognizing that people get angry, critical, resistant and frustrated is to understand that they have reasons to feel or act in these ways. People express themselves in different ways and with different levels of confidence, but there are good reasons to accept the narratives that people offer about their own lives. If someone is invited to express her feeling (rather than instructed to correctly name or quantify it), she makes it into a social phenomenon. Once people are critical or angry, they can also be critical or angry *about* something which is external to themselves. Whether or not they are considered an articulate or expert person is scarcely relevant. This is already a less lonely, less depressive, less narcissistic state of affairs than one in which people wonder how their minds or brains are behaving, and what they should do to improve them.

Against psychological control

Imagine if just a small proportion of the political will and financial capital that pushes the behaviourist and happiness agendas were diverted elsewhere. What if just a chunk of the tens of billions of dollars that are currently spent monitoring, predicting, treating, visualizing, anticipating the smallest vagaries of our minds, feelings and brains were spent instead on designing and implementing alternative forms of political–economic organization? The laughter which this would no doubt be met with in the higher echelons of business, university management and government is a sign of how politically important the techniques of psychological control have now become.

Would an enlightened mental health practitioner or social epidemiologist find it equally funny? I suspect not. Many psychiatrists and clinical psychologists are entirely aware that the problems they are paid to deal with do not start within the mind or body of a solitary individual, or even necessarily within the family. They start with some broader social, political or economic breakdown. Delimiting psychology and psychiatry within the realms of medicine (or some quasi-economic behavioural science) is a way of neutering the critical potential of these professions. But what would they and we demand, given the chance?

The demand that misery be de-medicalized, in explicit opposition to the interests of the pharmaceutical industry (and its representatives within the American Psychiatric Association) is one that is gathering momentum.[25] Even Robert Spitzer, the chief architect of the DSM-III in 1980, has argued that the extension of medical diagnosis to ordinary everyday troubles has now gone too far. The phenomenon of 'social prescribing' is one of the possible borderlands between medicalization and efforts to build alternative social and economic institutions. This could of course go either way: while it could mean seeking different models of social and economic co-operation, for mutual benefit, it can also unleash even greater medicalization of social relations, where both work and leisure are evaluated in terms of their private physiological or neurological utility.

Businesses which are organized around a principle of dialogue and co-operative control would be another starting point for a critical mind turned outwards upon the world, and not inwards upon itself. One of the advantages of employee-owned businesses is that they are far less reliant on the forms of psychological control that managers of corporations have relied on since the 1920s. There is no need for somewhat ironic HR rhetoric about the 'staff being the number one asset' in firms where that is constitutionally recognized. It is only under conditions of ownership and management which render most people expendable that so much 'soft' rhetorical effort has to be undertaken to reassure them that they are not.

Any faintly realistic account of organizations must recognize that there is an optimal amount of dialogue and consultation, between zero at one end (the Frederick Taylor position) and constant deliberation. Arguing for democratic business structures cannot plausibly mean the democratization of every single decision, at every moment in time. But it is not clear that the case for management autarchy still works either, even on its own terms. If the argument for hierarchies is that they are efficient, that they cut costs, that they get things done, a more nuanced reading of much of the research on unhappiness, stress, depression and absence in the workplace would suggest that current organizational structures are failing even in this limited aim.

If unhappiness is costing the US economy half a trillion a year in lost productivity and lost tax receipts, as Gallup calculates, who is to say that, on the spectrum between 'Taylor' and 'constant deliberation', the economically optimal amount of co-operation and dialogue in the workplace isn't considerably closer to the latter of those two poles? Consultation or dialogue which is purely there to make employees feel valued is useless and repeats the same error yet again. The goal is not to make employees feel valued, but to rearrange power relations such that they are valued, a state of affairs that will most likely influence how they feel as a side effect.

Organizational structures which privilege deliberation are very difficult to get right, but this is largely due to lack of practice, professional advice and experimentation. Writing in 1961, the cultural critic Raymond Williams suggested that the practice of democratic dialogue was something people may need help learning so it could be imported into the management of businesses and local communities. 'This is the real power of institutions,' he wrote, 'that they actively teach particular ways of feeling, and it is at once evident that we have not nearly enough institutions which practically teach democracy'.[26] Examples of successful co-operatives confirm the truth in Williams's insight: over time, members become more skilled in deliberating about the collective and less likely to use democratic structures as a vent for their private grievances and unhappiness. But they need to be supported in this learning curve.[27] It is a telling indicator of how our political culture has changed in the past half century, that the contemporary equivalent of Williams's suggestion is that we teach resilience and mindfulness: silent relationships to the self, rather than vocal relationships to each other.

Stress can be viewed as a medical problem, or it can be viewed as a political one. Those who have studied it in its broader social context are well aware that it arises in circumstances where individuals have lost control over their working lives, which ought to throw the policy spotlight on precarious work and autarchic management, not on physical bodies or medical therapies. In

2014, John Ashton, the president of the UK Faculty of Public Health, argued that Britain should gradually move towards a four-day week, to alleviate the combined problems of over-work and under-work, both of which are stress factors.[28]

At the frontier of utilitarian measurement and management today is a gradual joining up of economics and medicine, into a single science of well-being, accompanied by a monistic fantasy of a single measure of human optimality. Measurements which target the body are becoming commensurable with those geared towards productivity and profit. This is an important area of critique and of resistance. As a point of principle, we might state that the pursuit of health and the pursuit of money should remain in entirely separate evaluative spheres.[29] Extrapolating from this principle yields various paths of action, from the defence of public healthcare, to opposition to workplace well-being surveillance, to rejection of apps and devices which seek to translate fitness behaviours into monetary rewards.

Markets are not necessarily the problem; indeed they can be part of an escape from pervasive psychological control. Traditional paid work has a transparency around it which makes additional psychological and somatic management unnecessary. In contrast, workfare and internship arrangements which are offered as ways of making people feel more optimistic or raising their self-esteem replace exchange with further psychological control, often coupled to barely concealed exploitation. As Chapter 5 argued, neoliberalism's respect for 'free' markets has, in any case, always been exaggerated. Marketing, which seeks to reduce business uncertainty, has long been far more attractive to corporations than markets. Suspicion of services offered for free, such as most social media platforms, is a symptom of a more general anxiety regarding technologies of psychological control, which is not simply reducible to traditional concerns about privacy.

Advertising is among the most powerful techniques of mass behavioural manipulation, since it first became 'scientific' at the dawn of the twentieth century. On this issue, advertisers have a vested interest in contradicting themselves. The customer is sovereign and cannot be conned; the advertisement is simply a vehicle for the product. On the other hand, spending on advertising continues to rise, and efforts to inhibit the power of brands and marketing agencies to flood the media, public space, sports and public institutions with imagery are vigorously attacked. If advertising is so innocent, then why is there so much of it around?

Campaigns for advertising-free spaces (against 'visual pollution') have had a few notable successes in various cities around the world. The Brazilian city of São Paolo has no public billboards, following the 'Clean City Law' introduced by the mayor in 2006. Other Brazilian cities have explored similar measures to reduce or ban the amount of advertising. Other campaigns have been more narrowly focused. In 2007, advertisements for luxury accommodation were removed in Beijing. The mayor explained that they 'use exaggerated terms that encourage luxury and self-indulgence which are beyond the reach of low-income groups and are therefore not conducive to harmony in the capital'. A US organization, Commercial Alert, runs an annual 'Ad Slam' contest, in which $5,000 is awarded to the school that has removed the most advertising from its common spaces.

Campaigns such as these are inevitably dependent on some quite traditional ideas of how to defend the public, and target some relatively old-fashioned techniques of psychological control. Product placement in 'free' media and entertainment content is a different type of problem altogether, while the internet enables marketing to monitor and target individuals in a far more subtle and individualized fashion. 'Smart' infrastructures, which offer constant feedback loops between individuals and centralized data stores, are assumed to be the future of everything from advertising, to health care, to urban governance, to human resource management. The all-encompassing laboratory, explored in Chapter 7, is a frightening prospect, not least because it is difficult to see how it might ever be reversed, should that be desired in future. But there is no reason to assume that practices such as facial scanning in public places must remain legal.

What would the critique of smartness look like? And what would resistance to it mean? Would it be a celebration of 'dumbness'? Would we simply refuse to wear the health-tracking wristbands? Perhaps. Some aspects of the Benthamite utopia can seem almost impossible to duck out of — the sentiment analyser who discovers the happiest neighbourhood in the city, through mining the geo-data of tweets; the instructions from one's doctor to exercise more gratitude so as to improve both mood and reduce physical stress. But remembering the philosophical contradictions inherent in these ventures, and their historical and political origins, may at least offer a source of something which has no simple bodily or neural correlate, and involves a strange tinge of happiness in spite of unhappiness: hope.

Acknowledgements

My interest in economic psychology, broadly understood, originated in 2009 when I noticed, to my astonishment, that behavioural economics and neuroscience were being presented as credible explanations of the global financial crisis. I subsequently spent two years as a Research Fellow at the Institute for Science Innovation and Society, University of Oxford, which allowed me to start reading the burgeoning literature in behavioural economics, happiness economics and the policy applications of both. This research resulted in a couple of articles, 'The Political Economy of Unhappiness', *New Left Review*, 71, Sept.–Oct. 2011, and 'The Emerging Neocommunitarianism', *Political Quarterly*, 83: 4, Oct.–Dec. 2012 (the latter was subsequently awarded the Bernard Crick Prize for best article published that year in *Political Quarterly*).

I also edited a series of articles for openDemocracy's OurKingdom section on the topic of happiness over the course of 2011. In early 2012, I was invited to the Tavistock Clinic by Bernadette Wren to discuss my work, which resulted in various valuable social and intellectual connections, some of which have been crucial for this book. Sebastian Kraemer was particularly helpful and insightful. I am grateful to all of the colleagues, discussants and editors who assisted me in my work over this period.

I began working on this book in late 2012, after fine-tuning the proposal with Leo Hollis, my editor at Verso. My colleagues at the Centre for Interdisciplinary Methodologies, University of Warwick, were always stimulating, and offered various ways of thinking critically about measurement and quantification. During the last months of working on the manuscript, I sent chapters to individuals who I knew were each far more expert on the given chapter topics than I was. All of them demonstrated admirable patience, even if they were not always sympathetic to the somewhat polemical style of the book. They were: Lydia Prior, Michael Quinn, Nick Taylor, Javier Lezaun, Rob Horning and John Cromby. I'm very grateful for the invaluable feedback I received from these readers. Julian Molina provided ample research assistance at a number of stages of the book's development, and I was lucky to have someone so enthusiastic and diligent to support me. There are numerous bits of the book which he influenced for the better.

Leo Hollis had a clear vision of this book throughout, including during those periods when I did not. Working with an editor like Leo was a remarkable learning experience for me, and I've no doubt it helped me to become a better writer. I'd like to thank him for all the tremendous energy and confidence he invested in this book.

I'd like to thank my family and friends, as ever, for all your support and interest in my work, especially to Richard Haines, one of my most reliable sources of happiness. Martha appeared joyfully and noisily in my life only a couple of months after signing the contract for this book with Verso, and there were days (or more often, nights) when I worried that she'd scuppered the whole thing. She didn't, and I think she actually improved it in some mysterious ways. In the last month, she has started to tell us when she is 'appy, confirming Wittgenstein's insight that 'appiness is not something we can be factually right or wrong about, but which we either know how to express or don't.

Finally, to Lydia, who supported me throughout all of the above, from buying me a glass of champagne in the Ashmolean Museum the evening I learnt that the *New Left Review* had accepted my article on happiness in spring 2011, to the bottle of champagne we drank when I finally submitted the book manuscript in summer 2014, thank you for everything. Many of the themes explored in this book are ones which we've read about and discussed together, and which you'll no doubt develop far more imaginatively over the coming years than I've managed here. The book is dedicated to you.

October 2014

Notes

Preface

1 Jill Treanor and Larry Elliott, 'And Breathe . . . Goldie Hawn and a Monk Bring Meditation to Davos', theguardian.com, 23 January 2014.
2 Robert Chalmers, 'Matthieu Ricard: Meet Mr Happy', independent.co.uk, 18 February 2007.
3 Matthew Campbell and Jacqueline Simmons, 'At Davos, Rising Stress Spurs Goldie Hawn Meditation Talk', bloomberg.com, 21 January 2014.
4 Dawn Megli, 'You Happy? Santa Monica Gets $1m to Measure Happiness', atvn.org, 14 March 2013.
5 For example, the Penn Resilience Project was designed by Martin Seligman and a team of positive psychologists at University of Pennsylvania, to bring cognitive behavioural therapy into classrooms. In 2007, three UK education authorities sent 100 British teachers to visit the Penn Resilience Project, so as to recreate it in the UK.
6 'Work for World Peace Starting Now – Google's "Jolly Good Fellow" Can Help', huffingtonpost.com, 27 March 2012.
7 Sarah Knapton, 'Stressed Council House Residents Get £2,000 Happiness Gurus', telegraph.co.uk, 9 October 2008.
8 Fabienne Picard, Didier Scavarda and Fabrice Bartolomei,

'Induction of a Sense of Bliss by Electrical Stimulation of the Anterior Insula', *Cortex* 49: 10, 2013; 'Pain "Dimmer Switch" Discovered by UK Scientists', bbc.com, 5 February 2014.

9 Gary Wolf, 'Measuring Mood: Current Research and New Ideas', quantifiedself.com, 11 February 2009.

10 Friedrich Nietzsche, *Twilight of the Idols and The Anti-Christ*, New York: Penguin, 1990, 33.

11 Campbell and Simmons, 'At Davos, Rising Stress Spurs Goldie Hawn Meditation Talk'.

12 See Richard Wilkinson and Kate Pickett, *The Spirit Level: Why More Equal Societies Almost Always Do Better*, London: Allen Lane, 2009. Work by Carles Muntaner explores this issue further.

13 Gallup, State of the Global Workplace Report 2013, 2013

14 Adam Kramer, Jamie Guillory and Jeffrey Hancock, 'Experimental Evidence of Massive-Scale Emotional Contagion Through Social Networks', *Proceedings of the National Academy of the Sciences* 111: 24, 2014.

15 F. A. Hayek, *The Road to Serfdom*, London: Routledge, 1944.

1 Knowing How You Feel

1 'Hume was in all his glory, the phrase was consequently familiar to everybody. The difference between me and Hume was this: the use he made of it was to account for that which is, I to show what ought to be.' Quoted in Charles Milner Atkinson, *Jeremy Bentham: His Life and Work*, Lenox, Mass.: Hard Press, 2012, 30.

2 See Philip Schofield, Catherine Pease-Watkin and Michael Quinn, eds., *Of Sexual Irregularities, and Other Writings on Sexual Morality*, Oxford: Oxford University Press, 2014.

3 Quoted in Atkinson, *Jeremy Bentham: His Life and Work*, 109.

4 Ibid., 222.

5 Jeremy Bentham, *The Principles of Morals and Legislation*, Amherst, NY: Prometheus Books, 1988, 20.

6 Ibid., 70.

7 Joanna Bourke, *The Story of Pain: From Prayer to Painkillers*, Oxford: Oxford University Press, 2014.

8 Junichi Chikazoe, Daniel Lee, Nikolaus Kriegeskorte and Adam Anderson, 'Population Coding of Affect Across Stimuli, Modalities and Individuals', *Nature Neuroscience*, 17: 8, 2014.

9 This is not undisputed, but for a convincing argument for Bentham's monistic philosophy, see Michael Quinn, 'Bentham on Mensuration: Calculation and Moral Reasoning', *Utilitas* 26: 1, 2014.

10 Bentham, *The Principles of Morals and Legislation*, 9.

11 Ibid., 29–30.

12 Immanuel Kant, 'An Answer to the Question "What is Enlightenment?"', in *Kant: Political Writings*, ed. Hans Reiss, transl. H. B. Nisbet, Cambridge: Cambridge University Press, 1970.

13 Paul McReynolds, 'The Motivational Psychology of Jeremy Bentham: I. Background and General Approach', *Journal of the History of the Behavioral Sciences* 4: 3, 1968; McReynolds, 'The Motivational Psychology of Jeremy Bentham: II. Efforts Toward Quantification and Classification' *Journal of the History of the Behavioral Sciences* 4: 4, 1968.

14 Gustav Fechner, *Elements of Psychophysics*, New York: Holt, Rinehart and Winston, 1966, 30–1.

15 He defined psychophysics as 'an exact theory of the functionally dependent relations of body and soul or, more generally, of the material and the mental, of the physical and the psychological worlds'. Fechner, *Elements of Psychophysics*, 7.

16 'No motive exists that is not directed towards creating or maintaining pleasure, or eliminating or preventing displeasure', quoted in Michael Heidelberger, *Nature from Within: Gustav Theodor Fechner and His Psychophysical Worldview*, transl. Cynthia Klohr, Pittsburgh: University of Pittsburgh Press, 2004, 52.

17 Relation between mind and body 'are like those of a steam engine with a complicated mechanism. Depending on how much steam

the engine develops, its kinetic energy can rise high or fall low', Fechner, *Elements of Psychophysics*, 35.

18 This is referred to in Bourke, *The Story of Pain*, 157.

19 Martin Lindstrom, *Buyology: How Everything We Believe About Why We Buy Is Wrong*, New York: Random House, 2012.

20 Richard Godwin, 'Happiness: You Can Work it Out', *Evening Standard*, 26 August 2014.

21 Gertrude Himmelfarb, 'Bentham's Utopia: The National Charity Company', *Journal of British Studies* 10: 1, 1970.

22 This understanding of 'government', as extending beyond the limits of the state, was discussed at length by Michel Foucault, who attached great weight to Bentham's influence. Subsequently, a number of Foucauldian sociologists have analysed how 'govern-mentality' works in liberal societies such as Britain. See Michel Foucault, *Security, Territory, Population: Lectures at the Collège de France, 1977–1978*, Basingstoke: Palgrave Macmillan, 2007; Nikolas Rose, *Powers of Freedom: Reframing Political Thought*, Cambridge: Cambridge University Press, 1999; Nikolas Rose and Peter Miller, *Governing the Present: Administering Economic, Social and Personal Life*, Cambridge: Polity, 2008.

23 Association for Psychological Science, 'Grin and Bear It: Smiling Facilitates Stress Recovery', sciencedaily.com, 30 July 2012.

24 Maia Szalavitz, 'Study Shows Seeing Smiles Can Lower Aggression', time.com, 4 April 2013.

25 Dan Hill, *About Face: The Secrets of Emotionally Effective Advertising*, London: Kogan Page Publishers, 2010.

26 Richard Layard, *Happiness: Lessons from a New Science*, London: Allen Lane, 2005, 113.

2 The Price of Pleasure

1 Andrew Malleson, *Whiplash and Other Useful Illnesses*, Montreal: McGill-Queen's University Press, 2002.

2 House of Commons Transport Select Committee.

3 House of Commons Transport Select Committee.

4 Harro Maas, 'An Instrument Can Make a Science: Jevons's Balancing Acts in Economics', *History of Political Economy* 33: Annual Supplement, 2001.

5 R. S. Howey, *The Rise of the Marginal Utility School, 1870–1889*. Lawrence: University of Kansas Press, 1960.

6 Anson Rabinbach, *The Human Motor: Energy, Fatigue, and the Origins of Modernity*, Berkeley: University of California Press, 1992.

7 Margaret Schabas, *A World Ruled by Number: William Stanley Jevons and the Rise of Mathematical Economics*, Princeton: Princeton University Press, 1990.

8 Darian Leader, *Strictly Bipolar*, London: Penguin, 2013.

9 Quoted in William Stanley Jevons, *The Theory of Political Economy*, London: Macmillan, 1871, 11.

10 Howey, *The Rise of the Marginal Utility School*.

11 Jevons, *The Theory of Political Economy*, 101.

12 'We labour to produce with the sole object of consuming, and the kinds and amounts of goods produced must be determined with regard to what we want to consume.' Ibid., 102.

13 Harro Maas, 'Mechanical Rationality: Jevons and the Making of Economic Man', *Studies in History and Philosophy of Science* 30: 4, 1999.

14 'Now the mind of an individual is the balance which makes its own comparisons, and is the final judge of quantities of feeling', Jevons, *The Theory of Political Economy*, 84.

15 Ibid., 11–12.

16 Rosalind Williams, *Dream Worlds: Mass Consumption in Late Nineteenth-Century France*, Berkeley: University of California Press, 1982.

17 Jevons, *The Theory of Political Economy*, 101.

18 Alfred Marshall, *Principles of Economics*, Basingstoke: Palgrave Macmillan, 2013, 53.

19 Jevons, *The Theory of Political Economy*, 83.

20 Quoted in Philip Mirowski, *More Heat Than Light: Economics as Social Physics, Physics as Nature's Economics*, Cambridge: Cambridge University Press, 1989, 219.

21 See Philip Mirowski, *Edgeworth on Chance, Economic Hazard, and Statistics*, Lanham, MD: Rowman & Littlefield, 1994.

22 David Colander, 'Retrospectives: Edgeworth's Hedonimeter and the Quest to Measure Utility', *Journal of Economic Perspectives* 21: 2, 2007.

23 D. Wade Hands, 'Economics, Psychology and the History of Consumer Choice Theory', *Cambridge Journal of Economics* 34: 4, 2010.

24 This case is discussed in Marion Fourcade, 'Cents and Sensibility: Economic Valuation and the Nature of "Nature"', *American Journal of Sociology* 116: 6, 2011.

25 See for example, Rita Samiolo, 'Commensuration and Styles of Reasoning: Venice, Cost-Benefit, and the Defence of Place', *Accounting, Organizations and Society* 37: 6, 2012. This paper explores how cost-benefit analysis was used to calculate the worth of Venice flood defences.

26 See Department for Culture, Media & Sport, 'Understanding the Drivers, Impacts and Value of Engagement in Culture and Sport', gov.uk/government/publications, 2010.

27 Andrew Oswald and Nattavudh Powdthavee, 'Death, Happiness, and the Calculation of Compensatory Damages', *Journal of Legal Studies* 37: S2, 2007.

28 Simon Cohn, 'Petty Cash and the Neuroscientific Mapping of Pleasure', *Biosocieties* 3: 2, 2008.

29 Daniel Zizzo, 'Neurobiological Measurements of Cardinal Utility: Hedonimeters or Learning Algorithms?' *Social Choice & Welfare* 19: 3, 2002.

30 Brian Knutson, Scott Rick, G. Elliott Wimmer, Drazen Prelec and George Loewenstein, 'Neural Predictors of Purchases', *Neuron* 53: 1, 2007.

31 Coren Apicella et al., 'Testosterone and Financial Risk Preferences', *Evolution and Human Behavior* 29: 6, 2008.

32 This argument was put forward by the former UK government chief science advisor, David Nutt. See 'Did Cocaine Use by Bankers Cause the Global Financial Crisis', theguardian.com, 15 April 2013.

33 Michelle Smith, 'Joe Huber: Blame Your Lousy Portfolio on Your Brain', moneynews.com, 17 June 2014.

34 Alec Smith, Terry Lohrenz, Justin King, P. Read Montague and Colin Camerer, 'Irrational Exuberance and Neural Crash Warning Signals During Endogenous Experimental Market Bubbles', *Proceedings of the National Academy of the Sciences* 111: 29, 2014.

3 In the Mood to Buy

1 Ruth Benschop, 'What Is a Tachistoscope? Historical Explorations of an Instrument', *Science in Context* 11: 1, 1998.

2 Jonathan Haidt, *The Righteous Mind: Why Good People Are Divided by Politics and Religion*, New York: Pantheon Books, 2012.

3 See Maren Martell, 'The Race to Find the Brain's "Buy-Me Button"', welt.de, 20 January 2011, transl. worldcrunch.com, 2 July 2011.

4 Robert Gehl, 'A History of Like', thenewinquiry.com, 27 March 2013.

5 Lea Dunn and JoAndrea Hoegg, 'The Impact of Fear on Emotional Brand Attachment', *Journal of Consumer Research* 41: 1, 2014.

6 Jeffrey Zaslow, 'Happiness Inc.', online.wsj.com, 18 March 2006.

7 Keith Coulter, Pilsik Choi and Kent Monroe, 'Comma N' Cents in Pricing: The Effects of Auditory Representation Encoding on Price Magnitude Perceptions', *Journal of Consumer Psychology* 22: 3, 2012.

8 Drazen Prelec and George Loewenstein, 'The Red and the Black: Mental Accounting of Savings and Debt', *Marketing Science* 17: 1, 1998.

9 Jonathan Crary, *Suspensions of Perception: Attention, Spectacle, and Modern Culture*, Cambridge, Mass.: MIT Press, 2001.

10 Robert Rieber and David Robinson, eds., *Wilhelm Wundt in History: The Making of a Scientific Psychology*, Dordrecht: Kluwer Academic Publishers, 2001.

11 See James Beniger, *The Control Revolution: Technological and Economic Origins of the Information Society*, Cambridge, MA: Harvard University Press, 1988.

12 Robert Rieber, ed., *Wilhelm Wundt and the Making of a Scientific Psychology*, New York: Plenum Publishing Company Limited, 1980.

13 Ibid.

14 The American psychologist Edward Thorndike wrote in 1907: 'Psychology supplies or should supply the fundamental principles upon which sociology, history, anthropology, linguistics and the other sciences dealing with human thought and action should be based . . . The facts and laws of psychology . . . should provide the general basis for the interpretation and explanation of the great events studied by history.' Quoted in Kurt Danziger, 'The Social Origins of Modern Psychology: Positivist Sociology and the Sociology of Knowledge', in Allen Buss, ed., *Psychology in Social Context*, New York: Irvington Publishers, 1979.

15 Rieber, *Wilhelm Wundt and the Making of a Scientific Psychology*.

16 See John Mills, *Control: A History of Behaviorism*, New York: NYU Press, 1998.

17 See nudgeyourself.com.

18 David Armstrong, 'Origins of the Problem of Health-Related Behaviours: A Genealogical Study', *Social Studies of Science* 39: 6, 2009.

19 John B. Watson, *Psychology from the Standpoint of a Behaviorist*, Memphis, TN: General Books LLC.

20 Kerry Buckley, *Mechanical Man: John Broadus Watson and the Beginnings of Behaviorism*, New York: The Guilford Press, 1989.

21 Ibid., 130.

22 Watson, *Psychology from the Standpoint of a Behaviorist*, 41-42.

23 Emmanuel Didier, 'Sampling and Democracy: Representativeness in the First United States Surveys', *Science in Context* 15: 3, 2002.

24 Sarah Igo, *The Averaged American: Surveys, Citizens, and the Making of a Mass Public*, Cambridge, MA: Harvard University Press, 2009.

25 Quoted in Igo, *The Averaged American*.

26 Stefan Schwarzkopf, 'A Radical Past?': The Politics of Market Research in Britain 1900–50', in Kerstin Brückweh, ed., *The Voice of the Citizen Consumer: A History of Market Research, Consumer Movements, and the Political Public Sphere*, Oxford: Oxford University Press, 2011.

27 Igo, *The Averaged American*.

28 Loren Baritz, *The Servants of Power*, Middletown, CT: Wesleyan University Press, 1960.

29 Thomas Frank, *The Conquest of Cool: Business Culture, Counterculture, and the Rise of Hip Consumerism*, Chicago: University of Chicago Press, 1997.

4 The Psychsomatic Worker

1 Gallup, Inc., *State of the Global Workplace: Employee Engagement Insights for Business Leaders Worldwide*, gallup. com, 2013.

2 Ibid.

3 David MacLeod and Nita Clarke, 'Engaging for Success: Enhancing Performance Through Employee Engagement, A Report to Government', Department for Business, Innovation & Skills, bis.gov.uk, 2011.

4 Fiona Murphy, 'Employee Burnout Behind a Third of Absenteeism Cases', covermagazine.co.uk, 26 June 2014.

5 European College of Neuropsychopharmacology estimates that 38 per cent of Europeans are suffering with a mental health problem. Sarah Boseley, ' A third of Europeans are suffering from a mental disorder in any one year', theguardian.com, 5 September 2011.

6 Royal College of Psychiatrists et al, *Mental Health and the Economic Downturn: National Priorities and NHS Solutions*, 2011

7 Ibid.

8 World Economic Forum, *The Wellness Imperative: Creating More Effective Organizations*, weforum.org, 2010.

9 Andrew Oswald, Eugenio Proto and Daniel Sgroi, 'Happiness and Productivity', The Warwick Economics Research Paper Series No. 882, University of Warwick, Department of Economics, 2008.

10 Robert Karasek and Tores Theorell, *Healthy Work: Stress, Productivity, and the Reconstruction of Working Life*, New York: Basic Books, 1992.

11 MacLeod and Clarke, 'Engaging for Success'.

12 Luke Traynor, 'Benefit Cuts Blind Man Committed Suicide After Atos Ruled Him Fit to Work', mirror.co.uk, 28 December 2013.

13 Daniel Boffey, 'Atos Doctors Could Be Struck Off', theguardian.com, 13 August 2011.

14 Adam Forrest, 'Atos, Deaths and Welfare Cuts', bigissue.com, 10 March 2014.

15 Izzy Koksal, '"Positive Thinking" for the Unemployed – My Adventures at A4e', opendemocracy.net, 15 April 2012.

16 Richard Layard, David Clark, Martin Knapp and Guy Mayraz, 'Cost-Benefit Analysis of Psychological Therapy', CEP Discussion Paper No. 829, Center for Economic Performance, London School of Economics and Political Science.

17 Department for Work and Pensions, 'Working for a Healthier

Tomorrow: Work and Health in Britain', gov.uk/government/publications, 2008.

18 Tim Smedley, 'Can Happiness Be a Good Business Strategy?', theguardian.com, 20 June 2012.

19 Kathy Caprino, 'How Happiness Directly Impacts Your Success', forbes.com, 6 June 2013.

20 Drake Baer, 'Taking Breaks – You're Doing It Wrong', fastcompany.com, 6 December 2013; Dan Pallotta, 'Take a Walk, Sure, But Don't Call It a Break', blogs.hbr.org, 27 February 2014.

21 Anson Rabinbach, *The Human Motor*.

22 Matthew Stewart, *The Management Myth: Debunking Modern Business Philosophy*, New York: W. W. Norton & Company, 2010.

23 Quoted in Richard Gillespie, *Manufacturing Knowledge: A History of the Hawthorne Experiments*, Cambridge: Cambridge University Press, 1993, 100.

24 See Harvard Business School Baker Library's own online history of this: Michel Anteby and Rakesh Khurana, 'The "Hawthorne Effect"', in 'New Visions', library.hbs.edu.

25 Stewart, *The Management Myth*, 117.

26 Megan McAuliffe, 'Psychology of Space: The Smell and Feel of Your Workplace', triplepundit.com, 31 January 2014. The issue of laughter, as a basis for more authentic communication at work, is something that Eric Tsytsylin of Stanford Business School specializes in.

27 Peter Miller and Nikolas Rose, 'The Tavistock Programme: The Government of Subjectivity and Social Life', *Sociology*, 22: 2, 1988.

28 Matthias Benzer, 'Quality of Life and Risk Conceptions in UK Healthcare Regulation: Towards a Critical Analysis', CARR Discussion Paper No. 68, Centre for Analysis of Risk and Regulation, London School of Economics and Political Science.

29 Hans Selye, *The Stress of Life*, New York: McGraw-Hill, 1970, 17.

30 Hans Selye, *The Stress of My Life: A Scientist's Memoirs*, New York: Van Nostrand Reinhold, 1979.

31 Selye, *The Stress of Life*, 1.

32 Hans Selye, *Stress Without Distress*, New York: Signet, 1974, 116.

33 See Cary Cooper and Philip Dewe, *Stress: A Brief History*, Chichester: John Wiley & Sons, 2008.

34 One of the most important studies on this topic was the so-called 'Whitehall Study', carried out between 1967 and 1977 in the British civil service. This indicated clear causal links between socio-economic status and health effects.

35 'Unilever Gets Down to Business with Health', hcamag.com, 18 May 2010.

36 Cf. Michael Hardt and Antonio Negri, *Empire*, Cambridge, MA: Harvard University Press, 2000; Adam Arvidsson and Nicolai Peitersen, *The Ethical Economy: Rebuilding Value After the Crisis*, New York: Columbia University Press, 2014; Jeremy Gilbert, *Common Ground: Democracy and Collectivity in an Age of Individualism*, London: Pluto Press, 2014.

5 *The Crisis of Authority*

1 'Full Text: Blair's Newsnight Interview', theguardian.com, 21 April 2005.

2 Richard Wilkinson and Kate Pickett, *The Spirit Level*.

3 ESPNcricinfo staff, 'We Urge the Development of Inner Fitness', espncricinfo.com, 1 April 2014.

4 'Competitiveness and Perfectionism: Common Traits of Both Athletic Performance and Disordered Eating', medicalnewstoday.com, 22 May 2009.

5 Tim Kasser, *The High Price of Materialism*, Cambridge, MA: MIT Press, 2003.

6 See Toben Nelson et al., 'Do Youth Sports Prevent Pediatric Obesity? A Systematic Review and Commentary', *Current Sports Medicine Reports* 10: 6, 2011.

7 This is according to the Gini coefficient.

8 Kim Phillips-Fein, *Invisible Hands: The Making of the Conservative Movement from the New Deal to Reagan*, New York: W. W. Norton & Company, 2009.

9 Jessica Grogan, *Encountering America: Humanistic Psychology, Sixties Culture and the Shaping of the Modern Self*, New York: Harper Perennial, 2013.

10 Hadley Cantril, *The Pattern of Human Concerns*, New Brunswick: Rutgers University Press, 1966.

11 Quoted in Jamie Peck, *Constructions of Neoliberal Reason*, Oxford: Oxford University Press, 2010, 117.

12 Andrew McGettigan, 'Human Capital in English Higher Education', paper given at Governing Academic Life, London School of Economics and Political Science, 25–26 June 2014.

13 Edmund Kitch, 'The Fire of Truth: A Remembrance of Law and Economics at Chicago, 1932–1970', *Journal of Law and Economics* 26: 1, 1983.

14 Ibid.

15 George Priest, 'The Rise of Law and Economics: A Memoir of the Early Years', in Francesco Parisi and Charles Rowley, eds., *The Origins of Law and Economics: Essays by the Founding Fathers*, Cheltenham: Edward Elgar, 2005, 356.

16 Milton Friedman, 'The Social Responsibility of Business Is to Increase Its Profits', *The New York Times Magazine*, 13 September 1970.

17 Will Davies, *The Limits of Neoliberalism: Authority, Sovereignty and the Logic of Competition*, London: Sage, 2014.

18 Nikolas Rose, 'Neurochemical Selves', Society, November/December, 2003; Nikolas Rose, *Politics of Life Itself: Biomedicine, Power and Subjectivity in the Twenty-First Century*, Princeton, NJ: Princeton University Press, 2007.

19 Peter Kramer, *Listening to Prozac*, London: Fourth Estate, 1994.

20 Alain Ehrenberg, *The Weariness of the Self: Diagnosing the History of Depression in the Contemporary Age*, Montreal: McGill-Queen's University Press, 2010.

21 David Healy, *The Antidepressant Era*, Cambridge, MA: Harvard University Press, 1997.

22 As has been widely researched and commented on, anti-depressants are only marginally more effective than placebos, and the effectiveness of placebos has been growing year on year. See B. Timothy Walsh, Stuart N. Seidman, Robyn Sysko and Madelyn Gould, 'Placebo Response in Studies of Major Depression: Variable, Substantial, and Growing', *Journal of the American Medical Association* 287: 14, 2002.

23 Thomas Szasz, *The Myth of Mental Illness: Foundations of a Theory of Personal Conduct*, New York: Harper Perennial, 2010.

24 D. L. Rosenshan, 'On Being Sane in Insane Places', *Science* 179, 1973.

25 Ehrenberg, *The Weariness of the Self*.

26 Healy, *The Antidepressant Era*.

27 Hannah Decker, *The Making of DSM-III: A Diagnostic Manual's Conquest of American Psychiatry*, Oxford: Oxford University Press, 2013.

28 John Feighner et al., 'Diagnostic Criteria for Use in Psychiatric Research', *General Psychiatry* 26: 1, 1972. This later became the most-cited paper in the history of American psychiatry.

29 Decker, *The Making of DSM-III*, 110.

30 The question of whether a syndrome such as depression was 'proportionate' to the circumstances of the sufferer was a crucial one for Meyerian psychiatry, and meant that there was a tacit and often explicit alliance between many psychiatrists and campaigners for social reform through the 1950s and '60s. This was broken by the DSM-III. See Allan Horwitz and Jerome Wakefield,

The Loss of Sadness: How Psychiatry Transformed Normal Sorrow into Depressive Disorder, Oxford: Oxford University Press, 2007.

31 Quoted in Decker, *The Making of DSM-III.*

32 The case is known as the Osheroff Case, after Raphael Osheroff, who won the case. He had been treated for narcissistic personality disorder in 1979 and prescribed psychotherapeutic treatment. Later that year, he was transferred to a different mental health institution, prescribed lithium, and immediately started to recover. In 1983, he was awarded $550,000.

33 Tara Parker-Pope, 'Psychiatry Handbook Linked to Drug Industry', well.blogs.nytimes.com, 6 May 2008.

34 Peter Whoriskey, 'Antidepressants to Treat Grief? Psychiatry Panelists with Ties to Drug Industry Say Yes', washingtonpost.com, 26 December 2012.

35 See for example Julie Kaplow and Christopher Layne, 'Sudden Loss and Psychiatric Disorders Across the Life Course: Toward a Developmental Lifespan Theory of Bereavement-Related Risk and Resilience', *The American Journal of Psychiatry* 171: 8, 2014.

36 For instance, the cost of depression to European employers has been put at $77 billion a year. See Sara Evans-Lacko and Martin Knapp, 'Importance of Social and Cultural Factors for Attitudes, Disclosure and Time Off Work for Depression: Findings from a Seven Country European Study of Depression in the Workplace' *PLOS One*, 9: 3, 2014.

37 The HR Leadership Forum to Target Depression in the Workplace, 'Depression in the Workplace in Europe: A Report Featuring New Insights from Business Leaders', targetdepression.com, 2014.

6 Social Optimization

1 University of California – Berkeley, 'Gratitude or Guilt? People Spend More When They "Pay It Forward"', sciencedaily.com, 26 November 2012.

2 Chuck Leddy, 'When 3+1 Is More Than 4', news.harvard.edu/gazette/, 24 October 2013.

3 I have explored this further in William Davies, 'The Emerging Neocommunitarianism', *Political Quarterly* 83: 4, 2012; and William Davies, 'Neoliberalism and the Revenge of the "Social"', opendemocracy.net, 16 July 2013.

4 This is the basic premise of the field of business strategy. See Michael Porter, 'How Competitive Forces Shape Strategy', *Harvard Business Review*, March 1979.

5 Karon Thackston, '7 Thank You Pages That Take Post-Conversion to the Next Level', unbounce.com, 2 April 2014.

6 Kate Losse, 'Weird Corporate Twitter', thenewinquiry.com, 10 June 2014.

7 Mo Costandi, 'Shared Brain Activity Predicts Audience Preferences', theguardian.com, 31 July 2014.

8 Peter Ormerod, 'Is Your Friend an Unpaid Branding Enthusiast?', theguardian.com, 13 January 2014.

9 Stephen Baker, 'Putting a Price on Social Connections', businessweek.com, 8 April 2009.

10 John Cacioppo and William Patrick, *Loneliness: Human Nature and the Need for Social Connection*, New York: W. W. Norton & Company, 2009.

11 Hospital for Special Surgery, 'Socially Isolated Patients Experience More Pain After Hip Replacement', sciencedaily.com, 27 October 2013.

12 University of Zurich, 'Brain Stimulation Affects Compliance with Social Norms', sciencedaily.com, 3 October 2013.

13 MIT Technology Review, 'Most Influential Emotions on Social Networks Revealed', technologyreview.com, 16 September 2013.

14 Guy Winch, 'Depression and Loneliness Are More Contagious Than You Think', psychologytoday.com, 9 August 2013.

15 Quoted in René Marineau, *Jacob Levy Moreno, 1889–1974: Father of Psychodrama, Sociometry, and Group Psychotherapy*, London: Tavistock/Routledge, 1989, 30.

16 Quoted in Marineau, *Jacob Levy Moreno*, 44.

17 Jacob Moreno, *Who Shall Survive?: Foundations of Sociometry, Group Psychotherapy and Sociodrama*, Beacon, NY: Beacon House, 1953, 7.

18 Linton Freeman, *The Development of Social Network Analysis: A Study in the Sociology of Science*, Vancouver: Empirical Press, 2004.

19 See 'Over 38 Percent of Americans Suffer from Internet Addiction', english.pravda.ru, 24 June 2013.

20 Dave Thier, 'Facebook More Addictive Than Cigarettes, Study Says', forbes.com, 2 March 2012.

21 Damien Pearse, 'Facebook's "Dark Side": Study Finds Link to Socially Aggressive Narcissism', theguardian.com, 17 March 2012.

22 Ethan Kross et al., 'Facebook Use Predicts Decline in Subjective Well-Being in Young Adults, *PLOS One* 8: 8, 2013.

23 Scott Feld, 'Why Your Friends Have More Friends Than You Do', *American Journal of Sociology* 96: 6, 1991.

24 Stephen March, 'Is Facebook Making Us Lonely?', theatlantic.com, 2 April 2012.

25 Jeremy Gilbert, 'Capitalism, Creativity and the Crisis in the Music Industry', opendemocracy.net, 14 September 2012.

7 Living in the Lab

1 Jennifer Scanlon, 'Mediators in the International Marketplace: US Advertising in Latin America in the Early Twentieth Century', *The Business History Review* 77: 3, 2003.

2 Jeff Merron, 'Putting Foreign Consumers on the Map: J. Walter Thompson's Struggle with General Motors' International Advertising Account in the 1920s', *The Business History Review* 73: 3, 1999.

3 Ibid.

4 Thomas Davenport and D. J. Patil, 'Data Scientist: The Sexiest Job of the 21st Century', *Harvard Business Review*, October 2012.

5 Viktor Mayer-Schönberger, and Kenneth Cukier, *Big Data: A Revolution That Will Transform How We Live, Work and Think*, London: John Murray, 2013.

6 Anthony Townsend, *Smart Cities: Big Data, Civic Hackers, and the Quest for a New Utopia*, New York: W. W. Norton & Company, 2013, 297.

7 Mark Harrington, 'How Social Intelligence Is Revolutionizing Market Research', business2community.com, 20 June 2013.

8 'Carol Matlack, 'Tesco's In-Store Ads Watch You – and It Looks Like You Need a Coffee', businessweek.com, 4 November 2013.

9 Mark Bright, 'Facial Recognition Ads Planned for Manchester Streets', salfordonline.com, 28 May 2013.

10 Rob Matheson, 'A Market for Emotions', newsoffice.mit.edu, 31 July 2014.

11 James Armstrong, 'Toronto May Soon Track Residents' Online Sentiments About City Services', globalnews.ca, 17 June 2013 ; Sabrina Rodak, 'Sentiment Analysis: An Emerging Trend That Could Give Hospitals an Edge in Patient Experience', beckershospitalreview.com, 28 June 2013.

12 Dana Liebelson, 'Meet the Data Brokers Who Help Corporations Sell Your Digital Life', *Mother Jones*, November/December 2013.

13 Adam Kramer, Jamie Guillory and Jeffrey Hancock, 'Experimental Evidence of Massive-Scale Emotional Contagion Through Social Networks', *Proceedings of the National Academy of the Sciences* 111: 24, 2014.

14 Robinson Meyer, 'Everything We Know About Facebook's Secret Mood Manipulation Experiment', theatlantic.com, 28 June 2014.

15 Ernesto Ramirez, 'How to Measure Mood Using Quantified Self Tools', quantifiedself.com, 17 January 2013.

16 Matthew Killingsworth and Daniel Gilbert, 'A Wandering Mind Is an Unhappy Mind', Science 330: 6006, 2010.

17 Mount Sinai Medical Center, 'Neuroimaging May Offer New Way to Diagnose Bipolar Disorder', sciencedaily.com, 5 June, 2013; Lucy McKeon, 'The Neuroscience of Happiness', salon.com, 28 January 2012.

18 Steve Lohr, 'Huge New Development Project Becomes a Data Science Lab', bits.blogs.nytimes.com, 14 April 2014.

19 Shiv Malik, 'Jobseekers Made to Carry Out Bogus Psychometric Tests', theguardian.com, 30 April 2013.

20 Randy Rieland, 'Think You're Doing a Good Job? Not If the Algorithms Say You're Not', smithsonianmag.com, 27 August, 2013.

21 Cass Sunstein, 'Shopping Made Psychic', nytimes.com, 20 August 2014.

22 Rian Boden, 'Alfa-Bank Uses Activity Trackers to Offer Higher Interest Rates to Customers Who Exercise', nfcworld.com, 30 May 2014.

23 'Moscow Subway Station Lets Passengers Pay Fare in Squats', forbes.com, 14 November 2013.

8 Critical Animals

1 Lizzie Davies and Simon Rogers, 'Wellbeing Index Points Way to Bliss: Live on a Remote Island, and Don't Work', theguardian.com, 24 July 2012.

2 Cari Nierenberg, 'A Green Scene Sparks Our Creativity', bodyodd.nbcnews.com, 28 March 2012.

3 In Spring 2011, the British Psychological Society published an

open letter, authored by clinical psychologists, criticizing the DSM-V.

4 See Richard Wilkinson and Kate Pickett, *The Spirit Level*.

5 One calculation produced by the British happiness economist Andrew Oswald suggests that an unemployed person would need benefits of £250,000 a year to compensate them for the negative psychological impact of unemployment.

6 Sally Dickerson and Margaret Kemeny, 'Acute Stressors and Cortisol Responses: A Theoretical Integration and Synthesis of Laboratory Research', *Psychological Bulletin* 130: 3, 2004; Robert Karasek and Tores Theorell, *Healthy Work: Stress, Productivity, and the Reconstruction of Working Life*, New York: Basic Books, 1992.

7 Ronald McQuaid et al., 'Fit for Work: Health and Wellbeing of Employees in Employee Owned Businesses', employeeownership.co.uk, 2012.

8 David Stuckler and Sanjay Basu, *The Body Economic: Why Austerity Kills*, New York: HarperCollins, 2013.

9 See the CIPD Absence Management Annual Survey, cipd.co.uk, 2013.

10 Tim Kasser and Aaron Ahuvia, 'Materialistic Values and Well-Being in Business Students', *European Journal of Social Psychology* 32: 1, 2002.

11 Miriam Tatzel, M. '"Money Worlds" and Well-Being: An Integration of Money Dispositions, Materialism and Price-Related Behavior', *Journal of Economic Psychology* 23: 1, 2002.

12 Rik Pieters, 'Bidirectional Dynamics of Materialism and Loneliness: Not Just a Vicious Cycle', *Journal of Consumer Research* 40: 3, 2013.

13 Andrew Abela, 'Marketing and Consumerism: A Response to O'Shaughnessy and O'Shaughnessy', *European Journal of Marketing*, 40: 1/2, 2006, 5-16.

14 S. M. Amadae, *Rationalizing Capitalist Democracy: The Cold War Origins of Rational Choice Liberalism*, Chicago: University of Chicago Press, 2003.

15 Nafeez Ahmed, 'Pentagon Preparing for Mass Civil Breakdown', theguardian.com, 12 June 2014.

16 These fees were quoted to the author by the speaker bureaus' of Ariely and Thaler.

17 On this point, see the work of the Wittgensteinian philosopher, Peter Hacker, including Max Bennett and Peter Hacker, *Philosophical Foundations of Neuroscience*, Hoboken: Wiley, 2003; and his unpublished paper, 'The Relevance of Wittgenstein's Philosophy of Psychology to the Psychological Sciences'.

18 'Strikingly, neuroscience ascribes to the brain much the same range of properties that Cartesians ascribe to the mind.' Bennett and Hacker, *Philosophical Foundations of Neuroscience*, 111.

19 Ludwig Wittgenstein, *Philosophical Investigations*, Oxford: Blackwell, 2001, book 1, para 384.

20 Rom Harré and Paul Secord, *The Explanation of Social Behaviour*, Oxford: Basil Blackwell, 1972.

21 John Cromby, 'The Greatest Gift? Happiness, Governance and Psychology', *Social and Personality Psychology Compass* 5: 11, 2011.

22 Richard Bentall, *Doctoring the Mind: Why Psychiatric Treatments Fail*, London: Allen Lane/Penguin, 2009, xvii.

23 Les Back, *The Art of Listening*, Oxford: Berg, 2007, 7.

24 Harré and Secord, *The Explanation of Social Behaviour*, 107.

25 See Horwitz and Wakefield, *The Loss of Sadness*; Mark Rapley, Joanna Moncrieff and Jacqui Dillon, eds. *De-Medicalizing Misery: Psychiatry, Psychology and the Human Condition*, Basingstoke: Palgrave Macmillan, 2011.

26 Raymond Williams, *The Long Revolution*, Cardigan: Parthian Books, 2011, 358. I am grateful to Jeremy Gilbert for pointing this out to me.

27 Will Davies and Ruth Yeoman, 'Becoming a Public Service Mutual: Understanding Transition and Change', Oxford Centre for Mutual & Employee-owned Business, 2013; Will Davies, 'Reinventing the Firm', demos.co.uk, 2013.

28 Denis Campbell, 'UK Needs Four-Day Week to Combat Stress, Says Top Doctor', theguardian.com, 1 July 2014.
29 Philosophically, the assertion that rival measures or value spheres should remain isolated from each other is an argument associated with Michael Walzer, *Spheres of Justice*, New York: Basic Books, 1983.

Index

A4e, 110, 111, 112
Abrams, Mark, 99, 101
Accenture, 119
Achor, Shawn, 114
Activity Savings Account, 240
Ad Slam contest, 275
addiction, 204, 207
Adorno, Theodor, 99
advertising, 73, 85, 86, 93, 95–6, 100, 101,
    102–3, 186, 188, 189, 215, 253, 256, 262,
    275
advertising-free spaces, 275
affect scales/questionnaires, 241
Affectiva, 72
affective computing, 222, 237
Affective Computing research centre (MIT),
    221
Airbnb, 188
Aldridge, Beren, 246, 247, 248, 250
Alfa-Bank, 240
algorithms, 6, 204, 220, 221, 226, 237, 239, 261
altruism, 131, 182, 191, 195, 211, 243
American Psychiatric Association (APA),
    167, 168, 169, 171, 172, 173, 174, 177,
    178, 271
American Psychological Association, 87
amitriptyline, 164
Anderson, Chris, 185
Andrejevic, Mark, 260
antidepressants, 143, 163, 164, 166, 175
anti-psychiatry movement, 168

Apple, 37, 135, 159
apps, 3, 5, 26, 64, 135, 221, 228, 230, 232, 274
Ariely, Dan, 238, 257
Aristotle, 5, 20
Ashton, John, 274
Atos, 110, 112, 113
attitudinal research, 100, 147
Ayd, Frank, 164

Back, Les, 269
Bain, Alexander, 48
Barclays Bank, 178
Basu, Sanjay, 252
Beating the Blues, 222
Beck, Aaron, 165, 175
Beck Depression Inventory, 165, 175
Becker, Gary, 149, 151, 160
behaviour, 31–2, 262. *See also* verbal
    behaviour
behavioural activation courses, 111
behavioural economics, 182–3, 184, 189, 210,
    214, 219, 256, 257
Behavioural Insights Unit (Britain), 88
behavioural monitoring, 38
behavioural psychology, 97, 234
behaviourism, 87–92, 93, 96, 97, 100, 101, 102,
    232, 233, 234, 236, 237, 255, 258, 259,
    264, 266, 267, 268
Beihang University, 196
Beijing, advertising-free spaces, 275
'On Being Sane in Insane Places', 168

Bentall, Richard, 268
Bentham, Jeremy
aim of, 56
and Chicago School of economics, 150
childhood, 14–15
as developer of utilitarianism, 13
distrust of language, 19, 32, 104
on emotion, 74
followers of, 232
as godfather of public sector outsourcing,
35
on happiness, 113
influence of, 48
as lawyer, 15
on measuring subjective feelings, 241
on measuring utility, 46
on minds as mathematical calculators, 56
on money, 57, 114
as monist, 33
on pain, 19–20
on pain and pleasure as measurable, 262,
263
as philosopher, 14, 16, 26, 48
on politics, 18, 23–6, 32, 37, 76–7, 155
on psychic optimization, 177
on psychology, 29, 230, 267
on punishment, 16, 19, 23, 179, 183, 239
and scientific politics, 77, 88
on sexual freedoms, 15
shaping of, 178
as technocrat/technician, 14, 16, 48
as theorist, 54
tyranny of sounds, 22, 32, 97, 147, 225, 261
Benthamism/Benthamites, 20, 22, 26, 48, 55,
64, 76, 84, 104, 145, 177, 183, 257, 261,
267, 276
Bethlehem Steel, 118
big data, 219–20, 222, 223, 226, 233, 237, 260
blackboard economics, 155, 158
Blair, Tony, 140, 141
Blink (Gladwell), 72
bodily-monitoring devices, 137
Booth, Charles, 98
Bourke, Joanna, 19
brain research, 255, 256
British Airways, 10
British Office for National Statistics, 245
Brookings Institute, 98

Brown, Gordon, 140, 192
Buddhism, 2, 38, 265
burn-out, 106, 113, 116, 133
Bush, George, Sr., 255
businesses
American psychology and, 85
craze for psychological analysis in, 97
democratic business structures, 272
as obsessed with being social, 187
power relations within, 273
as producing, managing, and influencing
social relationships, 190
as professionally managed, 82
relationships of with universities, 82
thank-yous to customers, 186–7
buy button, 73, 256
buzz, 189

Cacioppo, John, 193–4
Cameron, David, 191
Cantril, Hadley, 99, 101, 146, 147
capitalism, 8–10, 25, 50, 51–2, 57, 58, 59, 103,
105, 107, 108, 116, 123, 210, 250
care farming, 246, 248
Carnegie Foundation, 97
CBS, 99
CBT (cognitive behavioural therapy), 2, 35,
111, 124, 165, 222, 258
celebrity endorsements/celebrities, 1, 95, 190
Cheltenham Literature Festival (Britain), 36
Chicago School of economics, 149, 150, 153,
154–5, 156, 157, 158, 159, 160, 161, 167,
177, 179, 223
chief happiness officers, 4, 113
choice, science of, 237
Christakis, Nicholas, 192, 194, 196, 203
Cialdini, Robert, 238, 257
Clausius, Rudolf, 115
Clean City Law (São Paolo), 275
clinical psychology, 250, 254
Coase, Ronald, 153–8
Coase's Theorem, 158, 159, 161
Coca-Cola, 187
cocaine, 68
cognitive behavioural therapy (CBT), 2, 35,
111, 124, 165, 222, 258
Cold War, 256
Commercial Alert, 275

Index

community psychology, 250, 254
competition and competitive culture, effects
    of, 141–3
competitive-depressive society, 148
complaints/complaining, 107, 133, 165,
    269–70
conservation of energy, principle of, 28–9,
    30, 115
consumer culture, 100, 104
consumer intelligence, 217
consumer neuroscientists, 74
consumer profiling, 216
consumer psychology, 74, 85
consumer voice, 102
consumerist philosophy, 76
consumption, as driven by emotions, 72
contagion, 189, 193, 196, 212, 225, 257
co-operation, 119, 125, 224, 271, 272
Cornell University, 257
Corporate Athlete Course, 112
cortisol, 133, 252
Crary, Jonathan, 79
Cromby, John, 267
Cumulated Index Medicus, 43
Curtis, Ian, 120

Damasio, Antonio, 72
Dartmouth College, 227
Darwin, Charles, 59
Darwinists, 84
data analytics, 102, 119, 223, 227, 230, 237
data collection, 218
data euphoria, 238
data mining, 220, 233, 260, 261
data science/scientists, 219, 230, 237
Davos meetings, 1–3
day reconstruction method, 64, 229
decision research, 256
Decision Science Research Group (UC
    Berkeley), 182
decision-making, 17, 68, 85, 182, 224, 235,
    237, 242, 243, 248, 252, 256
Decline of the West (Spengler), 121
deliberation, 88, 102, 260, 268, 272, 273
Denny's, 187
Department of Veterans Affairs (US), 227
depression, 141, 142–3, 164, 165, 166, 171,
    175, 176, 178, 194, 208, 231

Depression Anxiety Stress Scales, 175
depressive-competitive disorder, 179
Descartes, René, 27, 30
Descartes' Error (Damasio), 72
desire, science of, 74, 96
Diagnostic and Statistical Manual of Mental
    Disorders V (DSM-V), 177, 178, 204
Diagnostic and Statistical Manual of Mental
    Disorders II (DSM-II), 167, 168, 171,
    172, 174
Diagnostic and Statistical Manual of Mental
    Disorders III (DSM-III), 173–4, 176,
    204, 271, 290–291n30
dialogue, 125, 132, 136, 225
digital monitoring/tracking, 135, 260
Director, Aaron, 149, 153, 156, 157, 160
Director, Rose, 149
disempowerment, 243, 250
dopamine, 66–7, 68
Du Bois, W. E. B., 98
du Plessis, Erik, 74
dualism, 27, 28, 30, 265
Durkheim, Émile, 200, 227
Durkheim Project, 227

ebay, 160
e-commerce, 96
economic inequality, 252, 254
economics
    as basis for broad public agreement, 63–4
    behavioural economics, 182–3, 184, 189,
        210, 214, 219, 256, 257
    blackboard economics, 155, 158
    Chicago School of. See Chicago School of
        economics
    divorce of from psychology, 61, 69
    evolution of discipline of, 54
    exceptional status attributed to, 26
    function of, according to Coase, 156
    happiness economics, 5, 74, 229, 252
    as mathematical problem, 51
    neo-classical economists/economics, 113,
        123, 181
    as phenomenon of the mind, 59
    pop-economics, 152
    reunion of with psychology, 64, 182
    subjective sensation and, 55
    as winner take all, 160

305

economies
  classical political economy, 49–50, 57
  knowledge-based economy, 136
  political economy, 50, 56
  sharing economy, 188
  social economy, 190
Edgeworth, Francis, 60, 84
Eisenhower, Dwight David, 255
Ello, 213
emotion
  definition, 75
  as market research industry's preferred
    version of happiness/pleasure, 74
emotional contagion, 225
empiricism, 27, 30, 152, 269
employee engagement, 106–9, 113, 126
employee fitness-tracking programmes, 240
employee-owned businesses, advantages of,
  272
end of theory, 237
Enlightenment, 7, 19, 23, 27, 47, 85, 251
ennui, costs of, 108
enthusiasm, 251
entropy, law of, 115
ergonomics, 50, 116, 137
Essay on Government (Priestley), 13
European Commission, 255
European Management Forum, 1
evidence-based policy-making, 17
existentialism, 38
experience medicine, 126
experienced utility, measurement of, 64
experimental psychology, 81
Exxon Valdez oil spill, 62–3
eye tracking, 72, 97
eyes, focus on by Wundt, 79–81

Facebook, 10, 74, 100, 189, 204, 206, 207, 208,
  209, 210, 213, 220, 221, 224, 225, 238,
  239, 257, 269
face-reading software, 222
facial coding, 76, 97
facial scanning/face-scanning technology, 72,
  222, 276
farm experiences, benefits of, 246
fatigue, businesses' concern about, 50, 116, 120
Fatigue Laboratory (Harvard Business
  School), 120, 122

FearFighter, 222
Fechner, Gustav
  as coining pleasure principle, 29
  distrust of language, 32
  dualism of, 28, 30, 265
  on energy, 29, 115
  as influenced by Hegel, 30
  as monist, 33
  as new age thinker, 28
  parallels in English psychology to, 48
  psychophysical methods of, 60
  psychophysical parallelism, 259
  as representing relationships between mind
    and world as numerical ratio, 35
  on solving mind–body problem using
    mathematics, 27, 28
  on theory of psychology, 29
  weight-lifting experiments of, 30–1, 38, 49,
    50, 59, 78
Federal Drug, Food and Cosmetic Act (US)
  (1938), 170
feedback loops/feedback mechanisms, 95, 103,
  230, 276
feelings, adjustment of, 31–2
Ferriss, Tim, 112
fit notes, 112
Fitbit, 240
fitness-tracking ticket machine, 240
fMRI, 32, 231, 237, 241, 261, 262
focus groups, 102, 125
Foucault, Michel, 280n22
FP7 research (European Commission), 255
Freakonomics (Levitt and Dubner), 152
free markets, 19, 49, 57, 69, 140, 154, 181,
  185, 274
Free: The Future of a Radical Price
  (Anderson), 185
Freud, Sigmund, 29, 164, 169, 198, 200, 203
Friedman, Milton, 149, 150, 154, 156–7, 159,
  160, 161
friendship, 186, 187, 188, 191, 197, 201, 205,
  208, 211, 212, 222, 225, 243, 258
friendvertising, 189

Gale, Harlow, 83, 85
Gallup (poll), 9, 106, 146, 219, 272
Gallup, George, 101
gaming, 205–6

Index

The Genealogy of Morals (Nietzsche), 84
General Adaptation Syndrome, 129
General Medical Council (Britain), 110
General Motors (GM), 215–16
General Phonograph Manufacturing
    Company, 200
General Sentiment, 223
generosity, 185, 196
Georgetown University, 142
German Automobile Manufacturers'
    Association, 217
Germany, influx of Americans taking
    university degrees and research training
    in, 83
Gershon, Michael, 231
Gilbert, Jeremy, 213
Gladwell, Malcolm, 72
global economic management, 3
Google, 37, 193
Graham, Richard, 205, 206
gratitude, 33, 131, 186, 187, 194, 196, 210,
    276
group identity, 123
group psychology, 124, 125
Growing Well, 246, 247, 248, 250
Guze, Samuel, 169

Hague, William, 139–40, 141, 142, 144
Haidt, Jonathan, 73
Hall, G. Stanley, 83, 84
Halo (game), 205, 206
Hancock, Jeffrey, 257
happiness
    accessing truth of, 229
    Bentham on, 18
    as biological and physical state of being,
        230
    current explosion of political and business
        interest in, 8
    current preoccupation with, 69
    Jevons on, 113
    as like a muscle, 114
    as measurable, visible, improvable entity, 3
    as not a single quantity, 242
    as objective, behavioural event, 257
    as preoccupation for economists, 66
    as preoccupation for mental health
        professionals, medical doctors,

pharmaceutical companies, and
    individuals, 174
proxies for, 24
pursuit of via relationships, 209
science of, 209, 230. *See also* happiness
    science
search for measure of, 24–5
as sitting somewhere in between
    quantitative science and spiritualism, 38
as ultimate purpose of government, 37
workplace happiness, 109, 113
happiness advocates, 260
happiness economics, 5, 74, 229, 252
happiness gurus, 113, 211, 219
happiness measurement, 6, 11, 36–7, 38, 251, 260
happiness science, 6, 7, 9, 11, 20, 38, 231, 250,
    258. *See also* happiness, science of
happiness studies, 5, 147
happiness surveys, 267
happiness value, of words, 226
The Happiness Advantage (Achor), 114
hard-wired, 90, 183, 205
Harré, Rom, 266, 269
Harris, Oren, 170
Harvard Foundations of Human Behavior
    Initiative, 88
Hawthorne Effect, 123
Hawthorne Studies, 122, 134
Hayek, Friedrich, 154
health, 126, 251
Health 2.0 policies, 228
Health 2.0 technologies, 135
Health app (iPhone 6), 135
health-tracking wristbands, 276
Healy, David, 171
heart-rate monitoring, 25, 37, 137
hedonimeter, 60, 64
Hegel, G. W. F., 28, 30
The Hidden Persuaders (Packard), 73, 74
Hilton, Steve, 191
homo economicus, 61–2
Hoover, Herbert, 100
HOPE (Hawaii's Opportunity Probation
    with Enforcement) programme, 235
Hospital Anxiety and Depression Scale, 175
Hsieh, Tony, 113
Hudson Yards real estate project (NYC),
    233–4, 235, 237

human capital, 126, 151, 160
human existence, ideal form of, 112
human optimality/optimization, 5, 129, 274
human resource management, 189, 238, 276
human resources profession, 108, 133
Hume, David, 14
Hyde Park (Chicago), 148

idealism, 27, 181
Ignite U, 134
imipramine, 162
income inequality, 34, 144. *See also* economic inequality
Increasing Access to Psychological Therapies programme, 111
indices, 176
individual choice, theory of, 59
Influence: The Psychology of Persuasion (Cialdini), 238
Infoglut (Andrejevic), 260
Ingeus, 110, 112
insurance fraud, 42, 44, 45, 46
intangible assets, 126
internet addiction, 204–5, 207
internships, 274
interventions, 17, 20, 35, 108, 111, 265
Introduction to the Principles of Morals and Legislation (Bentham), 22
introspection, 22, 48, 63, 64, 78, 86
iPhone 6, 26, 135
iproniazid, 162

J. Walter Thompson (JWT), 93, 94, 95, 97, 215–16, 217, 218, 220, 225, 242
James, William, 83, 84, 86
Jawbone UP, 240
Jennings, Richard, 49, 50, 51
Jevons, William Stanley
and Chicago School of economics, 150–1
childhood, 47–8
on commodities, 58
as converting economics into form of psychological mathematics, 116
on decision-making, 59
as fascinated with machine-like qualities of the mind, 56

on happiness, 113
on how we experience pleasures and pains, 65, 66
as imagining mind through metaphors of geometry and mechanics, 62
introduction of to economics, 60
on the mind as mechanical balancing device, 264
on money as yielding happiness, 114
and natural sciences, 59
as obsessed with understanding fluctuations in pleasure, 84
as one developer of theory of utility maximization, 62
on pleasure and pain having own discernible quantities, 61
reading of economics, 50, 55
representation of capitalism, 57
on true comprehension of Value, 54
as turning market into mind-reading device, 57
vision of calculating hedonist, 56
weight-lifting experiments of, 49, 59
Jobs, Steve, 161
Johns Hopkins University, 92
Johnson & Johnson, 94
Jourard Self-Disclosure Scale, 165
Jung, Minah, 182
just noticeable difference, 30, 36, 37
justice, theory of, 62
JWT (J. Walter Thompson) (advertising firm), 93, 94, 95, 97, 215–16, 217, 218, 220, 225, 242

Kahn, Robert, 132
Kant, Immanuel, 23, 27, 28, 30
Karma Kitchen, 181
Kasser, Tim, 132, 253
Kefauver, Estest, 170
Keynesian thinking/policy, 149, 154, 160
Kline, Nathan, 161–4
Knight, Frank, 149
knowledge-based economy, 136
Knutson, Brian, 74
Kraepelin, Emil, 169
Kramer, Peter, 163
Kuhn, Ronald, 161–4

Index

Lamplighter health and well-being
programme, 134–5
language
of behavioural and neuro- sciences, 259
behaviourism as doing violence to
language we use to understand other
people, 264
Bentham as ridiculing language of law, 15
Bentham on natural sciences avoiding
meaningless use of, 17
Bentham's distrust of, 19, 32, 104
of gratitude, 186
limitations of, 33
metaphysical language, 84, 90
metrics and prices as, 64
of natural science, 17
numbers as means of recreating common
public language, 146
politicization of, 145
powerful and powerless as speaking
different languages, 260
quality of psychological language, 263
shift from conceptual language to scientific
one, 80
Wittgenstein on nothing prior to, 265
Wundt as refusing to purge psychology of
philosophical language, 81
Layard, Richard, 38, 111, 260
Lazarsfeld, Paul, 99
Leader, Darian, 52
learned helplessness, 165, 262
Lenin, Vladimir, 119
Lewin, Kurt, 198
Lieberman, Matt, 195, 213
Lindstrom, Martin, 32
Lloyds TSB, 186
Loehr, Jim, 112
Logical Abacus, 56
London School of Economics, 64, 98, 228
loneliness, 147, 193, 194, 196, 209, 253, 258
Lornitzo, Franz, 199
Losse, Kate, 187
Lynd, Helen, 98, 99, 101
Lynd, Robert, 98, 99, 101

Madison Avenue, 92, 93, 215
management
aim of in 1930s, 124

autarchic management, 272, 273
global economic management, 3
human resource management, 189, 238, 276
opposition to, 127
psychological management, 38, 141
psychosomatic management, 128
scientific management, 118–19, 120, 136–7,
235
somatic management, 274
therapeutic management, 125, 128
managerial class, 82
Mappiness (app), 228
market deregulation, 1, 144
market exchange, theory of, 62
market price system, 60–1
market research, 72, 73, 74, 75, 83, 97, 99, 100,
101, 103, 221, 223, 251, 261
marketing, 188, 193, 210, 274
markets, 57, 155, 156, 157, 158, 159, 160. *See
also* free markets
Marshall, Alfred, 58, 61
Martineau, James, 48
Marx, Karl, 55, 214
Maslow, Abraham, 146
mass psychological measurement, 217
mass psychological profiling, 216
mass surveillance, 193, 224, 236, 238
The Mass Observation Project, 100
materialism, 211, 253
mathematics, 47, 49
Mayo, Elton, 121–5, 128, 131, 132, 133, 134,
136, 189
McGill Pain Questionnaire, 175
McKeen Cattell, James, 83, 84, 85, 86
McKinsey & Co., 119
McNamara, Robert, 235
measurement
apparatus of as continually growing, 242
bodily-tracking devices, 240
of experienced utility, 64
happiness measurement, 6, 11, 36–7, 38,
251, 260
of human optimality, 274
as indicating quantity not quality, 146
mass psychological measurement, 217
no single measure of happiness and
well-being, 241
objective psychological measurement, 268

309

of ourselves, 232
of pain, 33, 249
of pleasure, 22, 33, 249
of politics, 145
of positivity, 165
psychic measurement, 59, 60
of punishment, 22
quality of life measures, 126
of speed of mental processes, 77
measurement tools, eighteenth century
    inventions in, 22–3
Mechanics' Institutes/Institutions, 47, 48
meditation, 32, 38, 68, 112, 260
Menger, Carl, 54
mental health/mental illness, 107, 108, 126,
    127, 252, 254
mental optimization, 242
mental processes, measuring speed of, 77
mental resilience, 135
Merck, 164
metaphysics, 31, 37, 78, 86, 89, 92
Meyer, Adolf, 93, 169
Meyerian psychiatry, 169, 290–291n30
Microsoft, 159
'Middletown in Transition', 99
'Middletown Studies', 98, 100, 101
Miliband, Ed, 191
Mill, John Stuart, 49, 53
mind, 7, 56, 57, 62, 68, 96
mind–body problem, 28
mindfulness, 32, 35, 259, 260, 265, 273
mind-reading technology, 33, 75–6
Minerva Research Initiative (Pentagon), 257
misery, 108, 115, 271
MIT Affective Computing research centre,
    221
money, 25–6, 27, 37, 39, 46, 51, 52, 57, 59, 61,
    65, 66, 67, 69
monism, 21, 29, 33, 34, 129, 131, 136, 176,
    241, 274
monopolies, 155, 158, 159
mood, use of term, 231
mood tracking, 5, 6, 228
Moodscope (app), 228
Moreno, Jacob, 197–205, 207, 208, 210, 214,
    264
motivation, 37, 112, 183
Munsterberg, Hugo, 84

Muntaner, Carles, 250, 254
Murdoch, Rupert, 213
Myspace, 213
mysticism, 259, 261

narcissism, 197, 204, 207, 220, 222
National Charity Company, 35, 109
National Health Service (NHS), 111, 247
National Institute of Mental Health, 169
national well-being, 4, 146, 245
Natural Elements of Political Economy
    (Jennings), 50
natural environment, 247
neo-classical economists/economics, 113,
    123, 181
neo-Kraepelinians, 169
neoliberal socialism, 212, 214
neoliberalism, 10, 34, 141, 144, 148, 149, 153,
    154, 160, 161, 177, 179, 210, 211, 213,
    223, 246, 258, 274
neurasthenia, 116
neurochemicals, 67, 68
neurological monitoring, 38
neurological reward system, 66
neuromarketing, 73, 76, 97, 102, 104, 188,
    256, 262
neuropsychology, 68
neuroscience, 4–5, 20–1, 73, 103, 176, 205,
    255, 257, 259
new age mysticism, 260
new age religions, 38
new age thinker, Fechner as, 28
New York Training School for Girls, 202
NHS (National Health Service), 111, 247
Nietzsche, Friedrich, 5, 84
Nike, 221
nucleus accumbens, 67
Nudge (Sunstein and Thaler), 88
Nudge Unit (UK), 235, 237
nudging/nudges, 90, 183

Obama, Barack, 255
Obama BRAIN Initiative, 255
occupational health, 132, 134, 254
O'Leary, Michael, 185
online advertising, 96
opinion-polling, 9, 101, 223
optimization

Index

definition, 243
human optimality/optimization, 5, 129, 274
managerial cult of, 137
mental optimization, 242
psychic optimization, 177
self-optimization, 213
social optimization, 181–214
well-being optimization, science of, 136
Osheroff, Raphael, 291n32
Osheroff Case, 291n32
outdoors, 245
oxytocin, 195, 256

pain, 19–20, 33, 50, 55, 66, 74, 249, 262, 263
Paine, Thomas, 17
PANAS (Positive and Negative Affect Scale), 228
Pareto, Vilfredo, 61
passivity, 249
paternalism, 90
pay-it-forward, 181–2, 184, 188, 191
Penn Resilience Project, 277n5
Pentagon, 255, 257
performance-related pay, 182
pharmaceutical industry/big pharma, 170, 171, 177, 178, 256, 271
physical activity, 247
physiological monitoring, 38
physiology, 195
Pinkser, Henry, 174
placebos, 290n22
pleasure, 21, 22, 33, 55, 65, 66, 249
pleasure principle, 29
political authority, 34, 63
political economy, 50, 56
politics, 18, 23–6, 32, 37, 76–7, 88, 145, 155, 259
polls, 9, 101, 146–7, 223
polymaths, 33, 121
pop behaviourism, 257
pop-economics, 152
positive affect, 175
positive psychology, 4, 6, 9, 11, 38, 74, 114, 165, 175, 194, 196, 208, 209, 210, 247, 250, 254, 259, 260
positivity, 11, 112, 165
Predictably Irrational (Ariely), 238

predictive shopping, 239
preferences, theory of, 61
price theory, 151, 152, 154
Priestley, Joseph, 13, 14, 47
The Principles of Scientific Management (Taylor), 118
'The Problem of Social Cost' (Coase), 156
Prozac, 163
psychiatric scales, 165
psychic energizers, 164
psychic maximization, 177
psychic measurement, 59, 60
psychic optimization, 177
psychological knowledge, 266
psychological management, 38, 141
psychological surveillance, 219, 223, 228
The Psychological Corporation, 86
psychology
  in America as having no philosophical heritage, 85, 86
  application of American psychology to business problems, 85
  association with philosophy, 80, 81
  behavioural psychology, 97, 234
  as being modelled on physiology or biology, 264
  clinical psychology, 250, 254
  community psychology, 250, 254
  consumer psychology, 74, 85
  economics divorce from, 61, 69
  experimental psychology, 81
  Fechner as key figure in development of, 28
  first laboratory for, 77–9
  first labs in American universities, 84
  group psychology, 124, 125
  neuropsychology, 68
  positive psychology. See positive psychology
  promise of practical utility of, 91
  reunion of with economics, 64, 182
  social psychology, 125, 189, 266
  theory of, as balancing act, 67
The Psychology of Advertising (Scott), 86
psychopharmacology, 162
psychophysical parallelism, 259
psychophysics, 29, 30, 31
psychosomatic interventions/management/ programmes/theories, 122, 124, 128, 135

psychotherapy, 124, 127
pulse rate, 25, 26, 27, 37, 79
punishment, 16, 19, 22, 23, 179, 183, 239
PwC, 119

Qualia, 36
quality of life measures, 126
quantitative sociological research, 98
quantified community, 233, 234
quantified self apps, 221
quantified self movement, 221, 228
quants, 237
questionnaires, 165, 175, 176

random acts of managerial generosity, 184
randomized sampling methods, 97
Rapley, Mark, 250
Rayner, Rosalie, 93
Reagan, Ronald, 144, 149, 159
Realeyes, 72
real-time health data, 137
real-time social trends, 224
recessions, 67–8, 252
Recognizing the Depressed Patient (Ayd), 164
reductionism, 27, 264
research ethics, 91–2, 225
resilience training, 35, 273
Resor, Stanley, 93–4, 95, 96
retail culture, 58
Ricard, Matthieu, 2, 4
Robbins, Lionel, 154
Robins, Eli, 169
Rockefeller Foundation, 97, 99, 121
Rogers, Carl, 146
Roosevelt, Franklin, 101, 146
Rowntree, Joseph, 99
RunKeeper, 240
Ryanair, 185

Salter, Tim, 110
sampling methods, 97–8
Santa Monica, California, 4
São Paolo, Brazil, Clean City Law, 275
scales, 146, 165, 175, 176
scanning technology, 75–6
scent logos, 73
Schrader, Harald, 44
scientific advertising, 215

scientific management, 118–19, 120, 136–7,
    235
scientific optimism, 242
scientific politics, 77, 88, 145
scientists, as source of authority, 147–8
Scott, Walter Dill, 83, 85
screen time, 207
second brain, 231
secular religions, 260
selective serotonin reuptake inhibitors
    (SSRIs), 163, 166
self-anchored striving, 147, 166, 175
self-anchoring striving scale, 146
self-forming groups, 200
self-help gurus, 210
self-help literature, 247
self-improvement, 212
self-monitoring, 258
self-optimization, 213
self-reflection, 211
self-surveillance, 221, 230
Seligman, Martin, 165, 277n5
Selye, Hans, 128–31, 133, 264
The Senses and the Intellect (Bain), 48
sentiment analysis/tracking, 6, 221, 223, 261
sexual orientation disturbance, 172
sharing economy, 188
shopping, 58, 74, 93, 188, 239
sick notes, 112
Sing Sing prison, 201
Smail, David, 250
smart cities, 220, 224, 239
smart homes, 239
smart watches, 37
smartphones, 10, 207, 222, 230
smiles/smiling, 36–7, 38
Smith, Adam, 49, 50, 52, 55
social, 1, 36, 184, 186, 187, 188, 190, 191, 203,
    204, 205, 207, 208, 211–12
social analytics, 188, 191, 193, 196
social capitalism, 212
social contagion, science of, 257
social economy, 190
social epidemiology, 9, 250, 254
social media, 188, 189, 199, 203, 207, 208–9,
    213, 224, 261, 274
social media addiction, 206, 207
social network analysis, 204, 208

Index

social networks, 193, 194, 195, 196, 213, 225
social neuroscience, 193, 195, 213, 214
social obligation, 184
social optimization, 181–214
social prescribing, 194, 212, 246, 271
social psychology, 125, 189, 266
social research, 98, 202, 226
social science, as converging with physiology into new discipline, 195
sociology, 254
sociometric analysis, 199
sociometric maps, 202
Sociometric Solutions, 239
sociometry, 199, 201, 202, 203
Spengler, Oswald, 121
Spitzer, Robert, 171–3, 176, 271
sponsored conversations, 189
sport, as virtue for political leaders, 140
sporting metaphors, 141
SSRIs (selective serotonin reuptake inhibitors), 163, 166
St Louis school of psychiatry, 169, 170, 171, 173, 174, 176, 179
Stanton, Frank, 99
Stigler, George, 150, 152, 153, 156–7, 158, 160
stress, 37, 129, 130, 131, 132, 133, 175, 250, 262, 272, 273
Stuckler, David, 252
subjective affect, science of, 6, 7
subjective feelings, relationship with external circumstances, 254
subjective sensation, 30, 45, 55, 61
Suicide (Durkheim), 227
Sully, James, 59, 84
surveillance, 231, 237, 238, 240, 242. *See also* mass surveillance; psychological surveillance; self-surveillance
surveys, 64, 97–8, 99, 100, 102, 165, 216–17, 219, 220, 223, 233, 266–7
Szasz, Thomas, 168

tachistoscopes, 71, 72, 75, 76, 79, 84
'Taking the Narrative Out of Pain' (Tracey), 32
talent analytics, 238
talking cures, 125, 127
Task Force on Nomenclature and Statistics (APA), 172

Tavistock Clinic (London), 205
Taylor, Frederick Winslow, 117–20, 133, 136, 218, 272
Taylorism, 119, 120, 123, 125, 127, 235
team-work, 251, 256
technology / technologies
  behavioural monitoring, 38
  bodily-tracking devices, 240
  computer programmes designed to influence feelings, 222
  digital monitoring / tracking, 135, 260
  employee fitness-tracking programmes, 240
  eye tracking, 72, 97
  facial scanning / face-scanning technology, 72, 222, 276
  fitness-tracking ticket machine, 240
  fMRI. *See* fMRI
  Health 2.0 technologies, 135
  health-tracking wristbands, 276
  heart-rate monitoring, 25, 37, 137
  impact of on happiness science, 10–11
  impact of on market research, 73
  impact of on psychology's claim to be objective science, 76
  mind-reading technology, 33, 75–6
  mood tracking, 5, 6, 228
  neurological monitoring, 38
  physiological monitoring, 38
  of psychological control, 274
  reverence for in Watson's agenda, 91
  scanning technology, 75–6
  self-monitoring, 258
  sentiment analysis / tracking, 6, 221, 223, 261
  for social network analysis, 204
  in Wundt's lab, 84
  telepathic brain-to-brain communication, 33
Tesco, 187, 222
testosterone, 68
Thaler, Richard, 257
Thatcher, Margaret, 139, 144
Thatcherism, 34, 140
The Theory of Advertising (Scott), 86
The Theory of Political Economy (Jevons), 54, 56, 59
therapeutic management, 125, 128
Thomas, William I., 93

313

Thorndike, Edward, 284n14
time and motion studies, 118
Townsend, Anthony, 220
Tracey, Irene, 32
Track Your Happiness (app), 228
truBrain, 68
Twitter, 187, 206, 208, 226, 267, 269–70
tyranny of sounds, 22, 32, 97, 147, 225, 261

Uber, 188
UK Faculty of Public Health, 274
unemployment, 107, 110–11, 116, 132, 144, 252
unhappiness, 9, 249–55, 269, 272
Unilever, 134–5
Unitarianism, 47, 48, 50, 55
universities, relationships of with businesses, 82
University of Chicago, 148
University of Michigan, 256
University of Pittsburgh, 226
University of Warwick (UK), 227
University of Zurich, 195
US military, on stress, 132
utilitarianism, 13, 19, 22, 24, 26, 27, 38, 56, 62, 65, 97, 103, 115, 129, 159, 177, 183, 184–5, 191, 195, 212, 228, 231, 232, 242, 255, 258, 269, 274
utility maximization, theory of, 62

Valium, 162
value, 52–5, 67
value for money, 64
verbal behaviour, 96, 223, 224, 253, 261
Viner, Jacob, 149, 152
viral marketing, 189
Virgin Pulse, 135
von Helmholtz, Hermann, 59, 77

Walmart, 159
Walras, Léon, 54

Watson, John B., 87, 89–96, 97, 102, 113, 152, 184, 215, 223, 233, 235, 237, 264
WEF (World Economic Forum), 1, 3, 6, 107
well-being, 4, 5, 64, 108, 146, 245, 251, 252, 274
well-being optimization, science of, 136
Wellbutrin, 178
wellness, 112, 113, 127, 129
Wharton Pennsylvania, 82
Whateley, Richard, 48, 54
whiplash, 43–5, 51, 69
Whitehall Study, 288n34
Who Shall Survive? (Moreno), 203
Wilkinson, Richard, 250
Williams, Raymond, 273
willingness to pay surveys, 64
Winch, Guy, 196
Winokur, George, 169
Winslow, Edward, 117
Wired magazine, 185
Wittgenstein, Ludwig, 263, 264, 265, 266
The Word of the Father (Moreno), 197, 201
work, 55, 106, 110, 116, 122, 128, 133, 252–3
work capability assessments, 110
workfare, 34, 109, 274
workplace disaffection, 108
workplace empowerment, 136
workplace happiness, 109, 113
workshop system, of Chicago School of economics, 152
World Economic Forum (WEF), 1, 3, 6, 107
World Health Organization, 107, 126, 167, 172
World of Warcraft (game), 205, 206, 207
Wundt, Wilhelm, 77–81, 83–4, 86, 87, 91, 217, 257, 265

Zak, Paul (Dr Love), 114, 195, 213, 255, 256
Žižek, Slavoj, 177